Spain and Portugal

—— Principal highways
—|—|— Railways

Statute miles
0   20   60   100

Kilometers
0   20   60   100

Sam Bryant

HALF OF SPAIN DIED

Books by Herbert L. Matthews

HALF OF SPAIN DIED

A WORLD IN REVOLUTION

CUBA

THE CUBAN STORY

THE YOKE AND THE ARROWS

ASSIGNMENT TO AUSTERITY
(with Edith Matthews)

THE EDUCATION OF A CORRESPONDENT

THE FRUITS OF FASCISM

TWO WARS AND MORE TO COME

EYEWITNESS TO ABYSSINIA

HALF OF SPAIN DIED

A Reappraisal of the Spanish Civil War

HERBERT L. MATTHEWS

Charles Scribner's Sons   New York

To Christopher,
when he grows up

PICTURE CREDITS

Black Star: 27 (By Dominique Berretty); Magnum: 1; Herbert L. Matthews: 18, 19; Sovfoto: 11; United Press International: 2, 3, 17, 20, 24; Wide World: 4, 5, 6, 7, 8, 9, 10, 12, 13, 14, 15, 16, 21, 22, 23, 25, 26

Printed in the United States of America
Library of Congress Catalog Card Number 72-1233
SBN 684-13079-3 (cloth)

ACKNOWLEDGMENTS

THE AVAILABLE DOCUMENTATION ON the Spanish Civil War has by now been thoroughly examined and used by historians. For new material one must await free access to the Nationalist (Franco) files and to some personal contributions, such as the papers of Dr. Juan Negrín, which will be made public in 1981.

Hugh Thomas's book, *The Spanish Civil War*, is so basic and complete that any new history must be heavily indebted to his indefatigable and patient spadework. I am grateful for his permission to rely on, and to quote from, his book.

The outstanding historian of the Spanish Civil War in the United States is Professor Stanley G. Payne, whose three books on the war and the Franco regime provide a rich mine of information. I disagree often with his interpretations and choice of facts, but it is impossible to write about the Spanish Civil War and not profit from his scholarship. He has kindly permitted me to quote from his works. Two of his books—*Falange: A History of Spanish Fascism* and *Politics and the Military in Modern Spain*—were published by the Stanford University Press, which has generously given me permission to quote passages. The third—*The Spanish Revolution*—was published by W. W. Norton.

A few books, like Professor Gabriel Jackson's *The Spanish Republic and the Civil War,* and Gerald Brenan's *The Spanish Labyrinth,* have become standard studies which are naturally useful to those writing about Spain. To such works must be added many specialized books, documents, novels, poems: an inexhaustible mass of material out of which an author like myself picks what seems important. My special contribution is to have been in Spain during nearly the whole of the Civil War as correspondent for my newspaper, *The New York Times.*

CONTENTS

PREFACE

IT IS ALWAYS QUESTIONABLE to what extent history, which is necessarily written after the event, truly reflects the ideas, emotions, and minds of the people and the country who made the history. A great deal of information has to be taken on faith. Historians assemble whatever facts and opinions are available and make a pattern out of them. The construction is artificial. The forces at work in any great event such as the Spanish Civil War are enormously complicated; much is lost at the time; sincere men make errors of judgment; some men lie. Statesmen of the time grope through a fog, never knowing for sure whether what they do will turn out the way they want.

No event of the twentieth century has suffered and profited more from history than the Spanish Civil War. Several thousand books have been written about it, many by the men and women who played leading roles at the time; many by observers like myself who lived through the war in Spain and wrote about it daily and in books; and many by a generation of young scholars working from books, documents, and interviews.

Out of the mass of information and opinions, a clearer picture has emerged than we could see at the time, for then we were too close to the events. Now we can step back a little and look the scene over from every angle. It is much too soon to grasp the whole picture, and it will never be possible to judge it without emotions or bias. Some subjects are like that. The French Revolution of 1789, for instance, is still a heated subject of controversy among historians and Frenchmen.

Nearly all Spaniards thought of their Civil War in national terms and nearly all the rest of us thought of it in international terms. Both were right. As a civil war, it inflicted such grievous wounds on Spain they have not yet healed. As an international conflict, it stands out as one of the significant historic events of the twentieth century, both in itself and because it set the stage for World War II.

Perhaps the most famous reminder that all of us were being caught up in the worldwide effects of the Spanish Civil War was Ernest Hemingway's novel, published in 1940, *For Whom the Bell Tolls.* The title was taken from the final sentence of a meditation by John Donne: "And therefore never send to know for whom the *bell* tolls; It tolls for *thee.*"

"It [the war] gave you a part in something that you could believe in wholly and completely and in which you felt an absolute brotherhood with the others who were engaged in it," Robert Jordan, Hemingway's hero in the book, muses to himself. "It was something that you had never known before but that you experienced now, and you gave such importance to it and the reasons for it that your own death seemed of complete unimportance."

When men fight with such heroism and disdain of life, as they did on both sides in Spain, it is partly because they believe they are fighting the one last, great fight in which good will triumph over evil. It was not to be; the Spanish Civil War is yet to end.

In this book, as Nietzsche's Zarathustra might have said, is *my* truth about the Spanish Civil War, as I lived it, saw it, felt it, studied it these many years, and brooded endlessly on what it meant to Spain and to the world.

It seems time for a reappraisal; time to think back in old age to "battles long ago" in the cities and fields of Spain, and to men who had ideals for which they died.

H.L.M.

July 1972

HALF OF SPAIN DIED

An early nineteenth-century Spanish critic, Mariano José de Larra, wrote an epitaph for his country:
HERE LIES HALF OF SPAIN: IT DIED AT THE HANDS OF THE OTHER HALF

1

THE MILITARY CAMPAIGNS

IN THE YEARS BETWEEN JULY 17, 1936, and
April 1, 1939, Spaniards fought one of the cruelest civil wars in
history.[1] It was also one of the most important, because while
it solved nothing permanently for Spain, which has changed
little since those years, it drew other nations into its vortex and
pointed the way to the greatest of all conflicts, World War II.
There is, of course, no need to say who won and who lost the
war. A Spain torn by internal strife after a century and a half
of misrule, social injustice, corruption, the hegemonies of
army, church, and reactionary capitalism and the revolutionary violence of the organized workers and peasants, exploded.[2]

A plot aimed at restoring law and order was engineered by
disgruntled Spanish generals, headed by Emilio Mola. A cautious, politically timid general made up his mind belatedly to
join the rebellion if he were given command of the only well-
trained and efficient fighting force in the Spanish Army––the
Moorish *Regulares* and the Foreign Legionaries *(Tercios)* who
made up the Army of Africa. His name was Francisco Franco
Bahamonde.[3]

No foreign power was involved in the uprising which, as
such, was a failure. The people of Spain[4]—not the Republican

1. Subsequent chapters describe in detail the general subjects mentioned
in this military summary.
2. Chapter 3, The Second Republic.
3. Chapter 4, The Generals.
4. Chapter 2, The Spaniards.

1

government, which hesitated almost too long—saved the nation. They held all the great cities except Seville and Saragossa, overwhelming army garrisons and Civil Guard barracks with fanatical bravery and at very high cost. On most of the warships, the crews mutinied and killed their officers, who were, or would presumably have been, with the Rebels. Hence, it was possible to block the Strait of Gibraltar and prevent General Franco from ferrying his Moroccan and Foreign Legion troops across to the mainland. General Mola had only one division to send down from Navarre to take the capital, Madrid, and it was short of ammunition.

Ill-armed and untrained but wildly enthusiastic militiamen from Madrid rushed up to the Sierra de Guadarrama northwest of the capital and held fast. In desperation both Franco and Mola sent to Berlin and Rome for help, and so the rebellion became a civil war, and the civil war a miniature world war. Hitler and Mussolini were at first reluctant to send aid, fearing that the democracies and Russia would be provoked into a European war. However, they did not hesitate long. It was clearly to their advantage to have a right-wing, friendly military government in Madrid instead of a Popular Front Republican government.

Hitler decided that Franco was the man to help, not Mola, and Mussolini concurred. The Germans sent Junker bombers and transport planes to carry troops across the Strait. The Italians sent planes, too, and also warships to drive away the bewildered crews of the Loyalist navy, who did not know what to do.

This allowed General Franco to get 9,000 men of the Army of Africa—disciplined, brave, and savage—across the Strait and into the peninsula in the first ten days of August. The equally brave but untrained Loyalist militiamen were no match for them as they drove a swath of terror and destruction through southwestern Spain. A trek began of frightened and embittered refugees, which was not to end until they, and hundreds of thousands more, swarmed over the Catalan frontier into France two and a half years later.

The Loyalist militia made a suicidal stand at Mérida, and

then fought fanatically to hold the Portuguese frontier town of Badajoz, but the Moors and Legionaries, now 20,000 strong, were just as fanatical and more experienced. They vented their blood lust in the conquered town in an incident which first made the world realize the ruthless way the Spanish war was being fought. About 2,000 unarmed militiamen and civilians were herded into the bullring and slaughtered. Franco's and Mola's armies were now linked. The Portuguese border was closed to the Republicans for the duration of the war, but was always open to the Nationalists for arms and supplies.

The generals seem to have called themselves Nationalists at the outset. They could hardly be expected to accept the label of Rebels or Insurgents, although this was what they were by any historic definition—until they won. Those who supported the Second Republic were, for obvious reasons, called Loyalists or Republicans.

The frontier with France, at Hendaye on the western end of the Pyrenees, had also been closed after Irún was taken by the insurgents on September 4, 1936. An undamaged San Sebastián was surrendered on September 13 by the chivalrous Basques, who did not want to see their lovely seaside resort destroyed. The ardently Catholic Basques fought throughout the war with a respect for human life unique in that cruel conflict. The equally ardent Carlists of Navarre were ruthless in their murder of leftists and Republicans but, at least, they usually did not kill prisoners of war, as the other Insurgents did.

Mola's forces could not take Irún until Franco had sent him 700 Legionaries in German Junker transport planes. Franco was, by then, the commanding general. His primary target was, of course, Madrid, whose capture would end the war. The main force of his Army of Africa drove relentlessly northward from Badajoz. However, the Generalissimo turned the army aside to relieve the besieged Alcázar of Toledo, thus probably losing his chance to capture the capital. In the old fortress of Toledo, a regular army commander, Colonel José Moscardó, had barricaded himself at the beginning of the rebellion, with about 1,300 men, mostly Civil Guards. With them were some 600 women and children, nearly all dependents, but Moscardó had also cannily taken 100 civilian hostages in with him, including the civil governor and his family. Arms were plentiful; food rather short. And there they held out for ten weeks with a bravery and fortitude which made the siege of the Alcázar, and its relief by Franco, one of the most famous incidents of the Civil War.

The Loyalist besiegers of the Alcázar were amateurish and badly directed. The fortress should have been taken, even though the Loyalists did not have cannons heavy enough to demolish the thick walls. On September 27, 1936, the National-ists entered Toledo, the Moroccans marring the occasion by their slaughter of the inhabitants, including the wounded in their hospital beds. The Insurgent troops went on to strike—belatedly—at Madrid.

Meanwhile, it had been the turn of the Republican govern-ment to seek aid abroad. Premier Léon Blum of France wanted to help and started to do so, but Prime Minister Stanley Baldwin of Great Britain and his Conservative government were deter-mined to keep clear, and at all costs to prevent the Spanish conflict from becoming a European war. The United States, led by the inexperienced Anglophile Secretary of State Cordell Hull, with an acquiescent but unhappy President Franklin D. Roosevelt, decided to follow British policy, declare neutrality, and impose an arms embargo. It was the height of American isolationism.

The Republican government, legitimately elected, was enti-tled by international law to buy arms to defend itself. No demo-cratic power would sell them arms. Madrid turned to the Soviet Union. Stalin was more than reluctant; he was persuaded to act by the Comintern and by his fear that a fascistic military gov-ernment would take power in Spain before he could intervene. Moreover, he had a terrible and, to him, more important task in mind. He was to begin his blood purge of the Old Bolsheviks in August 1936, one month after the Civil War began.

The Madrid government established diplomatic relations with the Soviet Union and the Comintern set up trading agencies in European capitals to buy arms and other supplies—with Spanish gold. An International Brigade of Volunteers (about 60 per cent Communist) from more than fifty countries was hastily assembled at Albacete, given a few weeks' training, and sent into battle in Madrid at a critical moment.[5]

The people of Madrid and the untrained militia had stopped Franco's Moors and Legionaries as they had earlier stopped Mola's Navarrese in the Sierra de Guadarrama. The Loyalist militia were always best at defensive fighting, where the courage and tenacity of the Spanish character had scope and where disciplined teamwork was not so necessary. There are no better guerrilla fighters in the world than the Spanish, as Napoleon's armies had long ago discovered.

When the Insurgent forces were stopped, Franco tried terroristic bombing of Madrid with his German planes—the first blitz of a European city—but this only increased the will of the infuriated Madrileños to resist. The militia (there were about 80,000 men, and women, too) had taken the main thrust of the Rebel attack.

In the crucial days of November 7 to 12, 1936, the Internationals—about 3,500 of them—were thrown into the breach at University City on the western edge of the capital. (Russian matériel—tanks and planes—finally began to arrive on October 14.)

The heaviest, and main attack, made by the Army of Africa, came on Sunday, November 8, in the Casa de Campo and against University City. The defenders were short of ammunition. Thousands stood their ground and, as they died, unarmed reservists rushed in to pick up their rifles and fight on, often to die in their turn. The Moors and Legionaries fought with their accustomed desperate bravery, at one time almost breaking through. General José Miaja, the Republican commander, there had his great moment of the war. Rushing to the breached lines, he threatened to shoot any militiaman who

5. Chapter 9, The Internationals.

retreated. The men rallied; the Moroccan vanguard was slain, and the line held. That afternoon the Internationals—mostly German and French—arrived from Albacete, parading with revolutionary songs on their lips through the capital to the front lines, where most of them died in the next ten days. On November 9 they took the main thrust of the drive on University City.

It was a defensive victory of enormous importance, for to have lost Madrid would have meant losing the war very quickly, not to mention certain diplomatic recognition of the Franco regime by the Great Powers. Germany and Italy went ahead with recognition anyway on November 18, 1936, but it was not until February 1939 that other countries followed suit.

Historians still argue about whether the International Brigade saved Madrid. The truth is that it helped to save Madrid. There was glory enough to go around. The Communist heroine, Dolores Ibarruri, known as *La Pasionaria,* echoed the cry of Verdun: "They shall not pass!"—*No pasarán!*—and the enemy did not pass.

At the beginning of August 1936, something called "Non-Intervention" had been concocted,[6] first put forward by—of all people—Léon Blum, the French Premier, who wanted to help the Republicans by cutting off *all* intervention of arms and men on both sides. Stalin was anxious to go along, since he was engaged in an urgent attempt to make an alliance with the British and French democracies against the Nazi and Fascist powers.

Thus began one of the most extraordinary games of power politics in modern times. Hitler did not want Franco to win, but he was determined not to let him lose. The longer the war lasted, the better for Nazi Germany. Mussolini wanted Franco to win, and in the course of the war sent not only great quantities of arms, planes, tanks, and submarines to sink ships going to Spain, but a whole expeditionary force which for much of

6. Chapter 6, Intervention . . . and Chapter 7, . . . And Non-Intervention.

the conflict numbered between 40,000 and 60,000 men.

Stalin, so far as his actions demonstrated, did not want to see a democratic Republican government win, and even less did he want to see a Communist takeover in Spain, which would certainly have brought on a European war. But for some time he was equally determined not to let the Loyalists lose if he could help it. The war was costing him nothing, since virtually everything he sent to Spain was being paid for by Spanish gold deposited in Moscow. But he could not send much help because, on the insistence of the British, the French frontier was closed except for four brief periods, and Russian and other ships were being sunk by Italian submarines and bombers. Russian aid began tapering off in mid-1937 and stopped in mid-1938. Stalin had in mind—and was quietly negotiating—the sinister alliance with Hitler which permitted Germany to launch World War II.

The real force behind "Non-Intervention" was, at all times, the Tory governments of Stanley Baldwin and the great appeaser, Neville Chamberlain. They forced the French to honor the Non-Intervention Agreement. The United States held to its neutrality and arms embargo.[7] The Spanish Republic could not buy arms and was receiving little help from the Soviet Union and none elsewhere, although Mexico, under President Lázaro Cárdenas, wanted to help and tried to do so. Washington blocked the Mexican efforts.

During this time a bitter war was being fought across the face of Spain, high in casualties and atrocious in the murderous terror exercised by the Nationalists as they gradually expanded their territorial gains. There had been a fearsome reign of terror on both sides when the war began[8]—spontaneous and uncontrollable on the Republican side as an embittered, furious people took class vengeance and vented their traditional hatred against the Roman Catholic clergy, burning many churches. In three months the government restored enough

7. Chapter 8, The United States.
8. Chapter 5, Terror and Revolution.

law and order to end the popular terror, but Russian and Spanish Communists set up their *chekas* (secret counterrevolutionary cells); Communists, Anarchists, and left-wing Socialists fought each other, and so a small, but steady, smoldering fire of terror went on below the surface in the Republican zone.

It did not affect the Spanish people. Where they suffered was from the terrorism of the conquering Nationalist armies. Since Generalissimo Franco (who became chief of state of a government in Burgos on October 1, 1936) never could trust the people, a deliberate policy of terror was considered necessary. As each village and town were conquered, all Republican officials, all trade unionists, virtually all who had played a role against the upper and middle classes or against the army and police were executed. This policy did not end with the war. Franco's postwar retribution was terrible, finally petering out in mid-1943 when it became evident that the Allies were going to win the war with Germany and Italy.

The Basques, because they had been promised autonomy, remained loyal to the Republic. Since they were a fervently orthodox Roman Catholic people, they were at all times an embarrassment to the Vatican and to Franco's Catholic supporters everywhere. They, with the miners of Asturias, who were left-wing revolutionaries, held a Republican beachhead on the coast of the Bay of Biscay. Because of its isolation and internal divisions, this position fell to the Spanish Insurgents and the Italian *Corpo di Truppe Volontarie* during June, July, and August 1937. (General Mola, incidentally, had been killed in a mysterious plane crash on June 3, 1937.) On the south coast, Málaga—disgracefully mishandled, deserted, and betrayed by the Largo Caballero government—fell to the Rebels and the Italians on February 8, 1937.

Franco persisted in believing that he could and must take Madrid. His first attempt had failed. His next move was to try to surround Madrid from the north by cutting across the Corunna Road and swinging east. This attack, in which the Internationals, bolstered by Russian tanks, took very heavy casualties, made little progress and was called off on January

9, 1937. But Madrid still was the great objective. Franco then looked south of the capital. On February 6, a heavy Insurgent force, with the Moors and *Tercios* as shock troops and the Condor Legion (as the German interventionist force was called) supplying artillery and airplanes, struck across the valley of the Jarama River. The objective was to cut the vital Madrid-Valencia highway and isolate the capital.

The foreign volunteers on the Republican side were handled with crass stupidity and incompetence by the Hungarian Communist from the International Brigade, General Gál, but what he lacked in competence was made up by the bravery and self-sacrifice of his soldiers.

In that fighting, American volunteers of the Abraham Lincoln Battalion had their baptism of fire. It was a withering, devastating, terribly costly battle for all concerned—Internationals and Spaniards—but the Nationalists were stopped.

February 27, 1937, was a black but glorious day for the American volunteers. General Gál sent them against Pingarron Hill into what Hemingway called "one single, idiotic, stupidly conceived and insanely executed attack in the hills above the Jarama." My figures were that of about 450 American volunteers who were sent into the battle, 127 were killed and 175 wounded. A small number of the Americans mutinied after the battle, but so did some Brigaders in the British and Franco-Belge battalions. The Americans were rank amateurs facing the best troops in Franco's army—and they stopped them. The next day the Insurgents once and for all gave up their attempts to encircle Madrid from the south. The Moors and Legionaries had taken such heavy losses that they were never again able, by themselves, to form the vanguard in battle. It is to the credit of the foreign volunteers that those who survived stuck it out and, with the wounded who returned, fought again. Discouragingly, it had to be another disastrous battle—Brunete—but they stayed and fought well every time.

So far as staff work was concerned, the Republican government's military successes on the edge of Madrid between November 1936 and January 1937 were due to two foreign Com-

munist commanders: the Russian Brigadier General Vladimir
Goriev, back at headquarters, and the Hungarian who went
under the name of General Emil Kléber and was believed to
have been General Lazar Stern of the Red Army. Unfortu-
nately, General Kléber became too conspicuous and famous for
Prime Minister Largo Caballero's comfort and he had to be
withdrawn. Generally speaking, the Russian and Eastern European Communist advisers were mediocre, although at various
times future Marshals Malinovsky, Konev, and Rokossovsky,
and Admiral Kuznetsov were briefly in Spain. When it came to
strategy, the Republic's advisers were no match for Franco's
German advisers—when he would listen to them. The Generalissimo had some of the top names in the Nazi armed forces at
his disposal: General Hugo von Sperrle, commander of the Condor Legion; his aide, the then Colonel Wolfgang von Rich-
thofen; Admiral Wilhelm Canaris, head of the German Military Intelligence; and Hitler's personal representative, General
Wilhelm von Faupel.

It was now Mussolini's turn to win the war for the Nationalists, as he hoped, by a drive down from the northeast toward the
provincial capital of Guadalajara, fifty miles from Madrid. The
Duce's air and naval forces had established a base in the Balearics in the first days of the conflict. Except for Minorca, the
islands were in effect an Italian possession for the duration of
the war. The Italian occupation of Palma de Mallorca was
blackened by a vicious swashbuckler, Arconovaldo Buonaccorsi, who called himself Count Rossi, and who headed what he
labeled the Dragoons of Death. He was a lecher and a sadist
who, it was reliably reported, had 2,000 men, women, and children executed in Palma in two days.

For the drive on Guadalajara, the Duce had amassed a wholly
Italian force of no less than four divisions of about 30,000 men,
supported by hundreds of tanks, mobile guns, trucks, a chemi-
cal unit, and dozens of fighter planes. The Italian corps was
supported on the right by 20,000 Spaniards, Moors, and Legionaries, under Colonel José Moscardó, the hero of the siege of the
Alcázar.

The Spanish flank began the attack toward Guadalajara on March 8, 1937, followed the next day by the Italians. An initial advance made the situation dangerous for the Loyalists. Spanish and International troops were rushed up from the Madrid sector. Among the Spanish commanders were two of the most famous soldiers of the war—Enrique Lister, a Galician stonemason who had been trained at the Frunze Military Academy in Leningrad after a miners' revolt in 1934, and Valentín González, called *El Campesino* (The Peasant).

With the Brigaders was the Italian Garibaldi Battalion which had distinguished itself at Madrid and Jarama. The Garibaldini met the Black Shirts in one of the most bizarre incidents of the war—exiles who hated Fascism and the Duce, fighting with ferocious bravery against bewildered conscripts and regular troops, many of whom had thought they were going to Ethiopia. It was a little civil war within a big one, but this time the Fascists lost, if only temporarily.

The Republican command at Guadalajara was still in Russian hands, for the Spaniards as yet had no army commander qualified to conduct an operation of such magnitude. On March 12 a detachment of Russian tanks under General Pavlov arrived at the front and spearheaded a counteroffensive. It was one of the few times in the war when the Russian, or Comintern, commanders proved superior to those of the enemy. The Italians were stopped and then routed in a counterattack on March 18. Nationalist Spaniards secretly rejoiced at the Italian disgrace. The battle ended on March 23 when the exhausted Loyalists had to stop. Two thousand Italians had been killed, 4,000 wounded, and 300 taken prisoner. The infuriated Mussolini vowed that the Italians would not leave Spain until General Franco, with his aid, had won.

The war around Madrid had reached a stalemate. The Insurgents could not take the capital; they could and did take the valuable Basque, Santander, and Asturian industrial regions in the north. Mussolini's Italian corps was given an easy victory at Santander. However, the German Condor Legion's planes, artillery, tanks, and advisers were the Nationalists' primary assets. It took the cautious Franco seven months to conquer the divided northern provinces.

It was in the course of this campaign that the most famous bombing of the Spanish Civil War took place. On April 26, 1937, the German air command experimented with the effects of a mass attack, systematically and completely destructive, of an open town. The town was Guernica, sacred to the Basques as their medieval capital. The bombing was a success, but it will forever live in infamy. Out of one man's anger came what many believe to be the greatest painting of our century, Picasso's "Guernica."

The Asturian miners knew that they could expect no mercy. They scorched the earth, fought to the death, or fled to the hills where many carried on guerrilla warfare for years.

A minor Republican offensive at the end of May 1937, aimed at Segovia, deserves mention because it is the battle which figures in Ernest Hemingway's *For Whom the Bell Tolls.* The Fourteenth International Brigade (French and Belgian) took part in the abortive attack.

After Jarama, those of the Internationals who were left, and the new recruits, had their first rest. So many American volunteers had arrived in Spain that a new battalion—the George Washington—was added to the battle-trained and decimated Abraham Lincoln. The government (it had fled the previous October to Valencia as the Insurgents neared Madrid) hoped to relieve the pressure on the north by a great offensive cutting behind the Insurgent forces holding Madrid. The plan was drawn up, and evidently imposed by the Russian advisers. Strategically it was good, but the tactical leadership was poor. The engagement is known as the battle of Brunete, from the name of the town west of Madrid, around which the fighting took place. The nominal commander was the loyal Republican army general José Miaja, who had been left behind in Madrid, to his surprise, when the government fled. He was a mediocre general, but he had the great virtue at that time of being absolutely trustworthy.

This was much the most ambitious Republican offensive yet

tried: two Spanish army corps of nearly 50,000 men and almost the entire International Brigade, then at its height in numbers and strength. The International Brigade was never again to be a great, unified fighting force, as it took dreadfully high casualties at Brunete and was in any event being distributed among predominantly Spanish units. The Americans suffered so heavily (500 casualties out of 800 men) that their two battalions were formed into one. Other International Brigade battalions suffered equally great losses, or even greater. Brunete was one of the two bloodiest battles of the Civil War. The Ebro was the other. Some Internationals mutinied; all grumbled, and the Communist leadership lost face. General Gál was recalled to Moscow, where he disappeared in the Great Purge.

About 25,000 Spanish Republican soldiers were killed. As much aircraft and artillery and as many tanks as could be mustered had been used and nearly all of them were lost. Enrique Lister, former commander of the Fifth Regiment, now leading the Eleventh Division, distinguished himself, as always, by taking Brunete on July 6, 1937, the first day, but there was much confusion, disorder, delay, and useless bravery. The Loyalist advance was halted a week after it started. Franco launched a counterattack on July 18 and recaptured Brunete on July 25. (Franco himself, incidentally, never took part in any battle, remaining at headquarters or in his various capitals throughout the war.) In this battle, some 10,000 Insurgents lost their lives.

Politics, which played virtually no role on the Nationalist side in the war, often dictated what the Loyalists did militarily and how they did it. The disunity among the Republicans was an important reason why they lost the war. The Anarchists were a disruptive force because they wanted to make a social revolution at the same time that they fought the war. The Communists, who now had about 300,000 members, were counter-revolutionary and concentrated on winning the war while fighting an underground war against the Anarchists and those whom they called the Trotskyites. The Socialists were split; a revolutionary left-wing faction under Premier Largo Caballero, in office since September 4, 1936, was anti-Communist and anti-Anarchist, although the Premier felt constrained to ally himself first with the Communists and then with the Anarchists. The bourgeois Republican parties and the moderate Socialists under Indalecio Prieto (although Prieto was soon to change) were aligned with the Communists, for they wanted to prosecute the war, not make a revolution.

These antagonisms exploded in an Anarchist uprising in Barcelona on May 3, 4, and 5, 1937, which was suppressed with much bloodshed. Largo Caballero had to resign. He was succeeded by a nominal Socialist, a noted physiologist and professor, Dr. Juan Negrín. The new Premier was a liberal with no ideology, but with a fierce determination to create a strong government, and to fight the war at all costs—and those costs meant accepting and using the Spanish Communists and maintaining a good relationship with the Soviet Union. Negrín moved the government from Valencia to Barcelona.

The next Republican offensive was along the still Anarchist-controlled Aragon front, which the Insurgents had neglected. On August 24, 1937, attacks were made all along the line from north of Teruel to Saragossa, which was a hoped-for objective. The Internationals played a major role, especially the Fifteenth Brigade, which contained the Americans. The fiercest fighting centered on Belchite, which the Abraham Lincoln Battalion took on September 6 with great bravery and heavy losses.

Hemingway could truly write of them after a trip he and I made to Belchite in September: "Those who are left are tough, with blackened, matter-of-fact faces, and after seven months, they know their trade"—which, of course, was soldiering. The Americans, incidentally, had done what Napoleon's forces could not do: they had taken Belchite.

But once again the advances could not be exploited and the Republicans returned to the defensive.

Franco was preparing a new attack on Guadalajara for December 18, 1937, with Madrid as the final objective. The Republicans forestalled him with a surprise attack at Teruel on December 15. No Internationals were used in the force of 40,000

Loyalists, although the Soviet General Stern, called Grigoro-vitch in Spain (not the General Kléber already mentioned), was an adviser. Teruel was a dominant mountain town south of Saragossa. The battle was fought in a fifty-mile-an-hour blizzard with the temperature 18 degrees below zero. There were more casualties from frostbite than from bullets, but Teruel was captured and Franco had to give up his planned offensive in order to make one more counteroffensive. He could not afford, politically, to take such a loss and, anyway, he had a fixed idea that the Nationalists must never give up terrain to the Loyalists.

"Franco has no idea of synthesis in war," wrote Count Galeazzo Ciano, Mussolini's Foreign Minister and son-in-law, in his diary. "His operations are those of a magnificent battalion commander. His objective is always ground, never the enemy. And he doesn't realize that it is by the destruction of the enemy that you win a war." It took a succession of hard and costly attacks with eleven crack divisions before Teruel was recaptured by the Nationalists on February 21, 1938. The Republic was forced to use Internationals in the defense, but the Loyalists could not stand up to the immensely superior German and Italian war matériel which the Insurgents were using. Russian military aid had been declining sharply since the middle of 1937, while German and Italian intervention had increased. The battle was typical—heroically fought on both sides, very costly in lives and matériel, but strategically indecisive.

The Republican government had shown it had offensive capability but not—in fact, never—enough strength and war material to exploit an advance. The Lincoln Battalion was again almost destroyed. The battle of Teruel resulted in exhaustion and bitter quarreling during which, as we shall see, the Communists turned on the now defeatist minister of Defense, Indalecio Prieto.

From then on, with one blazing exception at the Ebro River battle in mid-1938, Franco and the Nationalists were on the offensive. The Generalissimo had built up an army of about 300,000 men—somewhat fewer than the Loyalists, but greatly superior in all types of arms, thanks to Hitler and Mussolini. His allies had achieved, and kept, command of the sky and sea for the Nationalists. They replaced the war materials which the Insurgents had used up in the Teruel counteroffensive. The Republicans had used up their supplies of war materials, too, but they could not replace them. The veteran Loyalist troops had all been involved in the fighting, and were worn out.

A great and, for the Republicans, devastating attack began in Aragon on March 9, 1938, with a tremendous German artillery and aerial barrage. The Nationalists used seven army corps of twenty-six divisions, including 50,000 Italians and 30,000 Moors. The front was broken at a number of places on the first day. Belchite, which the Americans had fought so hard to win, was lost the following day. The Fifteenth Brigade was the last to leave. It retreated toward Caspe, where it made a valiant stand, but Caspe, too, was lost, and the Brigade all but wiped out. The re-formed Abraham Lincoln Battalion, more than three-quarters Spanish, was caught outside of Batea, scattered, and temporarily destroyed. About 125 Americans and Spaniards saved themselves by swimming the Ebro River. The remnants of the American, British, and Canadian battalions were reassembled, rested, and their battalions reorganized into a largely new Fifteenth Brigade in which there were three and a half Spaniards to every foreigner. The new commander was a fine and respected Spanish officer, Major Valledor.

Individual units of Loyalists and Internationals had fought with customary bravery during the Aragon offensive, holding one place after another for some days, but such units would always find themselves being flanked, and would have to retreat. German air superiority played a major role. The relentless drive continued until, on Good Friday, April 15, 1938, the Fourth Navarrese Division took the Mediterranean fishing village of Viñaroz, cutting the Loyalist zone in two. Franco's headquarters—not for the first time—announced: "The war is won."

It did seem that the war was over, but it was to last for another year. All that the Republic needed was one man who counted. He was the Premier, Don Juan Negrín. His slogan was:

Resistir es vencer! (To resist is to conquer). His Minister of Defense Indalecio Prieto was still hopelessly defeatist and Negrín forced his resignation. President Manuel Azaña had as good as given up.

Stalin, it seems, wanted the Spanish Communist ministers to resign. However, a new government was formed with Communists in many important posts. Spanish Communists were still the best, most disciplined, and most loyal officers and officials, and they held most of the key military posts. Negrín had no choice but, at least, the Anarchists had rallied to the government in the crisis and the Republicans were at all times loyal. The Republic fought on. When the Nationalists turned south and tried to drive to Valencia they met an impenetrable resistance. The large but isolated central southeastern zone, with Madrid as its heart, settled down for a quiet (too quiet—defeat and treachery were below the surface) autumn and winter.

In still Loyalist Catalonia, the Catalans had little enthusiasm for the war, but the army had new Russian-bought weapons, determined (mostly Communist) leadership, and plenty of fighting spirit. The French opened their frontier briefly to let arms, food, and oil through. The Republic was ready for its last and most dramatic offensive: a desperate gamble so nearly successful in its aims that it briefly created the possibility of bringing the Spanish Civil War to an inconclusive stalemate.

This was the sudden and unexpected drive across the Ebro River, north of the Nationalists' Mediterranean beachhead, which began at midnight, July 24–25, 1938, the day after I had cabled *The New York Times* that the drive on Valencia had been halted.

This time the plan was not Russian or Comintern, but the idea of the Spanish Chief of Staff, General Vicente Rojo, one of the few high army officers who remained loyal to the Republic.

The "Army of the Ebro," 70,000 strong, was commanded by the Republic's most brilliant military leader, a Communist who, along with Enrique Lister, had received some training at the Russian Frunze Military Academy. Colonel Juan Modesto, an ex-woodcutter, had seen some military service in the Moroccan Foreign Legion, which was then commanded by Franco, but he was essentially a nonprofessional who was a born military genius. Unlike Lister, who was always up at the front with his men, Modesto, who had taken the highest Spanish command post after Teruel, was a headquarters man with the rare ability to command large bodies of men in battle—in this case three army corps. He had a Russian "adviser," but an obscure one who was never identified. All the top field commanders were Spanish Communists.

Among the first International units to cross the Ebro was the Abraham Lincoln Battalion with the Fifteenth Brigade. The surprise was complete and the assault so successful that a large bridgehead was quickly established. Lister almost captured the important town of Gandesa; 4,000 Nationalist prisoners were taken, but Franco rushed up reinforcements and by August 2 the advance had been stopped.

Strategically, it was the old story for the Republicans: advance, bog-down, a Nationalist counteroffensive, a return to the original positions with both sides exhausted, but with Franco always in a position to replenish his losses quickly through German and Italian aid and the Republic unable to do the same. The Insurgents had to fight long and hard and at great cost to reconquer the lost ground. Once again, it was complete artillery and aerial superiority—mostly German, partly Italian —which gave Franco the edge.

Great events were also happening elsewhere in Europe. The Czech crisis reached its climax with the Spanish government briefly hopeful that it might spark a European war which would save the Republic. Negrín, before and after, kept seeking a negotiated peace in vain, behind the backs of the Communists. Franco, then and always, would settle for nothing less than unconditional surrender.

But the Ebro offensive had jolted the Nationalist regime as nothing else had in the war. Ciano wrote in his diary that an angry Mussolini told him: "Put on your record book that today, August 29th, I prophesy the defeat of Franco. . . . The Reds are fighters—Franco is not." The Duce, wrote Ciano, thought that

Franco had lost his chance of victory and "will come to a compromise with the other side."

"The Republican offensive across the Ebro caused gloom everywhere in Nationalist Spain," wrote Hugh Thomas, the leading historian of the Spanish Civil War. "Defeatism was talked even at Burgos."

The Battle of the Ebro was also historic in being the last engagement in which the Internationals fought. It was as great a fighting performance as any they had given in the war—which is saying much—and a proud record on which to end their service. The price, to be sure, was appallingly high. Of the 7,000 Brigaders who entered the battle, three-fourths were killed or wounded.

Premier Negrín (not Stalin, as nearly all historians seem to believe) made the decision to withdraw the Internationals. He announced it at the League of Nations Assembly during the Munich crisis. The Fifteenth Brigade's last fight was on September 23, 1938.

Eight days later Franco launched his counteroffensive against the Ebro bridgehead with his usual overwhelming superiority in artillery and his complete command of the air. The French had closed the frontier again on May 5. Enrique Líster supervised a stubborn, hard-fought withdrawal, which was completed on November 8. It had taken Franco nearly four months to regain what he had lost in a few days. The Republican army of the Ebro—the last and only army left in Catalonia—was as good as destroyed.

The Republican gamble had failed, but even then the situation within Spain had reached a stalemate. The Nationalist army was exhausted, too short of matériel to launch an offensive; and none too high in morale. Munich changed the picture. That diplomatic victory made Hitler realize that he no longer need fear a European war growing out of Spain whatever he did. It made Stalin realize that he could no longer hope for an alliance with the British and French democracies against the Axis. He wrote off Spain and began to woo the Nazis.

Meanwhile, Franco, desperate for new supplies, yielded to

German terms in order to get the war matériel he needed. He gave the Germans a major participation in the Spanish and Moroccan mines and agreed to pay the costs of the Condor Legion. As Hugh Thomas wrote, this was "the most important act of foreign intervention in the course of the Spanish Civil War. It enabled Franco to mount a new offensive almost immediately, and so strike the Republic when they had exhausted their supplies. Had it not been for this aid . . . a compromise peace, despite all Franco's protestations, might have been inevitable." Negrín, however, was blamed, not praised, by his associates.

Franco mobilized an army of 350,000 men along his whole Catalan line from the French border to the sea. It included his best Spanish divisions, four divisions of Italians, and the usual masses of German and Italian artillery, tanks, and planes. The Republicans still had a few hundred thousand men, but Catalonia was demoralized and quarreling; and arms, ammunition, and warplanes were pitifully short. The outcome could never be in doubt.

The Nationalists struck on December 23, 1938, with their Navarrese and Italian troops, across the River Segre. In this campaign, the Italians fought well against stiff opposition. Lister's Fifth Army Corps—the cream of the Republican army— which was intended as a reserve, had to be thrown right in. He made a typically tenacious stand for two weeks before Borjas Blancas, but he had only men while the Italians and Navarrese had tanks, guns, and planes. Lister had to give up the unequal battle. It was January 4, 1939, the start of the year in which the powers embroiled in Spain were to find themselves involved, despite all their appeasement and chicanery, in a far greater war.

Borjas Blancas was the last stand of the Republican army. From then on the lines were wide open, the troops generally retreating in disorder. I saw the quiet, scholarly division commander, Manuel Tagüeña, before Tarragona. "I sent for some guns," he said, "but they told me they had none." Tarragona fell on January 14.

Barcelona was no Madrid. As General Vicente Rojo later wrote, it was "a city of the dead." It had had its blaze of glory in the first days of the rebellion when the people held the Catalan capital for the Republic. Now it was unfortified, demoralized, and choked with the swarms of the million and more refugees who had been fleeing for months as the dreaded Nationalists advanced. Most of them moved on to flow over the frontier into inhospitable France. Barcelona gave up without a struggle on January 26, 1939.

There was no further attempt at making a stand, but there were loyal *Carabineros* (Customs Guards) to keep a semblance of order. The troops of Modesto, Lister, and Tagüeña fell back toward the French frontier in orderly fashion, holding a line briefly below Figueras so that the remnants of Negrín's government could convene a last session of the Republican Cortes (parliament) on February 1 in the dungeons of the old castle there. The Spanish Republican army, and those Internationals for whom no transportation or visas had been arranged, marched quietly across the French border. The Nationalist troops began reaching the frontier by February 9 and were in complete control of Catalonia the next day.

But not yet in control of Spain![9] There was the central zone, still under Loyalist control, with an army of 300,000 men theoretically capable of fighting for weeks or months. Premier Negrín was not giving up. He and his Foreign Minister, Julio Álvarez del Vayo, a Socialist who might as well have been a Communist, flew from Toulouse to Valencia a few days later, where Lister, Modesto, General Diego Hidalgo de Cisneros of the air force, and other Communist military and political leaders joined them. *La Pasionaria* was already there.

They found confusion, low morale, and a defeatism which was to turn into treachery against the Negrín government. The civilian loss of heart and spirit was as serious as the military defeatism. Militarily, the situation was clearly hopeless, except

9. Chapter 10, The Fighting Stops.

for the possibility of hanging on until the forces threatening to drive the major European powers into war consolidated. Negrín continued to hope that Franco could be induced to agree that in return for surrender he would not take reprisals against those who had fought against him or supported the Republic.

The Communists did not want to surrender on any terms. Negrín was working against their desires and without consulting them. Later they were to accuse him bitterly of vacillation and deceit. Negrín had always played a double game in the sense that he gave the Communists great power, since only in that way could the war be prosecuted, but he would never let them dictate to him or control the government at the top. This policy could work only so long as he, Don Juan Negrín, was personally powerful enough to command obedience as if he were a dictator, as Franco could on the Nationalist side. The unending disunity on the Republican side made this policy enormously difficult and never 100 per cent workable. Now, it broke down.

Negrín was not his normally decisive self to begin with. The people in the Loyalist zone were utterly weary of the war, and had been suffering appalling hardships, especially in Madrid. Most important of all, the key commanders in the Madrid sector were not Communists and had been plotting to make a peace, partly through defeatism and partly in the hope (which they should have known was vain) that they could make some kind of compromise terms with Generalissimo Franco. If the Caudillo (Spanish for Duce or Fuehrer) had not been so fanatical in his determination to purge Spain of every taint of "leftism"; if he had been willing to offer mercy and forgo massive reprisals, the Spanish Civil War would have ended a year or more before it did. As with the Allied "unconditional surrender" terms in World War II, the enemy had nothing to lose by fighting to the bitter end.

The leader of the antigovernment plot in Madrid was a prewar officer, a lukewarm Republican named Colonel Segismundo Casado, commander of the Army of the Center. Anti-Communism, always a powerful factor in the Republican camp, was now decisive, for one of the best fighting units in the central zone, the Fourth Army, was commanded by an Anarchist, Cipriano Mera. He went over to the Casado camp. Negrín, inexplicably, tried to placate Casado. He made him a general and, it seems, agreed to let him seek a negotiated peace. According to Hugh Thomas, he even "added that he would remove the Communist party from the government if necessary." The Communists said they would support Negrín in whatever he wanted to do. He evidently told them that he saw no possibility but to continue to resist.

The bewilderment and confusion were complete and, meanwhile, the Madrileños were starving and freezing. At a meeting of all the Republican military leaders on February 26, the Premier still preached resistance, but by then most of the military, naval, and air force officers (General Miaja, the hero of the early defense of Madrid was a surprising, but temporary, exception) were against Negrín. The Communists wanted to fight on and the Premier tried to give them the commanding power to do so.

It was too late. Casado came out openly against Negrín and the Communists on March 4, 1939. Miaja joined him. So did some Socialists, headed by the famous old moderate intellectual, Professor Julián Besteiro. And, of course, so did the Anarchists. A junta was formed which "deposed" the government of Dr. Negrín.

The next day a confused struggle began as the Communist divisions moved on Madrid. Negrín, Vayo, and all the Communist and Republican leaders in Negrín's quarters flew to Dakar. (There were still a few Russian advisers who were evidently as bewildered and helpless as the Spaniards, and they left, too.)

The Communist troops at first seized control of the key points in Madrid, but their leaders had fled and they did not know how to exploit their victory. There was a little civil war within the Civil War—Franco's enemies destroying themselves. The once-crushed Fifth Column was coming to life again. Casado's forces and the Anarchist division of Mera regained control. The colonel still tried, in vain, to get some kind of terms from General

Franco, who obviously did not need any longer to make the slightest concessions.

Casado had done no better than Negrín and, in fact, had deprived those who wanted to go down fighting of their chance to die more honorably than before Franco's firing squads. Moreover, the international situation was forcing the democracies to stiffen their stand against Hitler. The Nazis had marched into Prague on March 15. Negrín had tried to make the only possible gamble by continuing to resist.

The Nationalist forces were now ready to move along all the fronts from the south coast and Estremadura to Madrid. Casado, Miaja, some Socialists, and the few remaining Communist leaders gathered in Valencia, Alicante, and Cartagena, and went out by ship or plane. Franco's only concession had been to indicate that the defectors would be allowed to leave. At eleven o'clock on the morning of March 27, Madrid was occupied. Spanish history has known many famous sieges. None was more poignant or tenacious or braver than the defense of Madrid.

On April 1, 1939, Generalissimo Franco, from his headquarters at Burgos, issued a communiqué: "Today, after having made prisoner and disarmed the Red Army, the Nationalist troops have reached their final military objective. The war is ended."[10]

10. Chapter 11, Franco Keeps the Peace.

2

THE SPANIARDS

THOSE OF US WHO WERE INVOLVED in the Spanish Civil War (I as a war correspondent for *The New York Times* covering the Republican side) had strong and positive feelings at the time. We all know a great deal more now about the inner workings of the two sides than we could have known during the conflict. The verdict of at least nine out of ten of the professional American and British historians who have written about the war—mine included—favors the Republicans. But many of the criticisms and fears expressed about the Nationalists during the war were unfounded and unfair. One can no longer, in honesty, draw a black or white picture.

No book can be written about the Spanish Civil War, even in the 1970's, which is not controversial. A historian searches for a middle ground, but finds none in the known facts or the several thousand books which have been written about the war. Men and women who lived through the Spanish conflict can never forget it, whatever it was to them—tragedy, adventure, dedication, crusade, hatred, horror, pity, or glory. There will come a time, with all passion spent, when the Spanish Civil War can be written about and read about like the War of the Spanish Succession (1701–1713, which brought in the French Bourbon line). But this day is still far off.

The war was seen at the time as a confrontation of democracy, Fascism, and Communism. This idea oversimplified and distorted the truth. The Civil War came out of uniquely Spanish circumstances and it never was anything but that to Spaniards.

They were reliving their past. The future President, Manuel Azaña, in a 1930 speech, said: "Just as there are persons who suffer from hereditary diseases, so Spain, as a country, suffers from hereditary history."

The 1936 military rebellion was carefully, although badly, planned as a response to an immediate situation, but the explosion really came out of a long accumulation of conflicts between Spaniards. One can trace "causes" of the war in centuries of feudalism, militarism, clericalism, regionalism, economic inequalities, and rural poverty and misery. Despite the general belief at the time, Germany, Italy, and the Soviet Union were, as I have said, in no way responsible for starting the war. All the Spanish political movements, except the Monarchists, who wanted King Alfonso XIII back (he had abdicated in 1931), had foreign labels—Republicanism, Fascism, Communism, Socialism, Anarcho-Syndicalism—but every one of them had been given a Spanish coloration.

This has misled or baffled many foreign historians. Not only Spain but also Spaniards must be understood on their own terms. If they do not seem reasonable to us, it may be because they have different standards of rationality. They have not, except briefly and on rare occasions in recent centuries, been a united people. Locality and region, not nation, win their allegiance, for these are what the people understand.

One cannot apply Anglo-Saxon criteria. Since her "golden" sixteenth century, when she dominated Europe and conquered a New World, Spain has been cut off from Europe by the mountain barrier of the Pyrenees. A true peninsularity was developed. There is an oft-quoted dictum by Alexandre Dumas: "Africa begins at the Pyrenees." The same thought is often expressed the other way around: "Europe ends at the Pyrenees."

The very configuration of Spain imposed basic regional differences and rivalries. Except for Switzerland, Spain is the most mountainous country in Europe, with extremes of climate, of natural wealth and barrenness, of differing character, language, and race. Her history was made by Iberians, Celts,

Phoenicians, Greeks, Carthaginians, Romans, Goths, Franks, Jews, and Moors, the last two remaining for eight centuries. Basques and Catalans still have their own separate regions and languages. Like the Balkans, Spain is a melting pot of races that were never assimilated and which often fought each other. Moreover, Spaniards, almost alone in the modern era, will fight for ideas. Give them a cause and they will sacrifice their lives with ferocious bravery, as they did in the Civil War.

When he was President, Azaña was quoted by a *New York Times* correspondent in 1936 as saying: *"Sol y sombra!* That is Spain."* (Seats in the bullring are so labeled, according to whether they are situated in the sun or the shade.)

Spaniards are poor, but this is because of inequalities, inefficiency, corruption, and the selfishness of the small, wealthy class of landowners, businessmen, and bankers. Spain is, to be sure, an infertile country in these modern times, although it was a granary for the empire in Roman days. It lacks rain, and deforestation has made great areas barren. The roots of Spanish economic troubles, today as in the past, lie in the agrarian problem: minifundia in the north, latifundia in the south, often run by absentee owners paying subsistence wages to slave labor. This is why so many peasants in Andalusia and Estremadura became revolutionary Anarchists.

In Saracen times, Spain was a great industrial civilization. Now most of the heavy industry—iron, steel, and shipbuilding—is concentrated around Bilbao in the Basque country. Catalonia is a great textile producer, but an inefficient one, protected by high tariff walls. There are valuable mineral resources, some of them dating back to pre-Roman days: tin, copper, wolframite, iron, and coal.

All these were to play a vital role in the Civil War, for Spain's minerals were coveted and developed by foreigners, mostly the British and French in modern times. The Spaniards, themselves, did not have the temperament. Economic liberalism never took root in Spain, nor private enterprise, nor modern capitalistic civilization. Spaniards, at least until recently, did not want them. They are not a race seeking money, wealth, or personal success; they are suspicious of get-rich-quick men and their philosophy. Compared to the rest of Western Europe, their businessmen and bankers lack enterprise. They have not, on the whole, adapted themselves to modern industrialism. The factory did not become rooted, or merged, into the Spanish community. It was something strange or hostile. "The famous individualism of the race," the British Hispanologist, Gerald Brenan, pointed out, "does not apply to economics." He believes that "liberalism failed in Spain because Spaniards are essentially anti-capitalist and uncompetitive."

From the turn of the century to the Civil War, strikes were often drowned in blood, thereby exacerbating the class struggle while the employers and landowners usually "won." Economics, like every other element in Spanish society, pointed toward revolutionary strife. Yet Spain was always outside the ferment of the revolutions, new ideas, and progressive changes in social life and political institutions which followed the Reformation, the Enlightenment, the French Revolution, and the Industrial Revolution in other parts of Europe.

Divisions between the working and ruling classes were more than just social and economic gaps which could be closed, as in the rest of Europe, by a vertical mobility; they were barriers which could not be crossed. The people took no part in politics for centuries. Where there was not indifference, there was a complete distrust of government. There was no grass roots growth of liberty and democracy as there was in England; no social revolution as in France; no Reformation to liberalize the church. Traditional forces—monarchy, bureaucracy, church, army, landowning aristocracy—retained their control. As late as 1931, when the Second Republic was proclaimed, it is estimated that no more than a few million of the population of twenty-six million could be called middle class. The vast majority of Spaniards were poor, illiterate peasants and workers. The peasant villagers, especially, lived a primitive, church-ridden, priest-ridden existence in poverty, ignorance, and fear. To other Europeans they seemed medieval, still unabsorbed into the twentieth century.

Yet every foreigner who has known and studied Spain—and Spanish scholars and sociologists, too—agree that the virtues of the Spanish race are to be found in the people, *el pueblo*. Spain is not a country whose best men, in the moral and spiritual sense, come to the top to form an élite ruling class. No government since Napoleonic times had the support of the people until they rallied to the Second Republic in 1936; none has really been an expression of the aspirations of the ordinary Spaniard—not even the Second Republic. All governments, even Generalissimo Franco's, have operated on the surface of Spanish life. It was the unique feat of the Spanish Anarchists to reach the depths where the true soul of Spain lay seething, but they would have caused a tidal wave that would have destroyed everything. They asked the impossible of life. The individual in Spain is always at war with society. He was anarchistic before modern political and ideological Anarchism was invented.

It is paradoxical, but true, that in a human sense no race in Europe is, by character, so profoundly egalitarian. Before 1700 (when the Bourbon dynasty came in) Spanish society was even socially egalitarian, without strong class distinctions. A tradesman or a beggar considered himself the equal of a grandee in his worth as a man. The Spaniard's pride, dignity, and independence of character are a heritage from the early Middle Ages and the struggle to oust the Moors. These characteristics never did—and do not today—mean that Spanish institutions, such as government, army, and church, cannot be tyrannical. But then, at some intolerable point, the wrath of the people will be terrible. The masses rise in irresistible fury and carry everything before them. Then the blaze subsides and Spain goes back to inertia and apathy. (This unique propensity to calm down after a tremendous surge of energy, incidentally, helps to explain the decades of internal peace under General Franco after the Civil War.)

The Spanish historian, Ramón Menéndez Pidal, wrote of "an element of instinctive stoicism" in the people. "Austerity is the basic quality of the Spanish character," he claimed. Even today the Spaniard contents himself with little. Seneca, who was Spanish and who has always been the favorite author of Spanish philosophical thinkers, held that contented poverty was not poverty. But every now and then the Spanish people do become discontented and, when they do, they tear their country apart.

The *Siglo de Oro*—the golden sixteenth century—remains embedded in the Spanish ethos. It has left a nostalgia, a yearning to return to that age of glory which shows itself in a certain pride and arrogance. Spanish nationalism has more than a touch of xenophobia.

"At that time," wrote Menéndez Pidal of the reign of the Emperor Charles V (1500–1558), "the history of Spain became the history of the universe in the old world as well as the new."

Charles V failed in achieving European spiritual unity, which to him meant to destroy Protestantism. He and Spain began an attitude of still unended isolationism. Philip II, his son, returned to Spanish tradition, except for the Lowlands, shutting out continental Europe. Intolerance took exaggerated form. The Duke of Alva, who devastated Flanders for Philip, was a typical Spaniard. One can imagine his famous justification being used, with minor changes, in the recent Civil War: "It is far better to preserve by war for God and the King a Kingdom that is impoverished and even ruined than, without the war, preserve it for the benefit of the devil, and the heretics, his disciples."

In the year 711, one of the warring factions of Visigoth nobility invited Mohammedans across from Africa to help it against its enemies. In a few years, the Saracens had overrun the peninsula. It took eight centuries to get them out.

There were periods of tolerance when Christian, Moslem, and Jew lived in harmony and mutual respect and when Spain was the most culturally advanced nation of Europe. The Catholic monarchs Ferdinand and Isabella ended this. The year 1492 was not only historic for the discovery of America. The same monarchs who financed Columbus expelled the Moors and the

Jews from Spain—or forced their conversion to Catholicism. There were about 200,000 Jews in Spain: financiers, diplomats, government officials, scientists, literati, merchants, and craftsmen. The British historian Hugh Trevor-Roper wrote that Jews were so influential in Spain in the Middle Ages that, "to Erasmus, the whole peninsula seemed to have become a Jewish colony." The Sephardi communities around the world still testify to the persistence of the Iberian heritage.

The *Reconquista* was a fierce and intolerant crusade against any kind of heterodoxy. The Holy See's new system of the Inquisition then set the final seal on the period of religious tolerance. Culturally and economically, Spain never recovered, but it is characteristic of the Spanish temperament that this did not matter. The Moors, incidentally, did not return to Spain until General Franco brought them back. The Jews never did return.

From Ferdinand and Isabella to Napoleon, the monarchy was a centralizing, solidifying national institution. When that most despicable of monarchs, King Ferdinand VII, died in 1833, Spain had the first of its three modern civil wars, this one lasting seven years. Ostensibly, it was a struggle for the succession—whether his daughter Isabella should ascend the throne or whether the male line, headed by Ferdinand's brother, Carlos de Borbón, should succeed.

But there was a deeper question involved which led straight into the 1936–1939 Civil War. It was whether the Catholic, traditional, agrarian, and centralized rule of the past centuries should continue, or whether the great issues which the French Revolution had resolved for France and for much of the Western world should be accepted—a capitalist industrialism, a strong but relatively liberal democratic government, civic freedoms of press, speech, and meeting, liberal universities free of church control, freedom of worship, separation of church and state, the division of the landed properties. Unhappily for Spain, this tug of war was not—and has not to this day—been settled in favor of either side. The struggle went on through succeeding generations, as it will after Generalissimo Francisco Franco dies.

The golden age is truly and forever gone. One of Spain's modern philosophers, José Ortega y Gasset, put it in poignant words: "Spain wasted away. Today we are like a cloud of dust in the air after a great people has galloped down the highway of history."

The conquest of the New World was the first great wave of European imperialism since Roman times. "The Spaniards," Menéndez Pidal wrote, "needed no more than the short space of fifty years to discover the lands and oceans forming an entire hemisphere of our planet; to explore, subdue and civilize immense territories, subjugating thousands of tribes and vast barbarian empires. Any other people less hardened to privations and risks would have needed five centuries, for they would have found it necessary to plan out their enterprises so as to reduce to the minimum the discomforts of the unfavorable contingencies. It took Rome 200 years to dominate the barbarian tribes of Spain alone."

However, Menéndez Pidal, like all students of Spanish history, noted that the moments of intensity came only at long intervals. The normal climate is one of apathy, an imperturbable tranquillity and calmness of mind noted by foreign visitors to Spain since the *Siglo de Oro*. Philip II's ministers, in the phlegmatic Madrid society of the time, were nicknamed Ministers of Eternity because of the slowness and delays of the Spanish officials in negotiating. Hitler and Mussolini, during World War II, found these same attributes in Generalissimo Franco, much to their dismay.

It is partly that no Spaniard believes he has anything to learn from foreign peoples. He tends to think that his opinion is the only possible correct one. However, he finds that other Spaniards differ from him. A disagreement degenerates into a vehement, irreconcilable contest of wills. Each side seeks a clear-cut solution. As Ortega y Gasset pointed out, there is no single organ of national life which can impose civic spirit, no "enlightened minorities" capable of leading the masses who, in Spain, are so refractory to discipline. This produces what he called, in a pungent book, *Invertebrate Spain*.

In our time we have seen examples in Spain of both a marvelous and a terrible burst of energy—the Civil War—and, since 1939, Franco's "Invertebrate Spain."

The blaze of glory in the golden century was magnificent, but it was debilitating. When her great empire in Latin America dissolved in revolution early in the nineteenth century and the last links—Cuba, Puerto Rico, the Philippines, and Guam— were lost in 1898, Spain was driven in on herself. Curiously, the process brought a great flowering of culture, which was not to wither until the dead hand of the Franco regime's censorship swept it away, but the shock of the Spanish-American War turned Spanish energies and frustrations inward. Dr. Franz Borkenau's description of Spain at that time (*The Spanish Cockpit*) is apt:

> In the upper stratum: decay, corruption, political in-capacity, as well as complete lack of creative power in any other respect. Below: fanaticism, capacity for self-sacrifice, spontaneity of action in a narrow, local prejudiced sense, without constructive capacities on a wider scale. Such was the structure of Spain at the beginning of the nineteenth century and such it has remained to this day [1937]. . . . Such a deep severance of the people from ruling groups, such a passing of the initiative to the lowest stratum of society, is always a symptom of deep decay and disintegration of an old civilization.

Nowhere were the extremes of passion, the fervor, the love, the hatred, and what has been called "the outbreak of pure unreason" shown more clearly than in the Roman Catholic Church of Spain and its relations to the people. There has been nothing comparable in the world of religion. Since the reign of Ferdinand and Isabella, the Spanish church has been more papist than the Pope, more orthodox than the Holy See. Church history in Spain is one of authoritarianism, intolerance, con-servatism, imperviousness to progress. Only today is the pic-ture changing.

As with so many aspects of Spanish life, the religious prob-lem came to a climax in the Civil War, but it was not solved, any more than was any other deep-rooted Spanish problem.

It is hard for foreigners to grasp how profoundly Catholicism enters into every personal life and every aspect of Spanish existence. This is true whether the individual is a fervent Catholic or a fervent anticlerical. Spain is officially more than 99 per cent Roman Catholic. Unlike Latin American countries, where so many priests are foreigners, the clergy of Spain is Spanish. The church has truly been called "the embodiment of the Spanish nature." For a millennium it was, after the monarchy, the most important of Spanish institutions; it was a state within a state. "Sancho," Don Quixote said to his faithful companion, "we have come up against the Church."

The Inquisition was a great national power only in Spain. It was not abolished until 1810. The last victim of the Inquisition was an old woman, burned at the stake in 1781 "for having carnal converse with the Devil and laying eggs that had prophecies written on them." As late as 1900, the Carlists of Navarre wanted to revive the Inquisition.

Yet until about 1700, when the Bourbons came in, the church was a popular national institution. It then became an appendage of the monarchy and aristocracy, always opposing the state when it wanted to make reforms or to encroach on the wealth and privileges of the church.

St. Ignatius of Loyola founded the Society of Jesus in 1533 to save and protect the church at a difficult and corrupt period and he did so by cultivating and winning over the rich and powerful. The Spanish Jesuits became immensely wealthy, with great interests abroad. Before the Republican revolution of 1931, the Society of Jesus was estimated to control one-third of the wealth of Spain. It was no longer in landed property, for the Society's Spanish land holdings had been confiscated in 1837. This meant that church properties were in banks, businesses of all kinds, real estate, utilities, stocks and bonds. It also meant that, being capitalists, the church hierarchy was naturally tied to the lay capitalists and, by the same token, were considered class opponents of the workers and peasants. The church (and especially the Jesuits) had been gaining in wealth and political power for more than fifty years before the Republican revolution. Holdings were always under cover names—

straw men—so that no one knew exactly how much the Society of Jesus had, but it certainly was the greatest capitalist in Spain. Spaniards say, *"El dinero es muy católico"* ("Money is very Catholic").

The village priests, on the other hand, were close to the people and as poorly paid as their poverty-stricken parishioners. They were usually badly educated, but they had a deserved reputation for honesty and devotion. In the Civil War, village priests, or parish priests in poor sections of the cities, were rarely killed unless they took sides openly with the rightists or "Fascists."

The Second Republic, contrary to popular belief, did not expel the Jesuits, as they had often been expelled in Spain, France, and Italy in the eighteenth and nineteenth centuries. Under Article 26 of the Republican Constitution of 1932, the Jesuit Order was dissolved and its property sequestrated. Franco restored the properties and privileges as quickly as he could. On March 22, 1938, before the Civil War ended, the Caudillo issued a decree turning the clock back to the days of the monarchy. After that, incidentally, Spanish Protestants were more restricted in Nationalist Spain than Catholic priests had been in Republican Spain.

The nation had a history of antichurch violence which long antedated the Civil War. Burning of churches and convents and the killing of priests and monks occurred in all the large towns of Spain in 1835. During Barcelona's *Semana Trágica,* the "Tragic Week" in July 1909, one-third of the city's churches and monasteries were burned by the people.

Yet, Azaña's sensational remark in the Cortes on October 13, 1931, that Spain had "ceased to be Catholic" was wrong. Spain *was* Catholic, but hardly one-third of the Spaniards were *practicing* Catholics, and of that third, the majority would have been women.

Spanish liberals had been in conflict with the church since a Liberal party was formed in the Cádiz Cortes of 1810. In fact, the word "liberal" and the philosophy of liberalism came out of the Spain of that time. The struggle became acute after 1900, for the church had become stronger and wealthier in the three previous decades. The main conflict was over education. Priests, monks, and nuns did most of the teaching. The church feared the effects of learning, especially after the French Revolution, so science, mathematics, political economy, and even history were banned except for trained theologians. Law, commerce, and medicine, and subjects like physics and engineering were considered safe. Gerald Brenan cites a famous address to King Ferdinand VII from the only university in Catalonia: "Far be it from us the dangerous novelty of thinking." When the Liberals took power after 1836, they changed this in the lay state schools, but governments had no resources to compete with church teaching. Spanish education is still the most backward and inadequate, and her illiteracy the highest in Western Europe.

The sharpest struggle centered in the elementary schools, because the church had previously prevented the poor from even learning to read. Until 1910, most teaching was on religion by the religious. As late as 1927, the church catechism asked: "What kind of sin is Liberalism?" Answer: "It is a most grievous sin against faith." The catechism added that liberalism was "a collection of heresies," and that to vote for a Liberal was "generally a mortal sin."

This was the attitude of the hierarchy four years later when the Second Republic began. In considering the antiliberalism of a Spaniard like Generalissimo Franco, one must keep in mind this long struggle, and the equating of liberalism by the church with sin. There was no middle ground, no meeting place for the moderates within the church and among laymen. The hierarchy and its enemies were both fanatical.

One reason "Europe ended at the Pyrenees" was that the church opposed European culture and parliamentarianism. Unhappily, the hierarchy condoned corruption, injustice, and oppression in and by the ruling classes. The people saw a negation of Christian morality in the Spanish church—and they were right, even though innumerable priests, monks, and nuns of the lower orders led exemplary, self-sacrificing lives.

Spaniards would cease to practice their faith. In many churches of rural Spain, priests had to say mass alone, or with a few parishioners in attendance. Marxism had nothing to do with this phenomenon. Socialism, Anarchism, and Communism simply made anticlericalism more violent, as it made the hierarchy more certain of the wickedness and heresies of its opponents.

The attacks against the church in the Civil War were a result, not a cause, of this religious situation. And it was a situation that could have come about only in Spain. The church there was, and is, a *Spanish* institution, not simply a Roman Catholic religious community dedicated to universal moral and doctrinal principles. The hatred of the fanatical Spanish anticlerical is that of an outraged son who feels betrayed and brutally treated by the father who should cherish and support him.

"At no time in the history of Europe or even perhaps the world," writes Hugh Thomas of the beginning of the Civil War, "has so passionate a hatred of religion and all its works been shown." I would make a distinction. The hatred was not against religion; it was against the Spanish church and the clergy as a social, political, and economic force. It is rare for Spaniards— even Communists and Anarchists—to be antireligious, or to be atheists, all their adult lives. *La Pasionaria* was typical. She ceased to be a practicing Catholic, but she did not cease to be a religious woman.

The Spanish church was innocent of any connivance in the generals' rebellion. The many reports of firing from churches were certainly false, except for some isolated cases in Navarre.

Nothing excuses the orgy of slaughter and arson on the Republican side when the war began. However, the Loyalist record, taking the war as a whole, was not as bad as it was painted, nor was the Nationalist record as good. The "fog of war" clouded what really happened—which was bad enough. All fifty-eight churches in Barcelona, for instance, were burned more or less completely. So were churches in all the *pueblos* of Catalonia.

Virtually all the executions of priests, monks, and nuns, and the church burnings in the Republican zone, took place in the first three months of the war. They were the work of maddened, passionately aroused peasants and workers and militiamen from left-wing political parties and unions, often formed into gangs. The reasons were never pillage; the churches and the clergy were seen as class enemies allied to those who had rebelled against the Republic.

It was significant that the few Protestant chapels and pastors in Spain were not touched and continued their ministrations in the Loyalist zone. In a joint letter published by 150 American Protestant clergymen, educators, and laymen in September 1937, it was alleged, among other things, that Catholic priests and nuns had been murdered by Nationalists, and that the Insurgents had destroyed Protestant missions. It is also on record that Generalissimo Franco had some Basque priests executed for treason.

It is a blot on the church's record in the Civil War that, so far as is known, the hierarchy made no objections to the "necessity" of the blood purge which went on uninterruptedly in the Nationalist zone. Certainly, there was no open criticism. High churchmen always appeared in public with Insurgent leaders and attended their ceremonies.

In September 1971 there was a dramatic augury of change. The majority of an assembly of Roman Catholic bishops and priests from all over Spain voted for a resolution which said: "We humbly recognize, and ask pardon for it, that we failed at the proper time to be ministers of reconciliation in the midst of our people, divided by a war between brothers." Only 78 of the 94 bishops and 151 priests from all the country's dioceses, presided over by the Cardinal Primate of Spain, Enrique Tarancón, voted against the resolution.

Ironically, as Professor Gabriel Jackson of the University of California wrote, the sadistic, secretly working Loyalist police organization, the *Servicio de Inteligencia Militar* (SIM) had a bright spot in its generally black record. "The SIM employed torture against the political enemies of the Communists, but it also protected some 2,000 priests who were conducting private services in Barcelona homes." Jackson says of the year 1938, "I learned from private Catholic sources that the SIM protected these priests."

It is curious that parish priests who escaped to France did not go back. There were no known Spanish martyrs, as in the French Revolution, and few cases of heroic self-sacrifice at a time when their flocks were fighting and dying for secular beliefs.

There has been abundant documentation and evidence since the Civil War to bear out what the Republican authorities—and we foreign journalists—said about the government's attitude toward the church and religion. Priests who survived the first ghastly explosion of killing were left unmolested in the Loyalist zone, but they could not wear cassocks or say Mass or prayers in churches. Hundreds practiced their calling in private homes.

Life or death generally depended on whether they had been friendly, honest, and sincere with the poor of their parishes, and not solely with the rich. However, in the confusion and passion of those early months, many a worthy priest was slain simply because he wore a cassock.

When Dr. Juan Negrín was Premier, he tried on several occasions to induce the Vatican to open some churches and permit public worship, but he was rebuffed. The Republican government, through its ambassador in Washington, Fernando de los Ríos, invited a mixed commission of American Catholics and Protestants to visit both warring camps in Spain so that "the whole question could be objectively clarified." A spokesman for the Protestant communities expressed a willingness to join such a commission, but the invitation was ignored by the Roman Catholic hierarchy. A second invitation toward the end of the war was rejected outright by a Catholic spokesman.

In Catalonia, Jackson writes, some bishops and the Cardinal Archbishop of Tarragona, Vidal y Baraquer, were saved and sent to France by the *Generalitat* (the provisional government). Vidal y Baraquer wanted to return, but the Vatican refused to let him do so.

The Holy See was always embarrassed by the moves taken in the Republican zone to re-establish religious practices, perhaps because this would have confused the black and white picture which was being drawn. Two months after the war began Pope Pius XI referred to the Republicans' "truly Satanic hatred of God." However, he refused Franco's request to condemn the Basques publicly. In fact, Pius complained of the execution of Basque priests by the Rebel troops. The Basques were among the most devoted church-going groups in Spain. The Vatican, incidentally, was one of the first states (August 28, 1937) formally to recognize the Burgos junta as the official government of Spain. An apostolic delegate was appointed.

Before the war, General Franco was not an especially religious man. Some say that he was even anticlerical in his youth. It was a bit out of character for him suddenly to assume the mantle of a paladin of Christianity leading a crusade against atheistic Communism. The Nationalists needed the help which naturally came to them from the church, and they cultivated this source of support. The Falangists (a militant Fascist organization) also suddenly displayed a religious fervor which they had never shown before.

The church was richly repaid. As the Insurgents moved along, religious teaching was resumed, properties restored, churches rebuilt, divorces and civil marriages annuled, censorship by the clergy of all forms of culture restored, and open worship by Protestants banned. (This is still the situation in 1972.)

Freemasonry again became the worst "heresy" of all—worse, if possible, than Communism. Masonry, in Europe, has been a political, not a social, organization as it is in the United States. In Spain it was always "freethinking" and anticlerical. During much of the nineteenth century it was the instrument through which the liberal and revolutionary middle classes and also the anticlerical conservatives worked. The Jesuits were always its fiercest enemies. Franco, to this day, has shown a greater antagonism toward Masonry than toward Protestantism or liberalism. At the beginning of the Civil War, the church hierarchy reacted as if the Insurgents were, above all things, fighting Freemasonry. "Our victory," said Franco in a speech at Burgos on February 27, 1939, as the war was ending, "has not been over our brothers, but over the world, over international forces, over Freemasonry."

The Nationalist victory was, of course, accepted by the Roman Catholic Church as a victory for the faith. The triumphant Franco received a cable from Pope Pius XII: "Lifting up our hearts to God, we give sincere thanks with your Excellency for Spain's Catholic victory."

Gerald Brenan believes that "without going far wrong one may say that all the churches recently [1936] burned in Spain were burned by Anarchists and that most of the priests were killed by them." He suggests that "the anger of the Spanish Anarchists against the church is the anger of an intensely religious people who felt they have been deserted and deceived." Such emotions, like love and hate, lie close together in the human heart. When what the Scriptures say is taken literally —that the rich are wicked and damned, and the poor blessed— the result can be revolutionary.

The Anarchist creed combined humanity, generosity, and self-sacrifice, with hatred toward the church and violence toward landowners and industrialists. To most Spaniards and all foreigners the idealism was dangerous and wholly impractical, but to half-starved peasants and oppressed town workers it held the promise of a better and more just life, and they believed in it passionately.

Spanish Anarchism was a remarkable exhibition of a people's revulsion against the tyranny of the modern machine age. Anarchists valued freedom more than wealth. Nowhere but in Spain could this have happened, at least in such a form. Perhaps there is some link between this sort of popular rebellion and the present-day type of popular worldwide revolt of youth against the Establishment. If so, Anarchism had a message for our times, but if the world profited, the Spanish *pueblo* lost, for the Anarcho-Syndicalists were rejected by the Republic and crushed by the Franco dictatorship.

The founder of Anarchism was a Russian aristocrat named Mikhail Bakunin. Some of his followers came to Spain in December 1868, and the movement caught on quickly. By 1873 (Bakunin had split with Marx in 1871) there were 50,000 Anarchists in Spain; by 1900 a million. Anarchism became a uniquely Spanish phenomenon. No modern ideology has had such an appeal to the Spanish character. This was tragic, because Anarchism is a hopelessly impractical political ideal. It begins with that most pathetically noble of all beliefs—that men are essentially good. Such being the case, the individual must be sovereign. This is one reason why the individualistic Spaniard found Anarchism so attractive. The goal is the freedom of the individual, or "libertarianism" as the Anarchists call it. Therefore, any and every source of repression, especially the "unholy trinity" of state, church, and capital, must be fought. Army and police are enemies, being organs of the state.

Confederations of free communes or municipal councils provide voluntary instruments of government. The forces of production are harnessed through economic planning. In its extreme form, Anarchism abolishes money. While Socialism and Communism say "Each one gives according to his capacities and receives according to his needs," Anarchism says "Each one gives and takes what he wants, and that presupposes abundance and love."

Theoretically, Anarchism "abhors violence," but since all government is oppressive and since capitalism exploits the worker, they represent forms of organized violence which can only be overcome by counterviolence. The Italian Anarchist, Enrico Malatesta, who had his greatest following in Spain, prophesied that in the day of revolution "popular vengeance is terrible and inexorable," but "terror is a danger that brings out the worst and least responsible elements." It did just that in Spain.

The Spanish tradition of village communities and regional

autonomy, the passionately religious Spanish character, the easy resort to violence, the self-sacrificing fervor of teachers and students preaching puritanism and carrying the rudiments of learning from village to village, the self-imposed discipline, the crusading idealism, and the fanatical bravery—where but in Spain could all these characteristics rise naturally from the race? Anarchism was like a language that only Spaniards could learn and speak.

The reaction to Anarchism was also typically Spanish in its cruel, sweeping ruthlessness. The authorities were like the clergy of the Inquisition, destroying heretics in the name of Christian law and order.

If the Anarchists had been less simple, less ignorant of the world, and less desperate, they would not have believed that they could build a new Jerusalem through assassination or the general strike, which was being so persuasively preached early in the century by Georges Sorel in France. Always, the enemies were the priest, the landlord, and the official. Three Prime Ministers were assassinated in twenty-five years: Cánovas in 1897, Canalejas in 1912, and Dato in 1921. The Anarchist movement became indelibly stamped as terrorist, although it always had a moderate wing in the syndicates which were developed early in the twentieth century. They were what we call vertical trade unions. The movement became known as Anarcho-Syndicalism.

The authorities, the middle class, the church, and the military lived in fear of, or anger against, Anarchist violence, but their excessively merciless repression brought a new and compulsive violence of despair in reaction. The historic symbol of the terror was the already mentioned Tragic Week in Barcelona in 1909, which was part of an insurrection and general strike. One outcome of its failure was the formation in 1911 of a nationwide Anarchist federation, the *Confederación Nacional de Trabajo* (CNT). It became the one genuinely revolutionary trade organization of large size in the world. It was not a trade union in the ordinary sense. There were no funds. Leaders were never paid, not even by 1936 when it had a million members. Its tactic was short and violent strikes and it often won in Catalonia, so much so that Catalan workers were the best paid in Spain.

Believers in the revolutionary general strike and terrorism won dominance of the movement after World War I. The CNT was too reformist and moderate for them. A more militant wing formed a secret society in 1927 called the *Federación Anarquista Ibérica* (FAI). The dictator, General Miguel Primo de Rivera, had driven the Anarchists underground. The FAI became the élite of the Anarchist movement, the purists who put revolution before all else, and even, for a long time during the Civil War, before the task of defeating the military rebellion. The FAI had a mixture of idealists and potential—or real—criminals.

Bakunin had argued that if the people have the spirit and decisiveness, a social revolution is possible at any time. This was the mentality of the Spanish Anarchists and it put them often in deadly conflict with the Socialists and Communists. The Communist *chekas* killed more Anarchists than they did Insurgents. A moderate Anarchist wing very reluctantly and half-heartedly entered the Madrid government in November 1936, and Anarchists later supported Dr. Negrín but they were never as good or as disciplined troops as the Communists, and in the end, as has been seen, it was an Anarchist division that sealed the fate of the last resistance in Madrid. Nothing was more disrupting to the Loyalist cause than the Anarchists' combination of high morality and high criminality, and all of it aimed more at making a revolution than fighting a war.

There was a species of "original sin" involved; something in the Spanish character which made the ruling classes and the people embrace extremes of religiosity and anticlericalism, of dictatorship and anarchy, of ruthlessly imposed order and revolutionary violence. Spain was "a house divided"; it was bound to fall.

It has been calculated that in the century and a half after the Napoleonic Wars, Spain had 109 governments, 24 revolutions, and three civil wars. There is a famous passage in Richard

Ford's *Gatherings from Spain,* published in 1846, which is forever apt:

> When Ferdinand III [thirteenth-century king of Castile] captured Seville and died, being a saint he escaped Purgatory, and Santiago presented him to the Virgin, who forthwith desired him to ask any favors for beloved Spain. The Monarch petitioned for oil, wine and corn—conceded; for sunny skies, brave men and pretty women—allowed; for cigars, relics, garlic and bulls—by all means; for a good government—"Nay, nay," said the Virgin, "that can never be granted; for were it bestowed, not an angel would remain a day longer in heaven."

3

THE SECOND REPUBLIC

A CONSTITUTIONAL STRUCTURE HAD TO BE created out of a vacuum in 1931 when the monarchy was overthrown. There was nothing in the historic background to provide material or guidance to make a viable Second Republic. Good government remained a will-o'-the-wisp.

For thirty-five years after Ferdinand VII's death in 1833 there was an uninterrupted series of military *pronunciamientos*—palace revolts in which one general succeeded another while the people hardly knew and did not care. The monarch was the weak, frivolous, lascivious Queen Isabella II. In 1870, Spaniards called in a liberal Italian prince, Amadeo of Savoy, the Duke of Aosta, who was the king of Italy's brother. He lasted three years. In 1873, a First Spanish Republic was tried, which had four presidents in less than a year. Finally, in December, 1874, Antonio Cánovas del Castillo, a conservative statesman, engineered another *pronunciamiento* to bring back a constitutional monarchy under the same Bourbons—King Alfonso XII.

The Constitution of 1876 established an elected Cortes with all sorts of democratic freedoms—on paper. Popular elections were meaningless because of limited suffrage and manipulated counting. Rural politics were controlled by *caciques* (bosses) acting for the landowners. Conservatives and Liberals alternated in power by mutual consent.

The next monarch, King Alfonso XIII, literally inherited this state of affairs before he was born, when his father died in 1885. His mother, María Cristina, acted as regent until 1902. King

Alfonso was a cynical, clever, selfish ruler who was rightly held responsible for the modern Spanish Army's worst disaster. The territorial gains of twelve years of campaigning in Morocco were lost at Anual in the summer of 1921 in two battles against the Riffs. Seventeen thousand soldiers were killed. The king had ordered the campaign over the heads of his cabinet ministers.

He temporarily saved himself by permitting a military coup in which the captain general of Catalonia, Miguel Primo de Rivera, proclaimed himself dictator in 1923. Primo gave Spain a peaceful interlude for seven years. His dictatorship was popular for a while, thanks largely to the economic boom which followed World War I, but Spain, like so many other countries, was extravagant and over-optimistic. The Minister of Finance was young and inexperienced. His name was a fateful one— José Calvo Sotelo, whose murder was the signal for the Civil War.

Primo de Rivera was an example of power corrupting. His promises of civic liberties proved meaningless. His bohemian, intemperate behavior and his lack of understanding were at first amusing, but in the long run intolerable.

The worldwide depression began. In the end Primo had no friends and gave up in January 1930. He went to Paris, a bewildered and embittered old man, where intemperance and diabetes killed him off in a few months.

Because Primo de Rivera had seized power to save King Alfonso, his unpopularity embraced the monarchy and built up the opposition which was to sweep Alfonso off his throne. After vainly trying a number of expedients, the King decided to hold municipal elections on April 12, 1931, to test his support. Much to everyone's surprise—Socialists and Republicans included— the results were overwhelmingly unfavorable to the monarchy in almost every city and town. The rural votes were still controlled for the landowners by the *caciques*. The city vote was free and honest, and its verdict was unmistakable.

When the army and Civil Guard officers withdrew their support, Alfonso had no choice but to abdicate. Ironically, a number of generals (Franco was one of them) who later led the 1936 rebellion would not defend the monarchy, perhaps scenting opportunities to get on top in the forthcoming Republic.

Republicanism had been an insignificant movement until 1930. The Second Republic was basically weak from the start. It had enemies on the Right—aristocracy, much of the bourgeoisie, and the church—and on the Left the Anarchists and Communists. Its chief support came from the moderate Socialists of the *Unión General de Trabajadores* (UGT), and the center radical intellectuals, who formed Republican parties. Most of the peasants and unorganized workers were apolitical.

The Republican leaders were good men with good intentions. If they had had their way, they would have given Spain a liberal democratic regime, but the government lacked strength and the people lacked unity. Yet, as elections for a Constituent Cortes in July 1931 proved, the government did have popular support. These were just about the fairest elections ever held in Spain. The results were a landslide victory for the two Republican parties and their Socialist allies. Many men of high quality and distinction were elected, among them Dr. Juan Negrín, who then made his entry into politics. The people showed that they did not want the monarchy back and that they did not want another military dictatorship.

The Second Republic began during the economic crisis following the depression, which started in the United States in 1929. The economic situation in Spain in 1931 was critical: high unemployment, low agricultural prices, poor wages. There was a flight of capital and distrust of the government in international financial circles. Measures to deal with economic crises which became common practice in the 1940's and 1950's were unknown then. Keynesian government interventions were labeled "Communism" when the Azaña regime tried them in 1931–1933. Politics, even more than economic factors, led to strikes and disorders. The historic gap between the wealthy few and the poverty-stricken masses was unbridgeable.

The vital need for agrarian reform was stubbornly blocked

by the landowning classes. Gerald Brenan and other historians rate this as "the most important single cause of the Civil War." There were relatively satisfactory conditions in parts of the north and along the eastern coast down to Valencia, where there were fertile smallholdings and a conservative peasantry. The trouble was in the almost feudal latifundia of Andalusia and Estremadura in the south, and the two Castiles in the center where peasants were thrown out of work if they agitated for higher wages or held "subversive" political ideas.

Rural misery made fertile ground for Anarchism. Landless, poverty-stricken peasants emigrated to industrial Catalonia, taking their Anarchism with them. The Republic's Agrarian Law of 1932 would have helped if it had been put fully into effect, but it never was. Even on paper, as Largo Caballero said, the reform was "an aspirin to cure appendicitis." Only about 50,000 peasants out of nearly a million received land.

The Constituent Cortes met in Madrid on July 14, 1931, and began drawing up a new Constitution, which was completed on December 9. It was the first—and so far the last—time in their history that Spaniards were granted democratic rights such as freedom of opinion, assembly, and religious worship, or that education was to a great extent taken away from the priests in a regime that separated church and state. It was this Constitution, drawn up by a legally and fairly elected Cortes, which gave the Second Republic the right to be considered democratic in its later struggle against a fascist-type military rebellion.

The democracy, however, was a gift from the government; it had no grass roots. The government that made the Constitution was a squabbling conglomeration of Socialists, Radical Socialists, Left and Radical Republicans, Federalists, Radicals, Progressives, Catalans, and Galicians.

Article 26 of the Constitution on the status of the Catholic Church alienated the hierarchy and practicing Catholics irretrievably. The church was subjected to general laws without special privileges. Church properties were confiscated. Religious orders, such as the Jesuits, were dissolved and barred from conducting educational activities. State subsidies for the clergy were ended (a most unwise blow against the poor parish priests). Civil marriage was permitted, divorce recognized, and cemeteries secularized. About a hundred churches and convents had been burned, adding that much more bitterness to the conflict. Pedro, Cardinal Segura, Archbishop of Toledo and Primate of Spain, issued a hostile pastoral letter on May 7, 1931, comparing the Second Republic to a Communist regime. More churches were burned on May 11. The government declared martial law the next day and the army had to restore order.

One of the first results of the draft Constitution was a political crisis. The Prime Minister, Niceto Alcalá Zamora, a conservative Republican lawyer and landowner, and the respected Minister of the Interior Miguel Maura, resigned. Alcalá Zamora accepted the post of President of the Republic, but the debates on the Constitution in the Cortes were highly emotional and helped to build up the antagonisms which were to split the country. There had to be a Constitution, but it did not have to be one which offended large sectors of the population and intensified the split between Left and Right. Moreover, it promised more than it could fulfill.

The new government was composed entirely of anticlericals, starting with Manuel Azaña, who became Prime Minister. Azaña was a literary figure, incorruptible, brilliant, and a fine orator, but he was also cold, arrogant, misanthropic, cynical, sectarian, and bitterly anticlerical—hardly the qualities required to pacify a turbulent nation. He was exceptionally ugly and sensitive about it, which some who knew him believed explained his abrasive character. His influence was divisive. He had intellectual, not physical, courage.

The government's power base was a combination of the Republican groups and the Socialists. The UGT swiftly grew to outnumber the Anarchist CNT and to become the largest trade union federation in Spanish history. The Socialist party also became the largest political grouping, although it was soon to split into warring factions. For the first two years of the Republic, the Socialists were evolutionary and legalistic. It was the Anarchists who resumed street murders and mob violence, especially in Catalonia.

The government replied by forming a new urban police force —*Guardias de Asalto,* the Assault Guards—and taking a strong line on public order. The rural constabulary, the hated Civil Guards, continued their brutal work. It was a bitter irony for the Republic to seem as harshly repressive as the monarchy. The government imposed censorship and filled the prisons. This, said the Centrist Republican Diego Martínez Barrio, was a regime of "mud, blood and tears."

There was a tragic incident at Castilblanco in Estremadura on December 31, 1931, where four Civil Guards were killed and their bodies hacked to pieces; even women joined in mutilating them. It was a collective crime, a primitive paroxysm of rage. The government seemed helpless. A year later in January 1933, an Anarchist uprising in Casas Viejas, Andalusia, was so brutally repressed that there was a nationwide wave of indignation against the government, from which it never recovered. Peasants and workers were outraged. There was an interminable series of strikes, with violence, sabotage, and clashes with the police. A revolutionary atmosphere was forming. The government, now discredited, resigned in September 1933, and new elections were called for November 19.

These, like the Constituent Cortes elections, were truly representative, with freedom of the press, assembly, and political discussion scrupulously honored. Moreover, they involved clearly understood national issues.

The new feature was the emergence of a clerical coalition, the *Confederación Española de Derechas Autónomas* (CEDA). Its leader, José María Gil Robles, a lawyer who headed a party called *Acción Popular,* sought to create a Christian Democratic movement of Social Catholicism, with the slogan of "Religion, Fatherland, Family, Order, Work and Property." There were two small, militant, antiliberal Monarchist parties—the Carlist *Tradicionalistas* and the pro-Alfonso *Renovación Española*. (Gil Robles, now an old man, is still, in 1972, a factor in Spanish politics as a tolerated "oppositionist" to Franco.)

The 1933 elections were a disaster for the Republican Left. The Republican parties were virtually wiped out and the Socialist representation halved. (The Anarchists, as usual, had abstained.) Women, who were voting for the first time, although the overwhelming majority were illiterate, followed priestly advice and voted for the CEDA.

No two authorities are in agreement as to how seats in the Cortes were to be gauged in any of the Second Republic's elections, and this was true of 1933. However, the general picture was clear. The Right won 185 to 190 seats, the Center 150 to 160 and the Left less than 100. Professor Payne gives Azaña's Republicans as five in one of his books and ten in another, but either way, Azaña had little left.

The CEDA won between 110 and 115 seats and became the largest party in the Cortes. In the next two years of the so-called Black Biennium the CEDA was the most powerful political group in Spain. However, it refused to endorse the Republican system. President Alcalá Zamora, in any event, distrusted Gil Robles. He opted for a minority Radical government under Alejandro Lerroux, a demagogic opportunist who promptly set about reversing much of what the previous government had done. He amnestied the political prisoners, reinstated military officers with full pay and arrears, returned the properties of the grandees and religious orders, repealed the separation of church and state, and abolished the divorce and civil marriage laws. In short, Lerroux turned the clock back, but his Black Biennium was a period of corruption, immobility, and frustration in the midst of violence. His government was so weak that there were ministerial crises almost every month. Except for unemployment, the economy improved in 1934 and 1935, but the driving force in Spain was ideology not economics. Largo Caballero—tragically for him and for Spain—turned to the Left and set about remodeling the Socialist party into a revolutionary movement. At the same time, extremists took over the

Socialist UGT. The Anarchist CNT always was extremist.

This was the year, 1933, in which Adolf Hitler rose to power in Germany.

The sensational publicity given to Communism and Anarchism in the Civil War has masked the fact that until 1937 Spain's largest and most important leftist party was the Socialist. Except for Manuel Azaña, whose political label was Republican, the dominant figures on the Loyalist side were at least nominally Socialist: Francisco Largo Caballero, Juan Negrín, and Indalecio Prieto. Their Socialism was not orthodox. Largo Caballero did not read Marx and Lenin until he had prison leisure in 1934. Negrín's adherence was purely intellectual; he never showed any interest in making Socialism a reality. Prieto, who was a wealthy man by the time of the Second Republic, never took his Marxism seriously.

The sincere ideologists were men like the late "grandfather" of Spanish Socialism, Pablo Iglesias, a typographer; some trade union leaders of whom the miner, Ramón González Peña, was a shining example; a few intellectuals like the saintly Professor Julián Besteiro and, of course, hundreds of thousands of workers and peasants. They may not have understood Marxism, but they believed in something called Socialism.

A Socialist party was not formed in Spain until 1879, and it was not until 1888 that a Socialist trade union confederation was created: the General Union of Workers (UGT), with headquarters in Madrid. It was unlike the Anarchist CNT organizationally, being formed of craft unions, not vertical industrial syndicates. Moreover, the Socialists were slow in trying to win over the peasantry, leaving the field for many years to the Anarchists. In the declining years of the monarchy, a Federation of Land Workers was formed which became a part of the UGT. The peasants, especially in the south, were an illiterate and primitive element, unsuited to gradualism.

Although the Socialist party devoted much effort to the education of the workers in *Casas del Pueblo,* there was no time, money, or organization to educate the peasants. In their simplicity, they were extremist. If the Socialist movement was to hold them, it would have to be as extremist as the Anarchists, which is what happened. In the first few years of the Republic, the Federation of Land Workers grew to 450,000 members. Since the whole UGT was about a million strong, the Land Workers naturally pulled the Socialist movement toward the Left.

Meanwhile, more and more university graduates and professional men were being drawn into the Socialist fold. Unhappily, the two elements—workers and intellectuals—were like oil and water. The Largo Caballeros and the Indalecio Prietos were social and political antagonists.

Theoretically, Spanish Socialism was in the line of European democracy or British Fabianism. Like them, it sought results in political action and parliament. It was never atheistic; in fact, a strong Catholic tradition influenced it, especially in Old Castile where liberalism and Anarchism were weak.

The right-wing Socialists were so moderate, legalistic, and nonmilitant—at least in theory—that they cooperated with the conservative military dictatorship of Primo de Rivera (1923–1930). While a narrow majority of the party voted to join the Third International (Comintern) in 1920, this was reversed the following year. Only a small minority group of young Socialists turned Communist in 1921.

This does not mean that as a Socialist movement the Spanish federation was weak or ineffective. From the time of their first bloody—and successful—strike of 1890, the Socialists were aggressive participants in Spain's constant labor unrest. No workers were tougher or more class conscious than the miners of the north or the railway workers.

At the time of the Republican Revolution in 1931 the party was still moderate, and so were its two rival leaders, Francisco Largo Caballero, the Madrid plasterer who had succeeded Pablo Iglesias in 1925, and Indalecio Prieto, one-time Bilbao newsboy who became a newspaper publisher. Prieto had been elected to the Cortes as a Socialist in 1919, where he proved to be an eloquent speaker and brilliant parliamentarian.

One of the many developments that contributed to the Republican defeat in the Civil War was that the two leaders and their followers went in different directions, splitting the Spanish Socialist movement and contributing greatly to the fatal lack of unity in the Loyalist camp. Prieto, who headed the party's executive committee, always remained a moderate; Largo Caballero turned to an extreme left, revolutionary position in 1933–1935, when the youth in the movement gave him the famous, but ludicrously unsuitable, label of the "Spanish Lenin."

Largo Caballero was driven into a revolutionary position by a mixture of muddle-headedness and the need to hold on to the peasants of the fast-growing Federation of Land Workers. They would not have understood reformism. Many more peasants would have been won by the Anarchists if they had been offered nothing but the promise of parliamentary reforms.

A paradoxical result was that the bulk of the Spanish Socialist movement found itself to the left of the Spanish Communists in the Civil War and more in tune with their traditional enemies, the Anarchists. From 1935 onward, the Communists embraced the bourgeois, democratic policies of the Popular Front.

The Socialist split became regional in July 1936, after the war began, when the Catalan Socialists and Stalinist Communists joined to create the *Partido Socialista Unificado de Cataluña* (PSUC). It was, incidentally, the first united party of Socialists and Communists formed in Europe. Since the Communists quickly assumed leadership, the PSUC was soon at odds with the revolutionary Socialists of Madrid and the south, deepening the general disunity.

Largo Caballero had many exemplary qualities. He was honest, decent, good-hearted, and a fine popular leader. But, alas, he was not very intelligent, nor a good administrator, nor did he ever achieve an understanding of military affairs. He always overestimated the strength and capabilities of the Spanish Socialist movement. Spain was not ready, economically, socially, or administratively for a Socialist government. As wartime Premier, Largo Caballero made an even more disastrous calculation—his belief that a social revolution could take place while a war for survival under desperate odds was being waged. While he was still Premier, he received some good advice from, of all people, Joseph Stalin, in a letter written September 21, 1936. Make an agrarian reform, Stalin wrote, reduce taxes, avoid confiscations, encourage trade, appease foreign capital, and work with the moderate Republicans in the government. The Premier had other ideas.

Spanish Socialism had its last fling under Largo Caballero. When he was ousted as Premier in May 1937, the Communists became the most important of the government parties even though another Socialist, Juan Negrín, took Largo Caballero's place. Negrín temporarily saved the party from extinction in 1937 and 1938, when he refused Communist pressure to merge the two parties. At first, Prieto was by his side but, as we have seen, the pessimism of the then Minister of Defense after the Insurgent breakthrough to the coast in the spring of 1938 led to his dismissal.

As a Socialist party, the movement ceased to function in Spain. Since 1939, it has had to work underground or in exile, but it is hard to conceive of a future democratic Spain without a Socialist movement. Anarchism remains impractical, and Communism never had a popular appeal in Spain. Communist strength in the Civil War was fortuitous, not natural.

The still-strong Socialists were the ones who deserved credit for one of the great proletarian uprisings of modern history. This was in October 1934, when the Asturian miners had a brief blaze of glory before being crushed in a bloody and cruel reprisal. It was one of the events that played a crucial role in the unfolding drama.

There had been an Anarchist uprising the previous December, but it was suppressed in four days without affecting the nation as a whole. The Anarchists, after all, were always potentially revolutionary by their very philosophy.

The 1934 uprising was aimed at preventing the CEDA from

joining the government after a political crisis on October 1. It was a nationwide plot which took the form of a series of unsuccessful general strikes and an abortive attempt by regionalists in Barcelona to establish a "Republic of Catalonia" within the federal Republic of Spain. There was also a planned uprising in Madrid which was a fiasco.

The order for the general strike was issued from Madrid on October 5. The miners alone were prepared. Asturias is a province of large-scale mining, heavy industry, and small farms. There had been great labor discontent and a militant social consciousness. Three-fourths of the workers were unionized— the highest proportion in Spain. While the uprising was overwhelmingly Socialist, the Anarcho-Syndicalists of Gijón joined in and so did the Communists after the uprising started.

The miners lived in isolation in narrow valleys running south from Oviedo. Their work was hard, dangerous, and ill-paid, and since they belonged, as all did, to left-wing unions, there was enmity between them and the police. They were tough and brave and, being without contact with the rest of Spain, could go on fighting long after the uprising had been suppressed elsewhere.

"As a revolutionary technique," the former Foreign Minister Álvarez del Vayo later wrote, "the revolt in Asturias was a model of timing, underground preparation, and fighting spirit. . . . In the space of two hours the workers seized the principal points of the mining valley, captured the Civil Guard Barracks . . . occupied the entire city of Oviedo and all the routes by which attempts might be made to bring in military reinforcements."

Gerald Brenan puts the number who fought at 70,000, of whom 60,000 were Socialists and the rest Communists and Anarchists. Professor Payne, whose accounts favor the government and Franco side, puts the figure at 30,000. The Lerroux government could not rely on the conscripts of its regular army to fight against men of their own working class. The unhappy decision which the cabinet took was to call on Generals Franco and Manuel Goded to direct the suppression of the uprising as they thought best. They advised the then Minister of War Diego Hidalgo to bring over the Foreign Legion *(Tercios)* and—for the first time since the reconquest of Spain ended in the fifteenth century—the Moorish *Regulares* from Africa.

There had been some atrocities from a small, primitive element among the miners, who probably murdered about forty civilians, some of them from personal vengeance. The principal victims, unhappily and shockingly, were twenty-nine priests. A number of churches were burned. These deeds were given lurid and greatly exaggerated publicity. There was ample evidence later that the great majority of the revolutionaries behaved humanely. Many priests and prisoners were saved from mob fury, but the murders, looting, and church burnings were what riveted attention.

The contest was unequal. Moors and *Tercios* took villages house by house, street by street, murdering and raping as they went along. Colonel Juan de Yagüe (who was to employ similar tactics in the Civil War) considered terror to be beneficial. General López Ochoa, an enlightened commander, did his best, in vain, to restrain the soldiers. It was all over by October 18—in Mieres, where it had started two weeks before.

An accurate picture of the Asturias uprising will never be obtained because of the passions aroused, the censorship that lasted for months, and the partisanship that colored every account—and which still colors the interpretations of historians. Gerald Brenan says that 3,000 revolutionaries were killed, Stanley G. Payne says 900—and both are careful scholars. Those Spaniards who conducted the slipshod investigations were, themselves, involved in the affair. Postwar Nationalist accounts are hopelessly biased.

The Spanish people knew little of what had happened until weeks afterward as personal accounts came in by word of mouth. The atrocities of the *Regulares* and Legionaries were then learned. As more weeks passed, the bestial tortures used in the prisons by Civil Guards gradually became known. But nothing was published in the censored press, and there was never any impartial documentation. This permits a hostile historian like Professor Payne to write that "concrete evidence" substantiating charges of extreme army and police ruthlessness was never presented. There were ample popular reports based on personal experiences or knowledge. It is a *reductio ad absurdum* of scholarship to demand "concrete evidence" when none was allowed. As Hugh Thomas wrote, there was "a terrible retribution."

The moderate Left, outside of the Asturias, condemned the revolt as mad and foolish. At first, the Lerroux government was praised, but when it lost control of its mercenary troops, and when the police also committed atrocities, including the torture of prisoners to extract confessions which were unbelievable, public opinion turned.

Gradually from 30,000 to 40,000 prisoners were tried all over Spain well into 1935, while the censorship continued. There was no impartial justice against the true culprits among the miners and the atrocities of the soldiers and police. Only left-wing revolutionaries and their Republican sympathizers were punished. Moderate public opinion was alienated. The Left and Left-Center were drawn together in what was to become the Popular Front. One odd result was that Azaña, who was arrested although he had nothing to do with the revolt, became the idol of the people. Largo Caballero was also unjustly imprisoned. The uprising saw the rise to fame and future prominence of the former miner and Socialist union leader, Ramón González Peña. He became Minister of Justice under Premier Negrín.

"Defeated armies are good schools," wrote Engels. Nothing like the Asturian revolt had been seen in Europe since the Paris Commune of 1871, which was also crushed with ferocity. During the Civil War, 1934 was referred to as "a preventive *putsch*." Like Dunkirk, it was a defeat that sowed the seeds of future victories. It was also a tragic portent for the Spanish people, for after the fears aroused among the rightists by the miners' revolt, and the retribution taken by the mercenary troops and police, a delayed fuse had been lit which was to explode two years later. The miners had shown the power of an aroused people, while the military had learned the ruthless way to re-store law and order and to retain them by terror.

The victory over the Asturian miners enhanced the reputa-tion of the military as the strongest power in the country. This was to prove fatal for the Second Republic. Thereafter, nearly all groups of the Center and Right competed for the army's favor. The anti-Republicans realized that only the army could provide the force needed to overthrow the Republic.

Premier Alejandro Lerroux, who headed the Radical party and now led a coalition with the right-wing, clerical CEDA, kept on good terms with the military. He tried to be pragmatic and moderate, but his regime was scandal-ridden and so weak that there were thirteen cabinet crises in twenty-five months. As has been stated, he reversed almost every major accom-plishment of the first two years of the Second Republic during his Black Biennium of 1933–1935. None of the sadly needed social reforms were made. Lerroux governed under a "state of alarm" which permitted censorship and other measures to maintain "public order." Yet it was a government that did not satisfy the Right and embittered the Left.

By the autumn of 1935 the Left had regained much of its strength. The brutal reprisals against the Asturian miners and the atrocities of the Civil and Assault Guards were now com-mon knowledge. The experience had united the forces of the Left before the famous Seventh Congress of the Comintern in Moscow during August 1935 made its historic tactical switch from "united front at the base" to "Popular anti-Fascist Front on the basis of the united proletarian front." *La Pasionaria* attended the meeting as one of the Spanish Communist repre-sentatives.

The name of *Frente Popular* was just about all that the Span-ish Communist party contributed to the Popular Front, which was hastily formed when Lerroux, on January 7, 1936, called for a general election to be held on February 16. The Commu-nists were numerically few at the time and their party was so weak that its support was not needed, but they had an international prestige and a domestically able and militant, if rather undistinguished, leadership.

The Popular Front pact of January 15, 1936, was made by Azaña's Republican Left, Diego Martínez Barrio's Republican Union, the Catalan *Esquerra* (Left), and the Socialists and Communists. The Anarchists, as a party, abstained, but many individual Anarchists must have voted for the Popular Front. The strongest unifying force was fear of "Fascism."

The Right was also fairly well united in a "National Front," although its leaders were at odds and the Monarchists were a discordant element. On both sides, the bitter memories of Asturias pervaded.

The Popular Front clearly won the elections of February 1936, although Nationalist historians were later to juggle the figures and claim fraud. It was recognized as a fair election at the time, especially the decisive first round. However, the popular vote was fairly close. The generally accepted figures were 4,700,000 for the Popular Front against 4,576,000 for their opponents. It is arguable that the Right and Center votes could have exceeded the Popular Front's, but there is no way in which the figures for the Right alone can be shown to exceed the Left's.

As with all Spanish elections, no two authorities agree on the results. Hugh Thomas's figures for seats in the Cortes are: Popular Front 278, National Front 134, Center 55. E. Allison Peers, in the same order, gave 256, 165, and 52. *The New York Times,* at the time of the election, gave 269, 132, and 72. Stanley G. Payne gives 271, 137, and 40. Gerald Brenan gave the Popular Front 256 and the National Front 165.

Whichever of these figures are picked, there is no disputing the victory of the Popular Front. The difference between the narrow popular margin and the wide pro-leftist margin in the Cortes was due to the fact that, under the electoral law, 80 per cent of the seats went to any list getting more than 50 per cent of the votes in an electoral district. The Socialists and Republicans, being united, did better than their opponents. These two parties held the largest number of seats in the Front. According to whose figures one prefers, the Socialists could muster between 84 and 99 seats and the Republican Left between 87 and 117.

The Communists won only 16 seats (Thomas gives 17). This was four times more than their popular vote warranted. They could also count on five members from Catalan Marxist parties.

The CEDA emerged with much the largest representation on the Right—86 to 98 seats. The Falangists did not elect a single member.

This was the last democratic election held in Spain; there has been none during the Franco regime. In theory, it seemed a vote for moderation and parliamentarianism. Nine and a half million people had voted out of a population of at most twenty-six millions—the highest proportion of voters in Spanish history. However, there was an ominous feature—the great drop in the Center vote. The nation was polarized into two almost equal antagonistic factions. The Popular Front triumphed in nearly all the large urban and industrial centers, in working-class districts, among poor or landless peasants (unlike 1931), and in nearly all the coastal provinces. The Right won in Navarre, León, Castile, and half of Aragon (where there was high literacy and a large Catholic lower middle class of smallholders). Catalonia and the Levant, although they possessed a middle class, voted Left. The Basques voted Center.

The Right had expected to win and there were many rumors of a coup. Prime Minister Manuel Portela Valladares resigned in fright. President Alcalá Zamora called on a reluctant Manuel Azaña to take his place. He came up with a cautious cabinet and a modest program: amnesty for the political prisoners, autonomy for Catalonia, no socialization. "We want no dangerous innovations," Azaña said. "We want peace and order. We are moderate."

Alas! They may have been, but the country was not. The agrarian reform was restored, but harassment, occupations, violence, destruction of property, and peasant strikes continued and even increased as spring advanced, especially in southern and central Spain. In the cities there were armed clashes, church burnings, assassinations, wholesale arrests, and bombs by the hundreds.

In those five months two extreme groups rose from insignificance to power and influence: the Communists and the Falangists. Both movements had paramilitary trained youths. Street fighting was often vicious, especially as it was widely believed that the Falangist *señoritos* (young gentlemen) hired *pistoleros* (armed gangsters) to fight for them. There was no pattern and no central direction for the violence, which the government could not control. Many well-to-do citizens left the country, smuggling their money out.

In April 1936 a constitutional crisis was brought on by the Cortes, which deposed President Alcalá Zamora, who had made enemies on all sides. He was well-intentioned, a true Republican, and a genuine moderate. His dismissal by a vote of 238 to 5 (the Right abstained) was a shock to the country. It seemed—and in truth it was—as if the last hope of moderation was gone. Azaña surprisingly put forward his name for President. He was not the man he had been and he was disillusioned with politics. Evidently he thought that he could block the revolutionary Socialists under Largo Caballero. However, by moving up from Prime Minister to President on May 10 he weakened the already shaky Popular Front, especially when he later named his timid and tubercular friend, Santiago Casares Quiroga, as Premier.

Prieto's moderate wing of the Socialist party was in a minority by the tense month of April. He had exiled himself in France after the Asturias uprising, returned secretly in October 1935, and then acted openly after the election amnesty. On May 2, 1936, he made the best speech of his career. "A country can survive a revolution," he said. "What a country cannot survive is the constant attrition of public disorder without any immediate revolutionary goal." Violence, he went on, could bring only chaos and Fascism. He foresaw the Right turning to Franco for a military dictatorship. Azaña offered Prieto the premiership, but Prieto did not feel that he could take it while Largo Caballero controlled the great majority of the Socialists.

In four months, according to Gil Robles of the CEDA, there had been 113 general strikes and many more partial ones. The fifth month—June—was worse. Casares Quiroga acknowledged that since the February election 170 churches, 69 clubs, and 10 newspaper offices had been set on fire and that many more attempts had been made to burn churches and buildings.

Quoting Gil Robles, the Madrid newspaper *El Sol* wrote on June 17, 1936: " 'A country can perfectly well live under a Monarchy or under a Republic, under parliamentary rule, Soviet rule or the rule of a dictatorship. But a country cannot live in a state of anarchy, and Spain is in a state of anarchy today.' "

But the government could not end the anarchy. The Popular Front was never a strong and unified movement. The parties had banded together to win the February elections, but unity could not be sustained. The Anarchists and Basque Nationalists never joined the Front. It was a mishmash of different classes, factions, interests, and political groups, which were involved in contradictions and conflicts at every step. The split in the Socialist party was disastrous. A million and a half men were involved in the UGT alone. The Republicans were anti-Communist and anti-left-wing Socialists. The Anarchists were anti-everything, trying harmfully to play a lone hand.

In the eyes of their right-wing enemies, all the Republican forces were *Rojos*—Reds. To ask Spanish (or foreign) businessmen, bankers, landowners, and military officers to make fine distinctions between Socialists, Communists, and Anarchists (who called themselves "libertarian Communists") was unrealistic. On the other side, the label of Fascism was applied to almost every right-wing party or movement—Catholics of the CEDA, Carlists, Falangists, right-wing radicals, Monarchists, army officers, tradesmen, businessmen, financiers, landowners. They had not sustained their electoral National Front, but they were united in sentiment against a common group of enemies.

The Falangists (of whom more later) were like the Italian Fascist *Squadristi* of 1919–1922—activists who believed in terrorism. They formed into small groups; beat up opponents; murdered judges who condemned them and journalists who criticized them. They went especially for the Socialists and deliberately sought to create chaos. Their leader was José Antonio Primo de Rivera, son of the former dictator, a man of charm, imagination, integrity, flair, courage—many virtues, in fact, but his movement was a Frankenstein's monster to him.

The government arrested him on March 15, 1936, and he was not to see the light of day again. His twenty-six-point program was like Fascism, and while he had not wanted violence he did not try to stop it. The Falangists were strong in Madrid and the southern cities. They were a sort of pendant or parallel to the Communists. As Communist strength rose, so did theirs, even more sensationally. The imported ideologies of Fascism and Communism aroused fears out of all proportion to the real size and strength of the movements in Spain. It seemed as if the nation had divided into anti-Fascists and anti-Communists, a distortion that carried over and into the Civil War and became a worldwide misconception. As is often the case in politics, the myth was stronger than the reality.

The Falange was by no means the only counterrevolutionary force in Spain. There were the fanatical Carlists (Traditionalists) of ultra-Catholic Navarre, and the Monarchists, whom Calvo Sotelo was now leading. He was an able, violent man who hated the Republic and all it stood for. (Thomas calls him "dangerous and unscrupulous.") Both groups were supporters of the secret society known as the *Unión Militar Española* (UME). The military officers, now plotting rebellion, were of course the greatest threat to the Second Republic.

The Spanish Communists, because of the bourgeois Popular Front policy, were as counterrevolutionary as the forces of the Right, but they could not stand aside while Socialists and Anarchists fought in the streets and attracted greater and greater mass support. They went into the streets, too, but sometimes fought Socialists and Anarchists as well as "Fascists." The lack of working-class unity—then and during the Civil War—has to be emphasized, for it was a fatal weakness.

The growth of the Communist party was phenomenal. In March 1936 party membership was no more than 30,000. In July, when the war began, it was probably 50,000 or even more (it claimed 100,000). It may well have had 200,000 members by January 1937, and 300,000 six months later. The sensational growth, it should be noted, came after the war started. However, Professor Payne argues that despite their smallness in the first half of 1936, the Communists, being organized and disciplined, directed from outside as well as inside, knowing what they wanted, and perhaps helped financially by the Kremlin or Comintern, exercised far more influence than their size indicated.

I do not believe that they knew what they wanted. The Popular Front policy was new and oriented toward parliamentary moderation. As Gerald Brenan wrote: "One may therefore dismiss the story that they were planning a revolution for that autumn as Fascist propaganda."

The Spanish Communist party was important only during the Civil War, but in that period it was very important, indeed. The history of the Spanish conflict is so enveloped in emotion that there has been a tendency to overemphasize this importance, especially by scholars too young to have lived through the war period.

Much depends on whether one is a Spaniard or a foreigner. Nationalist propaganda, during and since the war, has distorted the picture beyond any reality for present generations of Spaniards. The Communists themselves, for obvious reasons, exaggerated their strength and accomplishments, and denied the evils and the sins by which they stained the Republican record. Whatever the future holds for Spain when Francisco Franco lies in his monstrous tomb in the Valley of the Fallen, it is most unlikely ever to take the form of a Communist regime.

The movement was born in Spain in April 1920, when some young admirers of the Bolshevik Revolution—mainly Socialist but some Anarchist—formed a miniature Communist party. The great bulk of the Socialist party and all the UGT would have nothing to do with the new Third International (Comintern). Some miners in Asturias and the Basque region were attracted, but as late as 1931, when the Republic began, the party had fewer than 1,000 members. (*La Pasionaria* gives a figure of 800.) During the preceding Primo de Rivera dictatorship, the Communists were so insignificant that the general did not bother to suppress the movement or close its newspapers.

Until the Popular Front was formed in January 1936 the Spanish Communists fought the Republican governments, the Socialists, the Anarchists, and all attempts at reforms. Right-wing and moderate Spaniards were frightened by Communism long before they had need to be. Communist strength in Spain was a result of the Civil War, not a cause. It is true that their propaganda was clever. Comintern advisers were in Spain well before the war. About 600 Spanish refugees from the Asturian revolt (mostly non-Communists to begin with) were getting military and political training in Russia. The party also did much inside Spain, through the Comintern's International Red Aid, to help the orphaned or jailed dependents of the militants. The other parties and the government did nothing. That was one reason why 1935 showed a sharp spurt in membership.

Neither then, nor at any time in the war, were there any truly outstanding political figures in the Communist party. The two famous early Leninist leaders, Andrés Nín and Joaquín Maurín, had left the party in 1932. They ended up in the dissident *Partido Obrero de Unificación Marxista* (POUM), partly Trotskyite, partly mongrel-Marxist, always revolutionary. (Nín was to die, secretly, under torture, in a Communist *cheka* cell in 1937—an atrocious act over which Premier Negrín, who was kept in ignorance, almost resigned.)

The most famous Communist of them all to this day (she is still alive in 1972 in Moscow) is Dolores Ibarruri, better known as *La Pasionaria*. As Dr. Franz Borkenau wrote about her early in the war: "The masses worship her, not for her intellect, but as a sort of saint who is to lead them in days of trial and temptation."

She was much the best orator in the Loyalist camp, or, at

least, she became so, for she had little education and little fo-
rensic training. She was born in the north in December 1895.
"All my family came from mining stock," she wrote in her
autobiography, ". . . a sad childhood and adolescence that was
not relieved by hope." She married an obscure Communist
miner trade union official. He and she were in and out of jail,
she giving birth to children of whom three died in infancy.
Until the Popular Front, her persecutors were the Republican
governments.

As a girl, she had been a devout Catholic but, like so many
Spanish Marxists and Anarchists, "My new faith," she wrote,
"was more reasonable and more solid than my religious faith
had been." Yet something remained, for one of the strange but
true stories of the terror in Madrid when the war began was
that *La Pasionaria* sheltered nuns, led them to safety in embassies, and helped them to get abroad. It was *La Pasionaria,* as
mentioned earlier, in the flaming first days of Madrid's defense,
who cried, "It is better to die on your feet than to live on your
knees. *No pasarán!"*

It is worth remembering that the period of the late 1920's and
the 1930's was a time when liberals everywhere in the Western
world were attracted to Communism, or admired the Soviet
regime. There were excellent reasons in those years to see in
Communism many of the crusading ideals of the early Bolshevik period. *The God That Failed* was an image of the late
1940's. Those who use hindsight to condemn the men and
women who entered the movement or who praised or tolerated
Communism, show an ignorance of the climate in which politically conscious people lived before and during the Spanish
Civil War. The true enemy of liberals, democrats, and human-
ists was Fascism, especially the German version. At that time
it was more creditable to be pro-Communist than pro-Fascist—
not that those who championed the Republican cause necessarily saw the war in the false terms of Communism versus
Fascism. The point is that to them the Communists were
fighting in a praiseworthy cause. To an overwhelming degree,

Spanish and foreign support and devotion went to the Republican government, not to the Spanish Communist party or to the Kremlin, and they went *against* Fascism. One had to live through the 1930's to understand the emotional force of anti-Fascism. The movement seemed the embodiment of all that was wrong and evil in a capitalistic and militaristic society.

One of the distortions still perpetrated by the Franco Nationalists and by some historians, as I mentioned, was that the Spanish Communist party had some special responsibility for bringing on the generals' rebellion. Fictitious documents were circulated "proving" that Russian, French, and Spanish Communists and the Largo Caballero Socialists plotted an uprising or revolution and the patriotic generals rose to save Spain from such a fate. Hugh Thomas, who at first thought these documents to be true, later wrote: "In fact it seems certain that these were forgeries, made before the rising and possibly really deceiving those who later propagated them." Two leading American authorities—Gabriel Jackson and David Cattell—have shown that these charges are utterly unbelievable and, in fact, impossible.

Communist complicity in bringing on the conflict was neither more nor less than that of the Socialists, Anarchists, Falangists, student organizations, and all the other tragically misguided organizations and men who created the atmosphere of violence and chaos which gave the generals the excuse to rise in the name, not of anti-Communism, which was hardly mentioned, but of law and order.

The failure to maintain law and order, except through military dictatorship, repeats itself in modern Spain, having discredited the Liberal governments of 1812 and 1820 and the First Republic of 1873. No sooner was the Second Republic established in 1931 than law and order began to break down. The people hated and feared the Civil Guard and, at times, the army. Liberal regimes were loath to call upon these institutions to repress and, too often, to kill other Spaniards. Yet, governments had no other instruments, not even in the Second Republic which had created a corps of Assault Guards, only to find in them replicas of the Civil Guards.

The violence increased blindly after the February elections. Some of the worst disorders were led by the youthful extremists of the Right and Left: the *Juventud de Acción Popular* (JAP, anti-Semitic, anti-Masonic, and anti-anything Left) and the *Juventud Socialista,* who were so extreme that they considered the Social Democrats to be "Social Fascists." There were also the smaller Federation of University Students (FUE, militant Marxist) and the equally militant Catholic Students.

Spaniards called them all *los exaltados.* They needed no drugs to make them "high." In southern and central Spain, where peasants were agitating, the atmosphere of class hatred was ominous. The Falange was officially dissolved on March 16, 1936 (the day after José Antonio Primo de Rivera was arrested), but it became even more active underground.

Throughout all this period no Socialist or Communist was a member of the government. The first cabinet in which both parties participated was formed by Largo Caballero on September 4, six weeks after the war began. The Republicans in charge before July 17 were amazingly lax and complacent. Everyone seemed to know that army officers were preparing an uprising, although no one knew just when, not even the plotters, headed by General Mola, who kept changing the dates.

Premier Casares Quiroga's optimism was inexplicable, unless one argues that he was a consumptive and euphoria is a symptom of the disease. He did not secure Seville or any of the big cities, or foresee the use of the Foreign Legion and Moors, despite what had happened in Asturias. Azaña played for time, which was working against him. Anyway, he was sure that rebellious officers could be handled as easily as he had suppressed General José Sanjurjo's uprising in 1932.

Largo Caballero, then sixty-eight years old, stubborn, proud, exalted, seemed to be inciting disorders. He had an exaggerated belief in the strength of the Left. Analogies to Russia in 1917 were being made, but they were false. What the moderate Socialist, Julián Besteiro, called "revolutionaries trained in the hard, cruel struggle of persecution," who had "the fibre and determination of violent revolutionaries" did not exist in the Socialist movement. There is no evidence that Caballero and his associates had worked out the technical and political problems of making a revolution. The moderate wing of the Socialist party did not want one, and the Communists, following Moscow's orders, were bourgeois. There were no Jacobins and no Bolsheviks to carry out the drastic upheaval of a social revolution. When a species of revolution came as the Civil War started, it was spontaneous, popular, and unorganized.

Professor Payne argues that the Republican regime failed because of its ideological sectarianism. This was just what the Second Republic lacked. Had it been able, and willing, to make a true social revolution there would have been no military rebellion. The Republican leaders never wanted a revolution. Professor E. Allison Peers, one of the soundest students of Spanish history, put it this way: "They failed in their main task for two reasons. First, like most of their race, they suffered from so intense an individualism that they were unable to maintain a coalition, such as that of April 1931, which represented fairly accurately the different views of Spanish progressives, and, had it remained united, would unquestionably have made numerous converts. Secondly, they were unable or unwilling to stop the pendulum, and the pendulum is the curse of Spain."

The Republic of 1931, it will be remembered, came upon an unprepared nation. It tried to carry Spain all at once into the highly advanced stage which a nation like France had reached after generations of experience. The Republican goals were those of the European Enlightenment—democratic, liberal, secular (separation of church and state); lay, not religious, education; the army controlled by a civilian government; freedom of speech and writing; land reform; equality for women; free trade unions; autonomy for the Catalans and Basques. The list was endless and, in the Spain of 1931, it was asking for utopia. Spain had never had any one of these features which seem so natural to other Western European nations and to the

United States. How could she get them all at once?

Traditional Spain wanted none of these things. Liberal and leftist expectations and hopes were disappointed; a powerful opposition was provoked. There was conflict at every level of Spanish society with no one element strong enough to impose law and order, and no grass roots democracy to unify the nation by popular consent or tradition.

Some scholars have argued (Professor Gabriel Jackson for one) that the Civil War was avoidable. However, such reasoning depends on a number of "if's." In dealing with history, the options are closed. Besides, every actor in the tragedy was playing the only role he knew or could play. The inevitability was the classic one of a Greek tragedy—each action leading to another and all of them to the catastrophic ending.

No force was present to change this disastrous progression, no outstanding and authoritative leaders, no suffiiciently powerful movement, no period when civilian government could bring law and order, and above all, no disposition by the major interests to solve the domestic problems through peaceful compromise or democratic processes. Except for a handful of political leaders, everyone was throwing fuel on the flames.

Spaniard faced Spaniard: one class faced the other—peasants against landowners, workers against industrialists, anticlericals against the church hierarchy, liberals against authoritarians—each fearing destruction by the other. How could Spain have escaped disaster? It had to be a war to the finish and, because outside powers intervened, it had to be a long war.

On July 4, 1936, a crowd emerging from a Socialist meeting in Madrid was fired on point-blank by gunmen in passing cars. On July 12, Lieutenant José Castillo of the Assault Guards was murdered by four men as he was leaving his home. The next day, the Monarchist leader, José Calvo Sotelo, was lured from his home by Republican Assault Guard officers and young leftists and murdered. This was the spark that set off the explosion.

4

THE GENERALS

THE SPANISH CIVIL WAR, it might be said, was a colossal mistake on the part of the generals and colonels. They intended to stage a quick palace revolt, just another *pronunciamiento* to save Spain from anarchy. They did not expect or want a civil war and were undoubtedly dismayed and astounded. A handful of men, without popular support, unwittingly stirred up the people of Spain in a way they had never been aroused in their history.

The long succession of *pronunciamientos* had created a popular image of military oppression. The rising by the army instinctively led workers, peasants, liberals, and progressives of all sorts to fight back in the name of liberty against a threatened tyranny. These Republican elements—whatever their political coloration—either saw their very existence at stake, or felt that life would not be worth living if the military triumphed. But the officers, in their different fashion, felt the same way. There had to be a fight to the finish. The victims were Spain and the Spanish people.

This does not mean that every Spaniard threw himself wholeheartedly into the struggle. The overwhelming majority of any people want nothing so much as peace and the opportunity to work and to live a normal family life. Those who truly wanted to fight it out in Spain were the minority, but an extraordinarily high proportion as such events go. In any case, no one was to be spared.

The Spanish Army, in modern times, was probably the most incompetent in Europe. Yet it had a glorious history and, as the stubborn resistance to Napoleon's forces proved, wonderfully courageous and determined fighters in the common people. Hitler gave a shrewd opinion of the Spanish soldier in his *Table Talk:* "Extraordinarily brave, tough against privations, but wildly undisciplined." Wellington, in his Peninsular campaign, had also noted how undisciplined they were—and what splendid fighting material.

The weakness then and later lay in the top-heavy officer corps. At the time of the Spanish-American War, there was one general for every hundred men. The *Anuario Militar* for 1930 listed 566 generals and 21,996 lesser-ranking officers. Many of the generals were retired or inactive, but when the Republic began in 1931 there were 195 active generals and 16,730 other officers for an army of less than 150,000 men. This was a ratio of one officer to eight men, compared to one to thirty-four in the French Army. The Spanish Army had more majors and captains than sergeants. The tiny Spanish Navy had more admirals than Britain's then great Royal Navy. Defense expenditures used up 30 per cent of the annual budget.

Spanish Morocco apart, the army was a police force, used politically to maintain order and keep the traditional ruling classes in their position of power and wealth. Traditionally, it was also the weapon with which power was seized. A Spanish scholar, Antonio Ramos Oliveira, counted eleven successful and thirty-two unsuccessful *pronunciamientos* between 1814 and 1923.

It was logical for the Second Republic to try to streamline and control this costly and potentially dangerous force. When Azaña became Minister of War in 1931, he set about the task enthusiastically, announcing rashly that he was going "to grind the army down to a fine powder." Azaña blamed the army (along with the church) for the nation's civic backwardness. He despised the army, calling it "inefficient, vulgar, and pretentious."

He aimed to reduce its size, cut its cost, and "democratize" it.

So, on April 25, 1931, he offered retirement with full pay. Half the officer corps accepted, most thereupon using their leisure time to conspire. One of Azaña's measures was to close the Military Academy at Saragossa, with its rigid, exclusive *esprit de corps*. The director happened to be Brigadier General Francisco Franco, who made his discontent clear in a farewell speech.

Azaña carried out a complete reorganization, cutting down the officers to 8,000 and the generals to eighty-four. As a result of his economies, the army was very inefficient and poorly equipped in 1936—one reason why foreign help was needed. The manner of Azaña's reforms—the obvious pleasure he took —offended the military hierarchy as much as the substance. They felt that he was deliberately humiliating them.

Azaña scattered the generals around, away from Madrid, sending Franco to the Canary Islands, Goded to the Balearics, and Mola to Pamplona in Navarre. He put staunch Republicans (at least he thought they were) in key spots, including General Miaja in Madrid. There were plenty of warnings of a coup, but no proof. Premier Casares Quiroga publicly proclaimed his trust in General Mola, the chief plotter.

The reputations of the generals who rebelled in 1936 were made in the hard, dangerous Moroccan campaigns. The Army of Africa had two principal components: the Foreign Legion *(Tercio de Extranjeros)* and the Moorish *Regulares.* The Legion was notorious for its fierceness and its apt, but absurd, motto: *"Viva la muerte!"* (Long live Death). The Moors, for their part, were noted for their savagery. These were the two forces first used under General Franco's command to repress the 1934 Asturian uprising, and later as the main shock troops of the Insurgents in the Civil War.

In the spring of 1936, there were still 425 generals, of whom eighty-four were on the active list. Few of them were to fight for the Second Republic.

Little need be said about the Spanish Navy. The government found itself in control of two battleships, seven cruisers, fifteen submarines, and twelve torpedo boats—after their officers had been killed or cowed. More were seized later in Cartagena. The battleship *España* and two cruisers defected to the Rebels. In all other vessels, officers who sided with the Rebels, or who were expected to, were slain, tossed overboard, or forced to flee. As a result the Loyalist navy at all times lacked experienced commanders. Not until some Russians arrived months later did it begin to function again, but never effectively. The Russians were not interested in the navy and sent little equipment and few advisers.

"While our soldiers were fighting for every inch of national territory against the Insurgents," *La Pasionaria* wrote sourly, "most of our ships remained safe and snug in Republican waters."

The air force, for the most part, remained loyal, but it was not of much use. The government found itself with 154 obsolete planes. The war in the air was fought by Germans, Italians and, for a while, Russians. Thanks to Hitler and Mussolini, the Nationalists almost always had overwhelming air superiority. Russian help in the air was relatively modest, and after some months what planes there were had newly trained Spanish pilots. The Republicans did little bombing.

In any consideration of the armed forces the different police corps deserve an important place: the Civil Guards, Assault Guards, Customs Guards (*Carabineros*), and the *Seguridad* (normal security forces).

The famous *Guardia Civil* was formed in 1844 to cope with highway robbery and rural disorders. By 1931, public order depended on the police to a high degree. The Civil Guard had long before become the instrument of landlords against peasant demonstrators and of employers against strikers. They numbered between 25,000 and 30,000. Being organized like a military force, their commander was always a general. In April 1931 he was General José Sanjurjo, hero of the Moroccan campaigns and, later, nominal chief of the rebellious generals.

The Civil Guards were disciplined, incorruptible, reliable picked men who lived in fortified posts in towns and villages. They were forbidden to mingle socially with neighbors or to marry local girls. They never walked alone, always in pairs and always armed. In their green uniforms, black capes, and tricornered hats they have long been among the most familiar sights of Spain and, to the people, a feared and hated sight. In the Civil War, they of course joined the generals' rebellion where they could. Where they could not, they were massacred, although a few units (in Barcelona, as an instance) remained loyal. Since they were always targets of the mobs, they shot to kill, being what Americans call "trigger happy." In their jails they frequently employed torture. Their reputation for brutality was only too well earned.

Police power disintegrated when the rebellion started as the great majority of the members deserted to the Insurgent cause. They were replaced at first in the Loyalist zone by *ad hoc* "revolutionary committees" and militia units. This explains why, in the early weeks, Premier José Giral's government in Madrid was impotent against terror, searches, arrests, summary executions, and church burnings. The remnant of the Civil Guard were purged and reorganized in a National Republican Guard. Those Assault Guards who remained loyal were reinforced. So were the *Carabineros,* especially when Dr. Negrín became Minister of Finance in September 1936. They were increased to more than 30,000 and became the most reliable and trusted of the police corps, being personally loyal to Juan Negrín. New revolutionary tribunals to administer justice were set up in November 1936.

The Civil Guard was abolished in the Republican zone on August 31, 1936, but of course they kept their name and organization in the Nationalist zone.

The rebellion of July 1936 was in no sense a popular or mass uprising—quite the contrary. It was a revolt of generals and colonels: Cabanellas, Queipo de Llano, Mola, Sanjurjo, Goded, Orgaz, Yagüe, Fanjul, and lastly—in point of time—Franco. There is evidence that some of them met in January 1936, a month before the Popular Front was elected, to talk over a military coup. Ramón Serrano Suñer, Franco's brother-in-law and a right-wing member of the Cortes, wrote in his memoirs later that he was *au courant* with the preparations in June 1936, weeks before the uprising. Sanjurjo was to lead the military forces and Calvo Sotelo the political. Each general or colonel was to mobilize a different section of the country.

Second in line to Sanjurjo was General Emilio Mola, and it was he who eventually organized the rebellion. Mola was born of a military family in a garrison in Cuba and had been an officer all his career. He was a rare character for a Spanish Army officer—an intellectual who wrote books of memoirs and even a manual on chess. Six feet tall, round-shouldered, homely, with thick eyeglasses, he hardly made a dashing figure. He lacked the human touch; a reserved man with few friends. Apparently, although not openly, he hated liberals whom he considered to be subversive and unpatriotic, and had quietly moved from a moderate position to extreme conservatism. He was one of a small and influential group of Spanish rightists who believed in an international conspiracy of Jewish financiers. Those were, after all, the years of Hitler's triumph.

The government, strangely, thought Mola to be one of the most loyal senior generals. In the spring of 1936, he was moved from command of the Moroccan Army (leaving the opening, as it turned out, to Franco) to Pamplona in Navarre. Carlists and Monarchists then made Pamplona the main conspiratorial center.

The Director, as his fellow-conspirators addressed Mola, realized that Madrid was the key to success. He was also hardheaded and ruthless enough to accept what would have to be done in the localities where the Rebels seized power. "It should be understood," he wrote in his first plot outline, "that the blow must be violent in the extreme in order to subdue the enemy. All the directors of political parties, societies or syndicates not in favor of the movement will be arrested, and exemplary punishments applied, so as to stifle strikes or rebellions." ("Exemplary punishments," of course, meant execution.)

His plan was probably completed by the end of May 1936. He needed only a handful of strategically placed high officers to launch the revolt, and he had them. In Morocco, he could count on Lieutenant Colonel Yagüe of the Foreign Legion and almost the whole corps of that élite, caste-conscious, combative group of *Africanistas.* Yagüe was known to leftists since 1934 as "the hyena of Asturias." He was a tough, typical Legionary, a good field commander, respected by his fellow officers, honest and ultrapatriotic. He had by then joined the Falange. (As the Civil War went on, he became sickened by its cruelty and hatred and was an outspoken, but not recalcitrant, critic.)

General Gonzalo Queipo de Llano joined the conspiracy after President Alcalá Zamora, a relative by marriage, was ousted. Sanjurjo was won over early in June. José Antonio Primo de Rivera, chief of the Falange, called on the military "to save the Fatherland," and on May 29 made contact from his prison cell with Mola. Calvo Sotelo, the Monarchist leader, was told of the plot by Mola early in June and pledged his support. So did Gil Robles of the CEDA, which gave Mola money, as did the Monarchists. Mola was shrewd enough to realize that he had to have some popular support. He and his military conspirators condescended to make common cause with the Falangists and other terrorists in order to provoke a popular explosion—"a state of violence," as he put it in one memorandum. They all realized that the Popular Front could not be deposed by political means, since it was too strong and had overwhelming mass support in the trade unions and the rural areas.

A few loyal officers urged President Azaña and Premier Casares Quiroga to act, but they did not dare to and, anyway, underestimated the danger. Azaña, normally so skeptical, relied on the loyalty of the commanding generals. He seems to have feared the extreme revolutionary Left more than the extreme Right.

It is ironical, in view of what happened and what the public image became, to realize that in this crucial period, when Mola and other officers had decided firmly on a revolt and were planning its details, Franco posed the greatest question mark of all the officers. This was typical of the general's caution, wiliness and shrewdness—the *Gallego* in him. Yet the conspirators could not hope to succeed without active support from Franco, who was still in the Canary Islands. He refused to make a move before he had to.

He maintained contacts with the plotters and no one doubted that he agreed with their aims. As early as February 1936, he was carefully but clearly moving away from the detached stance he had taken in previous years. After the election that month he argued for martial law to forestall a leftist revolution, which he feared. His feelings were only too clear to Azaña, who soon sent him to the far-off Canary Islands, with headquarters at Santa Cruz de Tenerife.

Nevertheless, the general believed enough in the continuity of the Republic to enter his name for a May 10, 1936, election in Cuenca. However, there was so much opposition that he withdrew before the polling day. José Antonio (as the young Primo de Rivera was always called) heard about it in prison and was so angry that he is supposed to have complained to his friends: "All the generals are chickens and Franco is the biggest chicken of all." Mola was so frustrated that he and his fellow conspirators are said to have called Franco "Miss Canary Islands of 1936."

Yet, Franco could not keep out. As Mola said, "He who is not with us is against us and will be treated as an enemy." If the plot failed, Franco would have been purged by the government as unreliable. Mola needed the Army of Africa and the obvious man to command it was its former respected leader, Francisco Franco.

Franco wrote a letter to Premier Casares Quiroga on June 23, 1936, which became famous and has been used by official biographers as evidence that the general was trying to warn the government of dire consequences if it did not change its policies. The army was loyal, Franco asserted, but its spirit was being undermined by the antimilitary campaign of the Left, and it was turning against the government. The situation, he wrote, was "grave."

To say that "the army was loyal" at the time really was numerically true. The trouble was that too many key officers were not loyal. Military coups, like revolutions, are always made by small, determined groups, who then carry the majority with them. If a majority of the officers had been actively engaged in the plot there would have been no need for a rebellion. The overthrow of the government would have been automatic.

General Mola set a target date of June 30, but there was such uncertainty that he postponed it. He became so discouraged at one time that he thought of dropping the whole business, but at the beginning of July Franco finally and definitely pledged his support, the price being the command of the Moroccan forces, the only really strong, effective units in the Spanish Army. This shrewd move guaranteed Franco a position at least equal to Mola's. Arrangements were made to fly the general from the Canaries to Tetuán in Morocco. Mola sent word to the rebel network to be ready for immediate action any time after July 15.

There was never, at any period of his life, anything quixotic about Francisco Franco Bahamonde. No Spaniard of modern history was less like the nation's most famous literary figure and, although physically Franco looked like Sancho Panza, he was equally far removed from that homely, good-hearted, down-to-earth character. Because of his role in the ruthless suppression of the 1934 miners' revolt, Franco had earned the reputation of an uncompromising enemy of the Left, not in the political sense, but in the name of law and order. He was the hero of the middle, as well as the upper classes. Asturias may well have shown him the road to fame and power.

He was born in 1892 in the naval port of El Ferrol, Galicia. The family had a long connection with the navy, but there was no place for young "Paquito," as he was incongruously called, and he reluctantly turned to an army career. He was at all times extraordinarily serious, austere, reserved, and hard-working. His career as a fighting officer was in Spanish Morocco, from 1912 to 1926. There he showed himself to be a remarkable administrator, a harsh disciplinarian, and an exceptionally brave soldier. In those years he eagerly sought action in the front line; in the Civil War he never took command in the field.

Because of his Moroccan record, he was successively the youngest major, lieutenant colonel, colonel, and brigadier general in any European army. His appointment as brigadier general took him away from Morocco and front-line duty. In May 1935 he was made army Chief of Staff by Gil Robles, who was then Minister of War—a post he lost when Azaña became Premier the following year. In the midst of his career, Franco married a devout Catholic Asturian girl named Carmen Polo. They had one child, a daughter.

Franco had been primarily responsible for bringing the Foreign Legion to a high level of discipline, armed power, and fighting spirit. The Legion was like a time bomb in the eyes of the Spanish Liberals. It was really "foreign," even though the officers and most of the troops were Spanish. Its loyalty was to itself and its commanders, not to the Spanish people or, obviously, the government.

The Legion, which was formed in September 1920, was an imitation of France's Foreign Legion, then eighty years old. The twenty-eight-year-old Major Franco was made second in command. The top commander was General José Millán Astray. By normal human standards, Millán Astray was half-mad and, because of terrible wounds, he looked like a figure from a horror film—one eye, one arm, one leg, and only a few fingers left on his remaining hand. He coined the Legion's absurd but very Spanish slogan: *"Viva la muerte!"*

The motto was shouted by the general at a ceremony in Seville on August 15, 1936, where the Monarchist flag was substituted for the Republican. He called on the crowd to shout it with him. Later, on the Day of the Race, October 12, at a great ceremony in the University of Salamanca he uttered the phrase that was forever to brand him and every Spanish officer like him: *"Abajo la inteligencia!"* ("Down with intelligence!") This was Millán Astray's answer to a last, noble protest by Spain's most famous living philosopher, Miguel de Unamuno, rector of the university and a Basque. Unamuno, who had at first supported the rebellion, expressed his sorrow and repulsion at Millán Astray's "outburst of vituperation" and bloodthirstiness, and he ended with a warning—using a play upon words—which was also to become famous: *"Venceraos pero no convenceraos"* ("You will conquer but you will not convince"). Unamuno was put under house arrest and died, a broken man, a few months later.

The Foreign Legion did, as I said, have many foreigners in it. What they had in common, in Franco's words, was that they were "shipwrecked from life." On the peninsula, in the Civil War, they found that the shore on which they had been cast was a Treasure Island. Discipline was extremely strict, Franco being noted for his harshness, although also for his justness.

"If they [the *Tercios*] were never hesitant to kill, often in cold blood, and customarily mutilated the bodies of their enemies to take proof of their prowess," wrote J. W. D. Trythall in his biography of the general, "this was partly the legacy of Franco's training." Looting, rape, arson, and slaughter were recognized and acceptable practices for the Moors and Legionaries, in Spain as well as Africa.

When the Civil War began, Franco was a Major General, forty-three years old, short (only five feet three inches tall) and plump, a "natural" for caricaturists and artists like the brilliant Luis Quintanilla. A shrill, high-pitched voice with a slight lisp and no resonance made him a poor orator and, in conversation, hard to understand, for he talked in a low voice, almost a whisper. However, he has always had complete self-assurance.

An American newspaperman who saw him at the beginning of the war wrote: "A less straightforward man I never met." The man who was to draw the most acidulous picture of the Generalissimo was Sir Samuel Hoare (later Lord Templewood), who was the British ambassador to Madrid in World War II. "It was always difficult to draw him into a discussion that involved the interplay of question and answer," he wrote in *Ambassador on a Special Mission*. "It was even more difficult to penetrate the cotton-wool entanglement of his amazing complacence." The ambassador refers to Franco variously as "this young officer of Jewish origin," "a slow thinking and slow moving Gallego," "a tortuous mind," "his Gallego cunning," "the belief in his own infallibility of judgment," and so forth.

"Franco is a man who declares himself, and then retracts; draws near and then steps back; vanishes or slides away; always vague and never clear and categorical," wrote Major Juan Antonio Ansaldo of the Nationalist Air Force. "He had seemed [during the Monarchy] to be the most monarchist of the young Spanish generals. . . . His constant declarations of loyalty to the Republican regime, and the celebrated speech given by him in the General Academy [of Saragossa] in which he defined, as the absolute and unquestionable duty of every officer, blind discipline to the established power, 'even more when the heart bleeds than when our natural impulses prompt us to it,' won him the confidence of successive Republican cabinets."

Of course, these traits, which were so disconcerting to his associates and opponents, can be interpreted as virtues, which they are for Franco's admirers. Caution, patience, deliberation, the willingness to change his mind—these are the traits that kept Spain out of World War II and, incidentally, drove Hitler and Mussolini frantic.

"The real tragedy of Spain," Hitler said in *Table Talk,* about the Civil War campaign, "was the death of Mola; there was the real brain, the real leader."

In the Civil War, Franco's slowness in making decisions and commitments was maddening for his military associates and subordinates and also for his German and Italian allies. The war was doubtless prolonged by these unusual features in the Generalissimo's character. He was not an imaginative or inspired commander, just a stubborn and determined one, with a traditional Spanish siege mentality and an obsessive compulsion to take Madrid.

On July 11, 1936, just before the assassinations of Lieutenant Castillo and Calvo Sotelo, a private, rented plane whose English pilot knew nothing of his mission, left London for Tenerife. The pilot was a Captain Bebb, who had been hired by Luis

Bolín, London correspondent of the Madrid newspaper, *ABC*. A Spanish military plane could not be used as the air force was known to be mostly loyal.

Although Franco had at last decided that it was safe for him to take action, he still thought it too risky to leave his wife and daughter behind. He put them aboard a German ship bound for Le Havre.

Before emplaning just after midnight, July 17, he declared a state of war in the Canaries and explained his motives in a radio broadcast. Anarchy, revolutionary strikes, and regionalism were destroying the nation, he said. The armed forces were being slandered; liberty and equality before the law could not survive; the Constitution had ceased to be operative; the army could not stand by. It would bring "justice, equality and peace" to all Spaniards and would uphold social gains and guarantee "for the first time, in this order, fraternity, liberty and equality." It would not act in a "spirit of vengeance." (Of all the things Franco said, this last was the least honored.) Curiously, the harangue was not anti-Republican or anti-Communist.

Captain Bebb then flew Franco to Casablanca in French Morocco. Franco reached Tetuán on July 19 and took supreme command of the Army of Africa.

He had to leave half his troops in Morocco to keep order. This gave him a force of maneuver of more than 15,000 Moors and Legioniares, joined on the mainland by an equal number of Civil Guards and about a thousand Assault Guards. The rank and file of the regular army where the Insurgents took over had no choice but to serve their officers or be punished—in fact killed. However, being conscripts they were men of the people, like the militias on the Republican side, and they could not be trusted. For much of the war, Franco used them for garrison duty and manual labor, not as fighting troops. More than half of the first Rebel infantry units, therefore, consisted of troops who were not Spanish—mercenaries of the *Tercio* and Moors of the native Regulars. Yagüe commanded the Moorish troops in the field throughout the war.

The Nationalists soon recruited tens of thousands of Carlists (*Requetés*) and Falangists, who were genuine volunteers and splendid fighting men. The *Requetés*—called *Boinas Rojas* because of their red berets—were taken into General Mola's northern army. They were ready to fight immediately for they had begun training their peasant militia as soon as the Second Republic showed its anticlerical slant. They were among the most backward people in Western Europe—arch-conservative, super-Catholic, adamant against change. They fought superbly for aristocratic privileges, church education, no freedom of worship, absolute submission to the Pope, complete devotion to the Carlist Pretender, and a fascist-type corporative system. This was more than Franco was bargaining for, but he knew the value of his Carlists, who heroically took very high casualties as shock troops.

The Falangists had to be trained with German help. Many former leftists and trade unionists sought safety in the Falangist movement (as many Falangists did in the Communist movement on the Loyalist side).

Starting in March 1937, an organization was created, with German assistance, to train Spaniards of the upper and middle classes in their twenties. They were made "temporary second-lieutenants" and casualties were so disproportionately high that the saying was "temporary lieutenant, permanent corpse." However, they contributed greatly to the Nationalist army. Even in the final year of the war, Franco was relying on certain élite divisions: three from Navarre, three from Morocco, and three from Galicia, plus his Italians and Germans.

All in all, General Franco's problems were easy compared to those of the Republican government in the early months of the war. But it is worth noting that except for Carlist Navarre and a few districts of Old Castile, there was not a single case where the people—the civilian population—rose and took power in the name of the Insurgents.

It is natural to write about "Franco's army" since everyone came to know it as such, but things had to happen before he became the Caudillo and Generalissimo. The first thing that occurred was the death of the nominal Rebel leader, General

Sanjurjo, in a plane crash on July 19. Five days later, General Mola formed a military junta in Burgos. He does not seem even to have consulted Franco, who did not become a member for a few weeks.

There were three important posts of command at the beginning—Mola in northern Spain, Queipo de Llano in Andalusia, and Franco in Morocco. Of the three, Franco was the most acceptable to all the other generals, with his legendary reputation, his safe political record, and his well-earned fame as a ruthless disciplinarian. Besides, the Army of Africa which he commanded was the strongest military force and was occupying the most important territory.

At a meeting in Salamanca on September 1, a *mando único* (single command) was established with Franco as the Caudillo —a title by which he has been known ever since. On September 29, the junta met again and made Franco "Head of the Government." In his first "law" he called himself "Head of the State" —a difference that was to mean much after the war ended. (He still is, in 1972, Head of the State.) Hugh Thomas called this "a real *coup d'état.*" The appointments were made formal on October 1, 1936, in Burgos, a date celebrated every year since. When a government with a cabinet was formed in Burgos toward the end of January 1937, Generalissimo Franco also became President of the Council (Premier) and the ministers took an oath of allegiance to him.

As if the fates were determined to give Francisco Franco a clear field, General Mola, as I wrote, was killed in a plane crash on June 3, 1937, eliminating the only possible rival and political dissenter, and probably the best of the Spanish military commanders, as Hitler said.

Queipo de Llano, incidentally, remained cooped up in Seville for the duration of the war. His nightly radio talks were the best propaganda the Insurgents had—vulgar, crude, undignified, often witty and personal, and always popular—but he could never aspire to national leadership.

On the Loyalist side, a near-miracle was being performed as the people—unorganized, without leadership, with hardly any arms—rose spontaneously to secure much the greater part of Spain, including all the biggest cities except Saragossa and Seville, and some smaller ones like Burgos, Pamplona, Segovia and Valladolid. However, the government stupidly hesitated at first to issue arms to workers and peasants, with results that in many localities were fatal.

President Azaña had acted reassuringly in the weeks before the outbreak, and the public was lulled. Thousands of wives and children left Madrid for the northern and eastern beach resorts and many were to be separated from husbands and fathers throughout the war. *La Pasionaria* confessed later that even the Communists were caught off guard. "Although the Communist party was the first to denounce the criminal plans of Franco and his crew and the clear danger to the Republic," she wrote in her memoirs, "perhaps it did not realize the full, tragic extent of that danger."

The government had lost control of Spanish Morocco in two days: July 17 and 18, 1936. The uprising and fighting started on the mainland on July 18. Republican officers and officials around the country, as well as in Madrid, were, almost unbelievably, caught by surprise. Some generals remained loyal, but if they were not in government-controlled territory, they were arrested and shot. The deadly, life-or-death aspect of the Civil War was unhesitatingly embraced from the first day by both sides.

The Rebels were immediately successful in Navarre, Aragon, Old Castile, and southern Andalusia. In those regions, the garrisons rose, with Rebel officers shooting unwilling associates. *Casas del Pueblo* of the workers were swiftly occupied and all known leftists executed. The peasants in Andalusia were heavily Anarchist and anticlerical, and they hated the army and Civil Guard. They naturally tried to resist, but even the loyal civil governors refused them arms, either foolishly believing past pledges of army loyalty or fearing the revolutionary spirit of the peasants and workers. Hundreds and, in time, thousands were killed.

Seville was the key to Andalusia. General Queipo de Llano

(then head of the *Carabineros*), hid his intentions, surreptitiously arrested the commanding general, civil governor, and police chief, and disarmed what loyal officers there were. He did this with a handful of officers who were in the plot and some two hundred soldiers. By nightfall he had won over the Civil Guard and Assault Guards. Workers belatedly called a general strike but the public, as elsewhere, had been surprised. Queipo now had the only armed troops and police and the army trucks. He had shown remarkable audacity, a shrewd use of terror, and a clever radio barrage of propaganda to the effect that Insurgents were in control. His victory was enormously helpful to the Rebels. Contemporary journalists and later historians justly credit him with an extraordinary feat.

The way the Republican government in Madrid hesitated, floundered, and dithered during the first twenty-four hours of the revolt is a controversial feature for historians. It made no sense, even when one says that the Republican leaders did not understand what was happening. The government may have been lulled by the fact that, in spite of Mola's efforts, the revolt seemed badly planned and lacked coordination. There were supposedly loyal ranking officers in most key centers of the peninsula. Actually, many had been playing both sides or had deceived the government. It was hoped that the air force and navy could prevent Moroccan units from crossing the Strait, which was briefly the case. An often overlooked, but critical feature was that the moderate, bourgeois government feared their own leftists and so refused to arm the working classes until almost too late. By the evening of July 18, the Republican leaders at last knew the worst.

The government then had about 60,000 soldiers, mostly ill-trained recruits. The Rebel forces were no more than half that size, but they included 4,200 *Tercios,* and 15,000 Moorish *Regulares.* If the Army of Africa could be ferried over to the mainland, it seemed that nothing imaginable could stop the Rebel forces. Nearly all the Civil Guards and many of the 18,000-strong Assault Guards had gone over to the Insurgents. The regular police—the *Seguridad*—obeyed whichever side got control in their localities.

Workers—the armed proletariat—spontaneously forming militia units, were the government's mainstay and, in many places, its only support. That they were strong enough to hold the cities and the territories they did against professional troops and police forces is one of the most remarkable popular military feats in history. It took fanatical courage and fearful losses to do it.

Had Madrid fallen, all would have been over. The turning point there was the belated distribution of 5,000 rifles by some young officers to men of the UGT and CNT labor federations. Fortunately, the conspirators hesitated, especially General Joaquín Fanjul in the Montaña Barracks. He stayed inside, expecting reinforcements which never came. Fanjul was a rabid rightist, almost senile and, many thought, unbalanced. General Miaja, after hesitating briefly, went with the government. Coming from a working-class family, he was hailed as "the people's general." Fanjul therefore found himself cut off with 2,000 soldiers and a few hundred Falangists.

After a day's preparation, the workers' militia, armed with pistols and rifles and two pieces of field artillery, attacked the Montaña Barracks with desperate bravery, suffering appalling casualties from the machine guns of the garrison. The defenders evidently quarreled. Some of them hoisted a white flag, but when workers advanced, others mowed them down. The maddened besiegers then broke through the main gate. Fanjul was rushed away to prison and later executed. Dozens of other officers committed suicide or were killed on the spot. Fifty thousand rifles and much ammunition were captured. The UGT, backed by the Communist party and the now Communist-dominated United Communist-Socialist Youth, took control of Madrid.

One of the leading plotters, General Manuel Goded, who was in Majorca, declared martial law and flew to Barcelona. The Catalan capital, it will be recalled, was an Anarchist stronghold and the scene of many sanguinary riots. Exceptionally, a large Civil Guard unit and some of the soldiers joined thou-

sands of recklessly brave Anarchist workers in overwhelming
Goded's forces and the security police. The attackers suffered
fearful casualties. It was all over by five in the afternoon when
General Goded and his staff surrendered. Goded made a radio
broadcast at seven o'clock in which he said, "Destiny has been
against me and I am a prisoner, wherefore I release all my
followers from their obligations toward me." The message was
read and reread over the Barcelona, Madrid, and Valencia sta-
tions. Within a week, all of Catalonia, with its important industries, was in the hands of some 50,000 militiamen, mostly industrial workers.

Unhappily for the Republic, the Rebels held the Balearic
Islands of Majorca and Ibiza where the Italians were to set up
their air and naval bases. Minorca remained loyal, but useless,
all through the war. Among the other important cities, Valencia, the biggest port on the east coast after Barcelona, wav-
ered tensely for two weeks and then was held for the government. There was no military revolt in Bilbao; the Basque
leaders just took over and remained loyal to the Republic.

In Oviedo, Asturias, center of the 1934 uprising, the commander, Colonel Antonio Aranda, hookwinked the people. He
was thought to be a loyal Republican and he certainly was a
Freemason. He always got on well with leftists and was distrusted by the Falangists. Through trickery he brought in Civil
and Assault Guard units, sent the armed miners off to Madrid,
and in their absence seized the city. On the way to Madrid the
miners were met at Valladolid (Aranda had sent word ahead)
and were massacred. However, other miners seized the towns
and villages of Oviedo Province. This situation was to remain
unchanged until the Franco forces conquered Asturias the following year, Aranda and his garrison meanwhile withstanding
a grueling and heroic siege.

The northern ports of Gijón and Santander were held by the
workers' militias. Franco's native province of Galicia, including the ports and El Ferrol naval base, fell to a typical combination of trickery and the superior arms of the soldiers and police.

The largest naval base, Cartagena, on the southeast coast,

was saved. The sailors mutinied, murdered their officers, and captured a battleship, three cruisers, a dozen destroyers, and ten submarines, which, added to other units, gave the Loyalists the bulk of the Spanish Navy.

Premier Casares Quiroga had foolishly ordered anguished civil governors around the country not to distribute arms. Yet it was the government's only hope. He was a timid man and resigned on the very first night, July 18. Azaña seemed bewildered. The next day he chose a friend and colleague, José Giral, a professor of chemistry, as his Prime Minister. Giral formed an all-Republican party cabinet which at last recognized the need to arm the people of Madrid but, tragically, it was not done on government orders elsewhere.

A loyal general, Luis Castelló, prevented a Rebel rising in Badajoz near the Portuguese frontier, thus separating the main Rebel area under Mola in the north (Navarre and Castile) from Andalusia in the south. The mutiny of the sailors and the loyalty of the air force prevented General Franco from transferring the bulk of the Army of Africa to the mainland.

One of the tantalizing "if's" of the Civil War was this: if the government had had the insight, courage, and trust to distribute arms to the people the first day in every province, it is conceivable that the rebellion would have been crushed. But this meant giving power to left-wing, revolutionary masses, which the government feared to do.

All the same, Madrid, Barcelona, Valencia, Bilbao, Gijón, Santander, Málaga, Murcia, Alicante, all of Catalonia and New Castile, and the entire Mediterranean coast from Gibraltar to the French frontier, were in government hands. Franco's Army of Africa was blockaded. Mola was held in the Sierra de Guadarrama passes by the suicidal courage of the untrained militia. The prospects were so gloomy by July 29 that, according to Mola's secretary, the general contemplated suicide.

The Popular Front not only controlled all the major urban and industrial areas but also held the huge national gold reserves of the Treasury. It had some loyal troops and trained security units. Above all, it had an aroused people who were hastily forming themselves into party militias. From every appearance, the uprising had failed.

Appearances were deceptive, of course. The government had no commander in chief comparable to Franco or with his authority. The few high-ranking Spanish regular officers who remained loyal—José Miaja, Hernández Sarabia, Sebastián Pozas, Vicente Rojo, Carlos Asensio, Segismundo Casado—were of mediocre quality. Casado, at the end, turned traitor. The effective Spanish military leaders came from the civilian ranks, although the two I mentioned earlier who played the greatest roles—Enrique Lister, the former stonemason, and Juan Modesto, the woodcutter—had some training. They had fled to Russia after the collapse of the 1934 Asturian uprising. (Lister, incidentally, is Manuel in André Malraux's novel, *Man's Hope.*)

Gustavo Durán, a musician, became a divisional commander. So did the former teacher, Manuel Tagüeña, and the swashbuckling *El Campesino.* He may once have been a peasant but, more significantly, he was a deserter from the Spanish Foreign Legion and had also fought in Morocco.

The leader who was to emerge as the strong man on the Republican side was to be the civilian, Dr. Juan Negrín. His Minister of Defense was the moderate Socialist, Indalecio Prieto, who had never read a military treatise. Previously, the Minister was the equally unmilitary Largo Caballero. There was no central General Staff at the beginning. The War Ministry, for instance, had no control over transport. Each political party and trade union had its own military headquarters and services.

For several months, the fighting was between the Insurgent regular army troops, bolstered by the Army of Africa, and the people, spontaneously banded into military forces. It then became necessary for the Republican government to create a disciplined army under central control. The process resembled what happened in the American and French Revolutions, although there was to be no Washington or Napoleon in Republican Spain.

The Loyalist militias came from the trade unions, labor organizations, and left-wing political parties. Those army officers in the government zone who remained loyal were mistrusted, at least for some time. Álvarez del Vayo, the Republican Foreign Minister, estimated that about 500 regular officers, including thirteen generals, served with the government forces. Other authorities give similar figures. Professor Payne says that about 3,000 regular officers actually served the Republic, although only 500 "ever held active field command of troops." A capable corps of junior- and middle-ranking officers was never formed on the Republican side comparable to Franco's "temporary lieutenants." Since there were some 15,000 officers in all when the war began, the proportion which was loyal was small, even counting those who were executed by the Insurgents. For some reason, virtually all the 8,000 noncommissioned officers went over to the Rebel side where they could. Most of the time the Loyalists had greater manpower, but this was more than offset by the quality of the Army of Africa and the Germans, plus the heavy armament and other equipment of the Italians and Germans.

The Republican militia made every mistake that could be made. It was undisciplined, with no coordination and even rivalry between units. It was completely ignorant of military technique and badly led, partly because it could not trust its staff officers. There was no lack of combativity or courage, especially in street fighting or in small engagements against a localized enemy. "Party pride seemed stronger than the feeling of common defense," Arturo Barea, the Spanish novelist, wrote of the Madrid front. The government found itself negotiating with Anarchists, Socialists, Communists, and Republicans, each speaking for themselves. Largo Caballero foolishly resisted the idea of a regular army as not being in the Spanish tradition. He believed in the guerrilla technique.

So every militiaman decided which post would be most suitable, and abandoned it when he changed his mind or when his ammunition ran out or, of course, when an enemy bullet settled his problems. Moreover, regionalism played a powerful role. The Basques fought only for their territory; Catalans were always reluctant and inefficient fighters on the Madrid front. Another national characteristic was that the militiamen were far more effective in street fighting than in the open where they were subject to sudden and incalculable panic.

It was obvious that such a militia, although it had saved the Republic, was no match for the disciplined, battle-hardened Army of Africa. The disorder, anyway, bordered on chaos. Major José Martín Blásquez, then in the War Ministry, in his book, *I Helped to Build an Army,* wrote despairingly: "Never in any war has there been so much waste as that committed by the militiamen of the Republic. They wasted everything—food, war material, transport vehicles—and lives."

The Anarchists were the greatest disciplinary problem because, philosophically and ideologically, their beliefs were based on the complete liberty of the individual. They firmly opposed submission to authority: no hierarchy of officers, no saluting, no regimentation, no distinctions. In the Anarchist "Iron Column" lots were drawn to see who should stand guard at night. Because of the Anarchist philosophy, and perhaps of the Spanish temperament, the government could not organize a cohesive revolutionary army as Cromwell did in England, Carnot in the French Revolution, and Trotsky in Russia. The Anarchists and other militiamen, too, could be very brave or very cowardly as the spirit moved them. Someone called it "organized indiscipline."

This state of affairs could not last, as even the Anarchists realized. There was a call for discipline. The Communists had understood the necessity from the beginning. One of their invaluable contributions to the Republican cause was that they put aside revolutionary ideals for a concentration on waging and winning the war militarily, and for that, discipline and organization were imperative. They already had Comintern advisers, one of them an Italian Communist, Vittorio Vidali who, in Spain, went under the *nom de guerre* of Carlos Contreras. He, among the foreigners, and Lister and Modesto among the Spanish Communists, were mainly instrumental in creating the Fifth Regiment.

It was a remarkable organization—one of the great revolutionary military units of all time. They took anyone who knew anything in the military line and made him an officer, whether he was a Communist or not. Vidali claimed that only 200 of the first 600 volunteers were Communist. In ten days, they had 6,000 men and a Communist ratio of one to four. Even Burnett Bolloten, who is a hostile witness, writes that the recruits were "Communists, Socialists, non-party workers and peasants." However, the core around which the Fifth Regiment was formed was the United Communist-Socialist Youth, and it was essentially a Communist force. The political commissars and the commanders were Communists. By December 1936 there were 60,000 members.

Enrique Lister had taken command of the Regiment in September. It was with them that he first earned his reputation as an outstanding field commander and a stern disciplinarian who made no bones about shooting soldiers who tried to turn back. Carlos, as everybody called Vidali, was even tougher for he was a real killer, but he was also an inspired organizer as well as a ruthless disciplinarian. Incidentally, he is now (1972) the Communist party leader in Trieste, Italy, and still a faithful Stalinist.

Many who were not Communists when they joined the Fifth Regiment became party members. The unit got preferential treatment in the distribution of Soviet arms when they began to come along. Some picked men were even sent to Russia for training as tank operators and pilots. The Fifth Regiment was not only a fighting force; it carried on propaganda, ran hospitals, repair shops, the incipient war industry in central Spain, homes for orphans, and training schools for aviators and tank drivers.

In October 1936, the militias were put under the General Staff by the government. The political commissar system was then extended to all units—a victory for the Communists, since nearly all of the commissars were party men. This, of course, was the system used by the Bolsheviks in the Russian Revolution when they could not trust their czarist officers. Commissars were given equal rank to the commanding officers of their units.

The basis of the Republican army was worked out at this time in the "mixed brigade"—a militarily self-sustaining unit, handling its own transportation, engineering, light artillery, antitank sections, munitions, communications, supplies, and medical detachments. The Insurgents reached the edge of Madrid before Largo Caballero could organize the "mixed brigades," so he reluctantly had to call upon the Fifth Regiment, which was mainly responsible for stopping the Rebel forces before the International Brigade could move in.

This Regiment, numbering between 60,000 and 70,000, could safely be disbanded on January 31, 1937. The rank and file were then about half Communist. The "mixed brigades" as it turned out, were mostly commanded by Communists. It was never possible to break down the conflicts and rivalries among Socialists, Communists, and Anarchists.

The Nationalists had no party coloration. Generalissimo Franco had to invent one. At least, he had to take what political odds and ends he had lying about and turn them into a "movement." For that purpose, the best material was the *Falange Española* which, thirty-five years later, is still the only officially sanctioned political party. It was launched in Madrid on October 29, 1933, by José Antonio Primo de Rivera. He said in a speech that if its goals "must be achieved by violence, there must be no shrinking from violence. . . . No other dialectic is possible save the dialectic of fists and pistols when justice or the Fatherland is offended."

This, indeed, became the tactics of his followers, although José Antonio was not, himself, a man of violence. He did not believe in achieving power through elections, but nevertheless ran for a Cortes seat in 1933 and was elected. He once denied that his movement was Fascist, but, as was stated, he put out a twenty-six-point program of "national syndicalism" in November 1934 which was a form of Fascism. He was a hopeless administrator, surrounded by incompetent sycophants.

Yet he and his movement filled an obvious, and to this day, enduring need. Many students joined. Professor Payne, who has written the standard work on the movement: *Falange: A History of Spanish Fascism,* says that 60 to 70 per cent of the Falangists were under twenty-one. Even José Antonio said that they had "more heart than head." They were superpatriotic and ultranationalistic—two Fascist traits.

This paradoxical man was, at first, more inclined to the Left than the Right. In vain he wooed Indalecio Prieto, whom he liked and admired. His movement was naturally rightist and, in the prevailing climate, it was sure to be militant. In fact, its significant role began when, against José Antonio's wishes at that time, it took to violence. To be sure, he did not seem to be trying hard to control his *pistoleros.*

José Antonio ran for parliament again in the February 1936 elections but he lost, and thereby lost his parliamentary immunity from arrest. By that time the Falange probably had 25,000 members, of whom at least a third fought in the streets. They were as tough and vicious as the Anarchist militants in the spring of 1936 and certainly contributed a great deal to the intolerable disorders. By July their numbers had increased to about 75,000. Most of these were what was known as "New Shirts" in contrast to the pre-1936 group of "Old Shirts." The shirts were blue. The analogy to Mussolini's Black Shirts and Hitler's Brown Shirts was obvious.

When the war began there was a rush to join the organization in the Nationalist territory. By the end of 1936, the Falange is believed to have had a million members.

The Blue Shirts were joined by the green-shirted JAP late in the spring of 1936. The JAP leader was Serrano Suñer, Franco's brother-in-law. To get results, it was realized that the Falange would have to join Mola's army plot.

José Antonio was arrested on March 15, 1936, for "the possession of arms without a license"—a mere pretext. He was kept at first in the *Carcel Modelo* of Madrid and moved in June to the Alicante prison. In both places he was able to keep in contact with his followers. He no longer opposed or regretted their shocking terrorism.

He was one of those men who seem marked for martyrdom. In all that has been said and written about him one gets the picture of the most impressive type of Spanish aristocrat and patriot: cultured, idealistic, gallant, and loyal to the memory of his dictator-father. Although he began as a liberal, he epitomized everything that was opposed to Republican ideals. He admired British imperialism and often quoted Kipling's "If" in English, for he knew it by heart. Like the Fascists, he was convinced of the decline of the West and believed in the *Fuehrer princip* (the leader principle) and in an élite, a hierarchy, and tradition. He despised materialism as bourgeois or Marxist. Like so many of the finest characters of the time in Spain, he was a confused man, torn by the complexities and contradictions of the society in which he lived. Spain is a country for the positive thinker who has no doubts.

All attempts to free him or get him released failed. He had said when he formed the Falange "Life is not worth the effort if it is not to be burned up in the service of a great enterprise." In his self-defense at the final session of his trial on November 17, 1936, he proudly said, "Life is not a firecracker which one lets off at the end of a garden party." Life was, for him, a sacrifice. He was condemned to death and executed on November 20, 1936. According to a member of the firing squad, he died bravely, crying, *"Arriba España!"* ("Rise up, Spain!"), the borrowed slogan of the Falange movement which was adopted by all the Nationalists throughout the Civil War.

José Antonio was executed without Premier Largo Caballero's consent and probably against his wishes, for it made a Nationalist martyr of a man who did not openly approve of Franco's policies. The Falange was not a part of Mola's *Junta de Defensa Nacional* set up in Burgos in July 1936. However, it was the only political movement available to the Insurgents. José Antonio was "canonized" by General Franco in 1938 as "the official symbol and patron saint of the new [Franco] dictatorship."

Yet the *Falange Española* was by no means the only right-wing organization backing the Nationalist cause; it was simply the most important, politically speaking. The Carlist *Tradicionalistas* were by far the best fighters, but politically they were a hopeless anachronism. Then there was a small but significant organization which, in fact, had originated Spanish "national syndicalism." This was the *Juntas de Ofensiva Nacional-Sindicalista,* known as the JONS. Its leader, Ramiro Ledesma, had been first with the slogan *"Arriba España!"* and an equally used motto: *"España, Una, Grande y Libre!"* ("Spain, One, Great and Free!")

The Falange statutes have a significant passage: "As creator of the Historical Era in which Spain attains the possibility of realizing her historical destiny and the goals of the Movement, the *Jefe* [Franco] assumes absolute authority in its utmost fullness. The *Jefe* is responsible before God and before History." This, not Fascism, is the key to Spain's governmental system during and since the Civil War.

On April 18, 1937, Franco issued a decree uniting the Falangists and Carlists into one organization along with the other minor parties which supported the Nationalist cause. The new movement had the awkward name of *Falange Española Tradicionalista y de las JONS.* The Monarchists were absorbed at the same time. The uniform was the blue shirt of the Falange with the red beret of the Carlist Traditionalists. They all used the Fascist salute. The Caudillo's move put an end to political speculations and rivalries for the duration of the war, which was an incalculable advantage over his Republican enemies.

Because of the overwhelming numerical superiority of the Falangists and their role in the street fighting, the FET (short for *Falange Española Tradicionalista*) became an essentially Falangist movement. In the Civil War, and afterward, it embraced all military officers, all government employees, social services, teachers' and students' organizations, employers, and workers.

In a speech on July 17, 1937, the first anniversary of the rebellion, Franco said that the FET "will follow the structure of totalitarian regimes such as Italy and Germany." Yet the Falange never was a totalitarian party in the Fascist or Communist sense of the one-party state. It has had no power, except as Franco delegated powers to it, or took them away. It was a convenient framework for the state and a shield, when desired, against army, church, bankers, businessmen, and Monarchists. Above all, it was a convenient fiction; a means of having a "Glorious National Movement" which existed as a political party in name only.

The system gave a most obvious and seemingly unanswerable label of "Fascism" to the Franco cause, arousing a whole world of liberals, democrats, and leftists to oppose and to fight to the death against this Fascism. Those who labeled the Insurgents as Fascist had every right to do so. After all, Franco himself had so identified his movement.

It was only later that one could see that the Franco regime was not Fascist in the new, classic and historic definition of the term, any more than the Republicans, even at the height of Communist influence, could rightly be branded as "Reds."

One can argue that there are various kinds of Fascist systems and that the Franco regime did become a variety of Fascism. However, Mussolini and Hitler had given the label a distinctive form at the time of the Civil War. The classic description is Mussolini's article on Fascism in the *Enciclopedia Treccani.* Franco's regime never has fit this mold. Generalissimo Franco, from 1937 to 1972, has had a straightforward military dictatorship with some Fascist characteristics, but no more. Although he became the Caudillo, there was no one-party rule and no totalitarian state in the sense of the Falange dictating every aspect of public and private life. There was no racism as in Nazi Germany, although the insignificant JONS was anti-Semitic. There were no militaristic adventures. Under true

Fascism the army is the instrument of the state working through the party. In Spain, the generals—Franco included—had no ideology or political philosophy and *they* ruled. In Italy and Germany, the church was not allowed to interfere in education or given powers of censorship.

Even José Antonio had denied that his movement was Fascist in a July 3, 1934, statement to the Cortes: "It so happens that we have grown up into the world at a moment when Fascism is prevailing, and I can assure Señor Prieto that this does us more harm than good, because Fascism possesses a series of external peculiarities which we do not intend to adopt for one moment."

After José Antonio's execution, the Falange had no outstanding leader and no coherent ideology. It was never a governing body. It was simply a means and an instrument of government under the Generalissimo's control, which it is to this day. The martyrized José Antonio Primo de Rivera could safely be worshipped; there was no living rival to the Caudillo.

The nearest thing to a political leader during the Civil War (and World War II) was Ramón Serrano Suñer, but he could not be rated higher, let us say, than Goebbels or Ciano. The *Cuñadissimo,* as everyone called him, making a play on the words *cuñado* (brother-in-law) and generalissimo, showed up in Salamanca in the winter of 1937 and immediately became Franco's trusted adviser. He had been trapped in Madrid, where his two brothers were shot, and he was imprisoned for several months until the Republican authorities foolishly and carelessly let him enter the Dutch Embassy, from where he escaped. He was an ambitious, shrewd, clever lawyer and politician, but highly emotional and burning with hatred for the *Rojos* who had killed his brothers.

Generalissimo Franco's brother, Nicolás, had been trying clumsily to form a political front. Serrano Suñer had much greater political talent. He became the most powerful civilian in the Nationalist camp. He admired Fascist Italy, where he had studied law and, for some unknown reason, he hated the British. Franco named him Minister of the Interior and *Jefe Nacional* of Press and Propaganda for the FET.

In 1936, Nationalist Spain began a regime by a military dictator, unchallenged, personal, autocratic, rigidly conservative—a man, not a movement or a Fascist system. The tradition went back to the "divine right of kings" and, indeed, on the postwar coins the head of Franco is rimmed with the ancient blessing: "By the Grace of God." Franco even took the rank of "Captain General of the Army and Navy" on July 19, 1938, a title previously held in Spanish history only by the king.

On December 9, 1936, I cabled to *The New York Times* a dispatch containing the following passage (which was, however, cut out by the cable editor and not printed):

> The use of the word "strength" in describing the positions of either side is only relative and that is a very important consideration which foreigners evidently do not take adequately into account. Neither side is strong enough to deliver a really smashing attack at present, which means that Franco cannot take Madrid and the Government cannot yet relieve Madrid. It will take bigger guns, more men, more planes, tanks and material than either side possesses to break this deadlock.

The generals were facing a long and bitter war against a majority of the Spanish people, a war that they could not win without foreign help. Franco was quoted by German Ambassador Eberhard von Stohrer, as saying in May 1938, with victory in sight, that 40 per cent of the population in Nationalist Spain was "unreliable." This could hardly have been an exaggerated figure. The generals had had to proclaim a "state of war" immediately and maintain it throughout the conflict, something the Republican government did not do until the war was ending.

The Germans and Italians in Spain were critical, and sometimes horrified, by the cruelty of the Nationalist repression and the reactionary, clerical nature of Franco's political measures. This was not, of course, the picture which the world was getting. Almost all the publicity had gone to the atrocities of the Loyalist militiamen. Time, and the patient work of scholars, were needed to shed the light of truth on both sides. The muse of history says: "A plague o' both your houses." It was a truly terrible war.

5

TERROR AND REVOLUTION

THE SPANISH CIVIL WAR BEGAN in an explosion of hatred; a haphazard social revolution in the Republican zone; and a reign of terror which, in different forms, went on throughout the war on both sides, and for four years afterward under the Franco dictatorship.

There is a near-unanimity of opinion among foreign historians of the Spanish Civil War on the atrocities committed by both sides in the first months of the conflict. In general terms, the outrages of the Republican side were carried out by an aroused, uncontrolled, spontaneous, class conscious and passionate people while the Madrid government, deprived of army officers and police, was distressed and helpless. The Nationalist atrocities were calculated measures of policy, spiced by revenge and a form of class hatred.

The judgment of the British scholar Hugh Thomas, whose work is as authoritative and objective as any history of the war can be, is typical. He points out that life in the Insurgent zone was at all times under complete and effective military rule. The workers and peasants—the vast majority of the people—were actually or potentially hostile, along with many liberal and professional middle-class elements.

"Hence," he writes, "not only did the rebels feel bound to act with extraordinary ruthlessness towards their enemies, but also they had to act openly, and expose the bodies of those whom they killed to public gaze. All that the Church officially insisted upon was that those killed should have the opportunity for confession. . . . There was this one difference between the executions on the Nationalist side and those on the side of the [popular] revolution: the great majority of the 'Red' atrocities, perhaps numerically more than those in Nationalist Spain, were carried out by irresponsible persons and were deplored by most of what remained of the administration of the State, without normal forces of law and order. On the Nationalist side, however, the killings were done in a society where the Army, the police and the Civil Guard survived, and which sponsored the massacres as a question of policy."

It should also be kept in mind that, with minor and sporadic exceptions, the atrocities in the Loyalist zone ended as soon as the government was able to assert its authority. On the Nationalist side they never ended during the war and they continued in the postwar reprisals.

"On the Republican side," Thomas continues, "there were public protests against the outrages. . . . On the Nationalist side there do not seem to have been any protests. . . . Among Republicans later there have been many admissions of regret at the extent of the atrocities; among the Nationalists apparently none."

The worst perpetrators on the Republican side were the revolutionary extremists—mostly Anarchists. On the Insurgent side, they were the military, the Civil Guard, and the old parties of the Right, especially from the CEDA. (The Moorish *Regulares* and the Foreign Legion acted like beasts as they conquered territory, but this was part of the military history of the war.)

Historians of all nations have indulged in a numbers game about those killed in the terror on each side. Both Republicans and Nationalists greatly exaggerated the figures. Thomas estimated the Republican executions at 60,000 and the Nationalists at 50,000 during the war, outside of the battlefields. Other authorities (Professors Payne and Jackson, for instance) do not believe that the totals for the Insurgents were less than for the Loyalists. To these figures must be added the thousands estimated to have been killed by the Franco regime between the end of the war in 1939 and 1943, when wholesale executions ceased.

The most persecuted single group, providing the highest proportionate number of victims, was the clergy—priests, monks, and nuns—killed in a brief and almost incredible outburst of popular fury in the first weeks of the rebellion.

After the war, the Franco regime issued a thick volume called *The General Cause,* purporting to be a scholarly and official description of "Red" crimes. It is such blatant and one-sided propaganda that no historian trusts it very far, but its figures on the clergy seem to have come from the National Sanctuary in Valladolid and are probably near the truth. (Incidentally, the Sanctuary gives a total of 61,000 violent deaths on the Republican side but does not mention those killed by the Nationalists nor does it mention the Basque priests executed by the Insurgents.)

"The total number of the assassinations which the Popular Front committed throughout the red zone," says the *Causa General,* "in the person of ministers of the Catholic religion and members of the religious orders, amounts to 7,937, including 13 bishops, 5,937 priests and 2,669 monks and nuns."

The rebellion had come after months of turbulence. Men were not only armed and, in many cases, trained, but also consumed with fears and hatreds. The atmosphere was so heated that what occurred was not a build-up but a violent explosion. The effective power in the Republican zone was, at first, in the hands of workers and peasants who pushed their weak, bungling government aside and took "justice" into their own hands. They were the ones who had defeated the rebellion in two-thirds of Spain, and it took a surprised and horrified government three or four months to put an end to their destructive passion. Between July and October 1936, workers' committees sprang up everywhere. They armed themselves, organized militias, and waged war—sometimes against other workers.

There was a form of juvenile delinquency, with youths given the power to requisition cars, use firearms, and kill in the name of patriotism or class hatred. Few people were killed in cold blood on the Loyalist side, but many on the Rebel side, for it was a matter of policy. The Republican leaders were not generals or colonels, but civilians, liberals, intellectuals or, in exceptional cases, labor leaders like Largo Caballero. Soldierly hardness or the deliberate use of terror was unthinkable to them.

The great wave of assassination and destruction on the Loyalist side was revolutionary in content because of its spontaneity and class hatred. Churches and convents were burned everywhere, not because the clergy had taken part in the uprising, but because of historic, anticlerical passions. To the militiamen, the churches were symbols of what we now call the Establishment. There was little pillage; art treasures were spared.

In addition to the clergy, the chief victims in the Loyalist zone were from the upper class and the bourgeoisie, especially in rural districts. Often to be wealthy was enough to be "guilty" of a crime against society, or—in the eyes of the Left Socialists, Communists, and Anarchists—to be enemies in the war. Some Anarchists (like their Carlist counterparts in Navarre) killed like crusaders destroying heretics or pagans. A few were sadistic butchers and criminals. Most simply gave way to an instinctive hatred and resentment which came out of generations of repressed passions.

The Republican leaders immediately realized that uncontrolled terrorism would destroy their government and their cause, but how to control the "uncontrollables," as they were called? They used what soldiers and police remained loyal. Thousands of right-wingers in Madrid were permitted to take refuge in embassies or houses made "extraterritorial" where many a Latin American minor diplomat, or Middle Eastern, or Finnish (one of the worst) made fortunes milking distressed victims, some of whom remained cooped up throughout the war. Leaders like Dr. Juan Negrín visited prisons at night to protect inmates and often to get them out to the safety of foreign embassies. One of the deadliest practices on both sides during the first months was for leftist or rightist groups to raid prisons with or without lists of names, taking victims on *paseos* (literally, "for a ride") from which they never returned.

Barcelona resembled Madrid, with the Anarchists committing most of the violence. The anticlerical abuses were even worse than in the capital. Hardly a church in the city escaped the torch. However, the Catalan government, the *Generalitat,* freely handed out thousands of passports to middle- and upper-class families, permitting them to get away in ships or planes. Rivalry between the leftist groups in Barcelona led to many deaths which were little more than gang killings.

When the news of the Badajoz massacre by the Moors (August 14) reached Madrid, the slaughter of political prisoners could be averted only by the government forming revolutionary, or popular tribunals. Justice was rough, but there was a certain honest legality about it. There were lawyers courageous enough to defend the accused. According to Professor Jackson, the "judges" were neither callous nor slipshod; they tried seriously to be fair on the whole, and far more suspects were freed than was realized. Many rebellious officers were shot, but some of those court-martialed had their sentences commuted. It was usually crude, quick work with the accused considered guilty unless he could prove his innocence—and fast.

Good men died by the hundreds because they were generals or colonels, factory managers or landowners; many of them unjustly, even by revolutionary standards. Sometimes prisoners were shot because the Insurgents were approaching, or because of an air raid, or because news arrived of some Rebel atrocity.

The *paseos* went on in Madrid through August, sometimes dozens in a night. It was always ostentatious—careening cars; the firing of guns where they could be heard; dead bodies left lying in the streets and fields. The sense of terror was real and justified.

Those who were saved, or just left alone, tried to avoid attention. Although nearly 300 nuns were killed, many thousands were saved. Some convents were turned into hospitals, with the nuns staying on as nurses. Augustinian monks in a Madrid school remained unmolested throughout the war. In a Salesian-run school, a regiment of Communist youths and Salesian friars lived side by side until the end of the war.

Among the most famous victims in Madrid were two brothers, the Dukes of Veragua and de la Vega, descendants of Columbus. (Fortunately, they were not the last of their line.)

The random killings in Madrid were just about brought to an end by a series of measures the government took at the end of August. All people were instructed to lock their doors at 11:00 P.M.; to allow no one in; and if militiamen tried to enter, to telephone the police.

Most of the extreme leftist leaders were serious, idealistic men. They saw no purpose in wanton killing and acted to stop it when they could. By the end of 1936 or beginning of 1937, the so-called Red Terror was entirely over. It has been argued that by that time every known rightist politician who could be caught had been imprisoned or killed or taken refuge in embassies. But it can be said that the Loyalist terror could and would have been much worse but for truly agonizing efforts on the part of many Republican leaders to stop it.

The terror, anyway, was so irrational and haphazard that it was ineffective; it did not get the fifth columnists or many of the worst enemies of the Republic. The terror in the Nationalist zone was far more effective.

One side effect of the terror in the Loyalist zone, which lasted throughout the war, was the operation of a large number of secret police organizations. They were all bad, but the Communists had by far the worst, especially when they got control of the *Servicio de Investigación Militar* (SIM) in 1938.

The objective supposedly was counterespionage against fifth columnists, spies, traitors, deserters, and the like. Unhappily, a great part of the activity was a murderous fight between Communists, Anarchists, Socialists, Trotskyites, POUMsters, and other varieties of left-wing factions. The struggle by the Communists for supremacy was at the heart of the conflict.

Each group had its *chekas,* where tortures and murders took place against the will and orders of the moderate men who ran the government. For much of the time, the authorities managed to restrain these activities. There were not many deaths from this internecine strife, and nine out of ten citizens probably did not even know what was happening. It was as though a lunatic fringe were at work. These were not the men who, by their thousands, formed the militias that fought the Rebels. The importance of the secret police, therefore, should not be exaggerated, but they played a nefarious role in the war which has naturally blackened all accounts of the Second Republic.

As early as September 1936 the Communists, under the direction of the Russian NKVD (People's Commissariat for International Affairs) representative, Alexander Orlov, began filling prisons with hundreds of *their*—not necessarily the Republican government's—enemies, torturing and killing many of them. There was not, as Burnett Bolloten, the former United Press correspondent on the Franco side, claimed, "an independent Russian police system" dominating all of Loyalist Spain throughout the war. There were many police organizations (Hugh Thomas counted nine) including some legitimate ones. Professor Payne, more accurately, concedes that the "Communist-controlled espionage network . . . never became absolute," since the government, army, *Seguridad,* trade unions, political parties, and regional governments all had their own police organizations.

The Communists worked secretly, but when they were detected committing excesses against their chosen enemies, the government stopped them, if only temporarily. At the same time, it was true that the most important and most vicious secret police work was done by the Communists, mostly Spanish but also Russian and Comintern.

The International Brigades likewise had their network functioning as a secret political police along the lines of the Soviet OGPU. Its first chief, suitably, was Vittorio Vidali (Carlos Contreras). It had *chekas* at Albacete, the International Brigade center, and several other places. A CNT prison official,

Melchor Rodríguez, had the courage and humanity to break the secret of the Madrid *chekas* in March 1937, causing a salutary scandal but not a lasting one.

The SIM had a laudable beginning in the autumn of 1937, when Indalecio Prieto, then Negrín's Minister of National Defense, yielded to Communist pressure to form a counterintelligence organization which would also hunt down and suppress the so-called uncontrollables. These were Anarchists and other left-wing revolutionaries, as well as spies, deserters, and agents of the Nationalists. The SIM soon became the most powerful—and also the most odious—of the secret police groups.

Prieto carefully arranged at the beginning to keep control out of Communist hands, but he could not do so for long. Like all the Spanish police, as Gerald Brenan remarked, the SIM was "extraordinarily incompetent." However, it did some effective work in detecting spies and fifth columnists. Yet the methods it used and its self-employment as a Communist instrument against their political enemies, deservedly gave it a black and bitter name. Hugh Thomas, writing of the desperate crisis which followed the Insurgent breakthrough to the coast in April 1938, gives a picture of the SIM in Barcelona which could be magnified for other times and places.

"The SIM," he writes, "undertook a brief private murder campaign of vengeance. Forty people had been 'taken for a ride' before the government intervened to end this development. The special prisons of the SIM in Barcelona, especially that in the convent of San Juan, nevertheless remained full of strange tortures which might have been devised by the ghost of Edgar Allan Poe. A spherical room painted in black with a single light at the top, gave a mad feeling of vertigo. Some cells were so small that one could not sit down. Such tortures were applied indiscriminately to Nationalist and Republican (or Anarchist and POUM) prisoners."

Premier Negrín either could not prudently do anything decisive about the SIM, or considered that stern measures of arrest and execution were necessary. The moderate cabinet ministers, who had insisted on fair standards of justice—Prieto, Giral, Irujo, Zugazagoitia—protested, but were powerless against the SIM and the Red *chekas*. Negrín, himself a middle-class liberal and democrat, was relying more and more on the Communists who, by 1938, saw no other way to keep the war going than through discipline, terror, and greater power for themselves.

This is a feature of the Spanish Civil War which admirers of Juan Negrín, who was Premier during the SIM's creation and existence, find difficult to understand. Dr. Negrín was a man of the highest principles of humanity, although stern and dedicated in his determination to prosecute the war. There was no doubt that he was kept in ignorance of the worst abuses of the SIM and the Spanish-Russian branch of the NKVD, and he was appalled after the war to discover how bad they had been and to learn about their torture cells.

But what did he know at the time? Could he have deliberately turned his back and shut his mind to what was happening in the belief that harsh police measures were unavoidable in such desperate straits? Certainly, when he learned how the Communists had secretly tortured and then killed Andrés Nín, the famous and respected POUM leader, he was so bitterly angry that he threatened to resign. But he stayed in office, judging that a showdown with the Communists would be harmful—perhaps fatal—to the prosecution of the war. There was only one way to fight the war at this stage and that was *with* the Communists. It is also too often forgotten that in addition to an army, Negrín had a Second Republic to administer, a great and complex government of a diminishing but always considerable portion of Spain, with many millions of people living their lives as all people do. Industry, agriculture, finance, jobs, family, education, health, justice, and the endless business of administration had to go on. The Communist terror was selective, and affected relatively few people.

Burnett Bolloten compiled a massively documented book which was intended to demonstrate that the Republican government's democratic structure was nothing but a "grand camouflage" (the name of his book) to hide a regime entirely run by Russian Communists and their obedient Spanish minions. Professor Payne, on the whole, agrees with him. Bolloten claims that the secret police in Spain became "a mere arm" of the Soviet police apparatus and that the Russian OGPU quickly "became the decisive force in determining the course of events in the anti-Franco camp." This is a wild exaggeration. Governmental power at no time got out of the hands of Spanish Republican leaders.

The problem remains of explaining how a man like Juan Negrín could accept the activities of a secret police organization as odious as the SIM became under Communist direction in 1938. My guess is that Dr. Negrín not only did not know the details of what was happening, but made a deliberate effort not to know. I am certain that he could never have sanctioned torture or murder. He understandably accepted the very summary justice of the popular tribunals and, later, the *Tribunales de Guardia* (military courts) which were set up at the end of 1937. The maximum sentence of these courts was swift execution by firing squads. The proceedings were open and there was no torture.

Whatever excuses are made, it is still part of the record that evil things happened while Juan Negrín was Republican Premier.

If one wonders whether Premier Negrín deliberately permitted a small amount of police terror, what should one say of Generalissimo Franco and the calculated, unremitting, callous use of terror from the beginning to the end of the war and then for years afterward?

It is true that Franco issued orders against the Moorish custom of castrating bodies and their invariable practice of raping the women as they went along (not that the latter practice was confined to Moors). The fact is that Franco's orders were not obeyed, and when his attention was called to this—incidentally by a German observer, Captain Strunk, fresh (as I also happened to be) from the Abyssinian War—he refused to believe him and did nothing to stop the soldiers. The Generalissimo approved of the wholesale and unending executions as a military necessity—and perhaps they were, in a strict, mechanical sense of the phrase.

Franco's forces were like an invading army. They were that in a true sense insofar as his Moors and Foreign Legionaries were his best shock troops; his German artillery, planes, and tanks gave him material superiority at all times; and his 50,000 to 60,000 fully equipped Italian expeditionary corps (backed by a large air force and submarines) swelled his infantry as well as other arms. His splendid Carlist troops could never provide more than the basis for three divisions. His Falangist volunteers had to be trained—by Germans, incidentally. In the circumstances, it is militarily arguable that Franco had at all times to employ terror as a tactic. He had to conquer a generally hostile country, which happened to be his own country.

John Whitaker, *New York Herald Tribune* correspondent with the Insurgent forces, wrote a damaging, and now famous, article for the October 1942 American quarterly *Foreign Affairs,* in which, among other things, he gave a good example of the Insurgent problem. When the Moors and Legionaries took Badajoz after a desperate struggle, they machine-gunned 2,000 militiamen and civilians in the bullring, as was mentioned in the first chapter. (Jay Allen of the *Chicago Tribune* was the first correspondent to break the story, for which he was vilified by Roman Catholics all over the United States.)

"Of course we shot them," Colonel Yagüe said to Whitaker. "What do you expect? Was I supposed to take 4,000 Reds with me as my column advanced, racing against time? Was I supposed to turn them loose in my rear and let them make Badajoz Red again?"

There were no spare Rebel personnel or officers to set up internment camps. The obvious tactic was to execute every Republican official and trade union or labor leader and imprison all others who might cause trouble. The rest of the populace would then, as they did, remain orderly.

Even in the field, the knowledge that the approaching Moors and *Tercios* were going to slaughter and mutilate the men and

1. Robert Capa's famous photograph of a Republican soldier falling mortally wounded at the beginning of the war.

2. Moroccan troops from France Army of Africa rest on the road Madrid.

3. A church in Seville reportedly burned by Loyalists as the war began.

4. José Calvo Sotelo, the deputy whose assassination was the spark that set off the Civil War.

Manuel Azana (*left*), President of the Spanish Loyalist government.   6. Dr. Juan Negrin (*right*), Republican Spain's Prime Minister and greatest war leader, as he looked on taking office in April 1937.

7. University City, Madrid (*above*), which took the full force of the Moorish troops' first desperate effort to conquer the capital.   8. (*Below*) One of the many hundreds of shells that landed in the early months on Madrid's Main Street, the Gran Via.

9. (*Left*) The bombing and shelling of Madrid by Franco's German planes was the first blitz of a modern city.

10. (*Below*) The courtyard of the Montana Barracks in Madrid whose surrender saved the capital for the Republican cause. No quarter was given.

11. La Pasionaria (Dolores Ibarruri), Republican Spain's most famous Communist figure. She is still (1972) in Moscow, the nominal leader of the Spanish Communist party.

¡NO PASARAN!
EL FASCISMO QUIERE CONQUISTAR MADRID
MADRID SERA LA TUMBA DEL FASCISMO 6

12. (*Left*) La Pasionaria's cry for all to see: "They shall not pass! Madrid will be the tomb of Fascism."

13. A part of the ancient Basque capital of Guernica after the German bombing in April 1937.

14. A red-bereted Carlist from Franco's crack Navarrese shock troops.

15. Generalissimo Francisco Franco, chief of the Spanish insurgent regime, is shown (*center*) with two staff officers as they studied their war map at headquarters. The picture was made just before the battle in which insurgent troops captured Alfambra in their drive to retake Teruel.

16. The defender of the Alcazar of Toledo, Colonel José Moscardo, is decorated by Generalissimo Franco after the siege of the fortress ends.

. Generalissimo Franco with General Wilhelm Faupel, Hitler's personal representative to the Nationalist Government.

18. Ernest Hemingway and Herbert Matthews standing on shellshattered floor of the Hotel Florida, Madrid, in 1937, where Hemingway wrote "The Fifth Column."

19. The author (*fifth from the left*) with Americans of the Lincoln Battalion of the International Brigade.

). Anti-Nazi Germans of the International Brigade on a Madrid Street during a lull in the fighting.

21. Veterans of the Abraham Lincoln Brigade parade on New York's 14th Street late in 1938 on their return from fighting in Spain.

22. Mussolini's expeditionary force returns to Naples for a triumphal march after the war.

23. Soldiers of Hitler's Condor Legion, marching through the Brandenburg Gate, Berlin, after their victorious service for the Franco cause.

24. Generalissimo Franco and his wife, Dona Carmen Polo, in the insurgent capital Burgos as the war was ending. The Nationalists used the Fascist salute througho the conflict.

25. A few victims of the 44-hour bombing of Barcelona by Italian aircraft from Majorca and Sardinia, March 17-18, 1938.

26. Closing in for the kill. The last Loyalist defender faces the rebels in a northern village.

27. Generalissimo Francisco Franco, the Spanish Civil War's greatest and most durable symbol, poses for history in 1970.

rape the women was terribly effective. Militiamen fearing to be cut off would flee. Peasants would take their women and children and whatever pitiful belongings they could transport and move on to the safety of the Loyalist zone—and then move again and again as the war progressed until thousands poured over the French frontier in January 1939 to an unwelcome and wretched exile. For the Republicans, it meant so many more mouths to feed and people to house and, often, obstruction of the troops on vital roads.

There is no question that the Nationalist policy of terror was a great military and practical success. That was, and still is for Spanish Nationalist and Francoist historians, its justification. Of course, censorship has hidden from most Spaniards the truth of what happened.

Aside from "military necessity," there was a politico-class type of terror on the Insurgent side comparable to similar atrocities on the Loyalist side. The only difference was that the Nationalists did not kill priests and nuns or burn churches. When the military coup failed to end the rebellion quickly, the Carlist and Falangist militias, who had prepared lists of victims on a great scale, went to work. In the north everyone connected with the Republican cause was shot, not only Communists, Socialists, and Anarchists but also middle-class liberals and Freemasons. In Andalusia, where the Rebels had only a small following, the advancing Nationalists left as few "Reds" alive as possible. The Seville countryside was hostile. Peasants had shot or imprisoned the priests, landlords, and municipal officials and, in their turn, as the Insurgent forces gained control, they were shot.

General Queipo de Llano instituted his own private and very effective reign of terror. The penalty for labor strikes, hidden arms, and the export of capital was death. "Marxists," loosely defined, were killed and Freemasons executed even faster, if possible. The prisons overflowed, but every night, between one and three o'clock, death lists of prisoners were compiled and the executions carried out swiftly—but audibly for terroristic reasons—on the edge of the city. The man who directed the repression for Queipo, by all accounts, was an alcoholic, a lecher and a sadist named Colonel Díaz Criado.

Queipo had begun his world-famous radio broadcasts, to which millions listened every evening. He was heard even in Paris and London. The talks were salacious and boastful, with revolting details, evidently true, of the sexual prowess and exploits of the Moorish soldiers. Arthur Koestler, in his *Spanish Testament*, quotes from a typical broadcast by Queipo on July 23, 1936, a week after the uprising began:

"Our own brave Legionaries and [Moorish] *Regulares* have shown the Red cowards what it means to be a man. And, incidentally, the wives of the Reds, too. These Communist and Anarchist women, after all, have made themselves fair game by their doctrine of free love. And now they have at least made the acquaintance of a real man, and not milksops of militiamen. Kicking their legs about and struggling won't help them."

Koestler considered Queipo de Llano to be a sexual psychopath. The general had a bluff, hearty, jovial manner which, according to Professor Jackson, made him "popular" with the workers, even though he had shot their leaders. He was popular with British businessmen, too, for he kept up the exports of sherry, olives, and citrus fruits, earning valuable foreign exchange for the Burgos government.

Each region had its own variation of the terror. In Navarre, Carlism was rampant and triumphant after a century of defeats. The Carlists felt like crusaders, killing for the love of Christ and their ideal of Spain. They especially hated the Basques, as traitors to their Roman Catholic religion, but all who were not fervently Catholic, monarchical, and conservative were suspect.

In Galicia, aside from trade unionists and Republican officials, the chief victims were in professional fields. Teachers and doctors were considered to be leftists; lawyers were spared as being rightists. Although starting slowly, the terror became ferocious, for Galicia had been a strongly Republican province and it was deemed necessary to strike terror in order to keep the people cowed.

Castile, with its long imperial traditions and sedate virtues, was relatively more restrained. The same sort of people were killed, but not so many, and justice had a certain summary legality about it, many more being jailed than executed. However, only too often, in every town, Falangists and/or Civil Guards would visit the jails, take out prisoners and shoot them just off the highways so that workers and peasants had "examples" of the need to behave. Falangists killed in a special way —a sort of signature—with a revolver bullet between the eyes.

Majorca, as I have already mentioned, had the unique distinction of an especially vicious terror under the direction of the Italian Fascist official, Arconovaldo Buonaccorsi. He was a flamboyant character in his Black Shirt, driving his racing car, announcing at the beginning of the war that "he needed at least one woman a day." He killed, or had killed, several thousand Majorcans.

One of the atrocities perpetrated by the Moors was mentioned by John Whitaker in his *Foreign Affairs* article:

> The men [Spaniards] who commanded them never denied that the Moors killed the wounded in the Republican hospital at Toledo. They boasted of how grenades were thrown in among two hundred screaming and helpless men. They never denied to me that they had promised the Moors white women when they reached Madrid. I sat with these officers in bivouac and heard them debate the expediency of such a promise. Some contended that a white woman was Spanish even if Red.
>
> This practice was not denied by El Mizian, the only Moroccan officer in the Spanish Army. I stood at the crossroads outside Navalcarnero with the Moorish major when two Spanish girls, not out of their teens, were brought before him. One had worked in a textile factory in Barcelona and they found a trade-union card in her leather jacket. The other came from Valencia and said she had no politics. After questioning them for military information, El Mizian had them taken them into a small schoolhouse where some forty Moorish soldiers were resting. As they reached the doorway a ululating cry rose from the Moors within. I stood horrified in helpless anger. El Mizian smirked when I remonstrated with him. "Oh, they'll not live more than four hours," he said.

Professor Stanley G. Payne, whose books, in some respects, favor the Franco side, is forthright and relentless in describing the Nationalist terror. Among other things he quotes extensively from Whitaker's article. He makes the point that "Franco was not responsible for initiating the killings" but he adds:

> Savagery was as widespread among Nationalists as among the leftists. . . . In his cold, calculating fashion, Franco apparently found it expedient not to thwart the blood lust of his followers, but to acknowledge it as one of the main unifying forces behind the rebel movement. It served to eliminate the enemies of the new regime, and it made large numbers of Nationalists participants in a common orgy so gruesome as to irrevocably bind them together.

Payne points out that because the Insurgents needed every soldier they could muster for the fighting, the rearguard was left to the mercies of the Civil Guards, right-wing militia groups, and Falangists.

> Thousands of killings were the doing [of the Falangists] but the ordinary conservatives and rightists often equaled or exceeded them in ferocity, and ultimate authorization came from the military dictatorship, which allowed a sort of limited anarchy to prevail for the better part of a year. During this time the various elements on the Nationalist side were, in effect, free to kill almost whomever they chose, so long as it could be said that the victim had supported the Popular Front.

This type of repression was gradually brought under control at the end of 1937. However, it did not make much difference, for the courts-martial which were set up condemned almost as many men as would have died without trial, and the advancing troops were usually murderous.

Stanley Payne's rather understated conclusion is that: "The inflexible policies of the rebels broke the spirit of part of the opposition, but could hardly promote the moral and spiritual unification of Spain."

The moral problem did disturb some notable Catholic liberals in Europe like Jacques Maritain, who coined the phrase "White Terror" for the Nationalist atrocities as a balance to what the world was calling the "Red Terror." Others who protested were François Mauriac, Cardinal Verdier of Paris, Don Luigi Sturzo in Rome, and the Spanish Catholic writer, José Bergamín. No American Catholic of their stature, except perhaps George Shuster, seems to have spoken out against the "White Terror."

The killing of priests and the burning of churches at the beginning of the war was understandably unforgivable to Roman Catholics, but for those who value life for purely human reasons, it is as reprehensible to murder a worker because he belongs to a trade union as it is to kill a priest just because he belongs to the Roman Catholic Church.

Some of the arrests, tortures, and killings on both sides were a naturally grisly aspect accompanying any civil war. It stood to reason that men and women were caught in each zone whose hearts and souls belonged with "the enemy." It was also part of the game that espionage was as easy as it was necessary and dangerous. Unlike a war between nations, the people involved were exactly like each other, all Spaniards. An intense degree of suspicion was natural, and with it, fear. No chances could be taken. If there were doubts, it was better, in Pancho Villa's macabre phrase, "to shoot him for the time being."

Both sides had well-organized military intelligence networks in operation throughout the war. The Republicans' was organized at a very early stage by Alexander Orlov, who later defected to the United States. "With the help of the Soviet long-standing network of spies in Berlin and Rome," he told Professor Payne, "and with my own network on the territory of Franco, I was able to provide Prime Minister Negrín and his Chief of Staff Vicente Rojo with the strategic plans of the Nationalist High Command and with the Order of Battle before and during each important engagement with the enemy."

The Nationalist intelligence system was expertly organized and supervised by the Germans. Moreover, the Nazis had a vast, secret network of police agents in Franco Spain easily comparable to the Russian and Comintern network on the

Republican side, but they did not have or need *chekas* for an internal political struggle.

In both cases, spying was also done for the foreign countries —the Soviet Union and Germany—as well as for Spain. The existence of the International Brigade and the German and Italian interventionist forces meant that there were many foreign spies at work. The paranoiac and sadistic French commander of the International Brigade, André Marty, saw spies wherever he looked, with often murderous, but sometimes tragicomic results when he could be stopped. His frustration would amuse his Communist associates, but his anger generally found victims.

Moreover, there was that forever famous "Fifth Column": a phrase that will never go out of the languages of the world. No matter who used it first, it was General Mola who gave the words to history. Four columns were converging on Madrid in October 1936. A newspaperman asked him which of the four he thought would capture Madrid. None, he said, for a fifth column of hidden Insurgent supporters would rise at the last hours within the capital and take over.

It was a careless, thoughtless remark which had a terrible sequel. On November 6 and the night of November 7–8, 1936, when the fate of Madrid hung in the balance, about a thousand prisoners were taken from the Model Prison and massacred in Madrid and surrounding villages. Professor Jackson ascribes the slaughter—the worst single atrocity of the war on the Loyalist side—"to a case of the prison guards, many of them criminals, taking justice into their own hands."

I believe, myself, that the orders came from the Comintern agents in Madrid because I know that the sinister Vittorio Vidali spent the night in a prison briefly interrogating prisoners brought before him and, when he decided, as he almost always did, that they were fifth columnists, he would shoot them in the back of their heads with his revolver. Ernest Hemingway told me that he heard that Vidali fired so often that the skin between the thumb and index finger of his right hand was badly burned. (Hemingway, it will be recalled, wrote a play in Madrid which was called *The Fifth Column.*)

There is no question that the extraterritorial embassy buildings in Madrid, which harbored thousands of refugees until the end of the war, also harbored fifth columnists working with the connivance of foreign envoys.

As the Nationalists conquered towns and cities, fifth columns would rise and often take terrible vengeance for their months of dissimulation or hiding. They would usually have a few names or lists of names.

"Which, if not victory, is yet revenge," as Milton wrote.

It is pure nonsense to think of the terror—its magnitude and ferocity, and on the Nationalist side its cold calculation —as the result of a cruel streak in the Spanish character. Spanish attitudes toward violence and death are not like those of Anglo-Saxons or, for that matter, other Latins like the Italians. The sixteenth-century Englishmen and Scotsmen were more callous, brutal, and murderous than twentieth-century Spaniards. Temperament, character, history, tradition molded the modern Spaniard in such a way that he did not feel the same sense of horror and revulsion over the atrocities that were felt by foreigners. There were innumerable honorable exceptions, of course, who were horrified and who were just as Spanish as an Anarchist killer or a Foreign Legion officer.

"In the second half of 1936," writes Gabriel Jackson, "the most profound social revolution since the fifteenth century took place in much of the territory remaining in the hands of the Popular Front."

In more or less strong terms, nearly every historian of the Spanish Civil War makes the same point. I would say that there was a revolution of sorts, but it should not be exaggerated. In one basic sense, there was no revolution at all, since the Republican government functioned much as it did before the war. It happened to have Socialist and Communist, and even Anarchist, ministers in the cabinet, but it was still the legitimate, elected and, within wartime limitations, democratic government of the Second Spanish Republic.

When one thinks of the classic social revolutions of modern times—the French, Mexican, Russian, Chinese, and Cuban—it is not possible to say that anything comparable happened in Loyalist Spain. There was no (to quote the Oxford English Dictionary) "complete change" or "turning upside down"; there were a number of local changes and upheavals of a spontaneous, unorganized, undirected and uncoordinated kind, some of them ephemeral, a few of a more permanent nature.

The successive governments accepted much of what happened, but by no means all, because there were some madly utopian Anarchist escapades and many cases where production fell so severely that the authorities had to step in. For international reasons, the policies of the government, even Largo Caballero's, had to be essentially liberal and reformist. This was all the more true, paradoxically, as the Communists gained greater power, for their tactics were bourgeois, democratic, and counterrevolutionary. The fundamental policy of the government was that the war had to be won—or at least fought—and a revolution put aside for later consideration.

The basis for statements like Gabriel Jackson's was that there was a sudden, spontaneous, and widespread movement to occupy factories and seize landed properties. There was also a widespread assumption of local and collective authority, although it could not be sustained, for obvious reasons.

Where factories were taken over, much went on as before. Wages went up and rents came down. In many rural areas, rents were abolished, property records burned, land confiscated and collectivized. But the collectivization was always local, without planning or control from provincial centers or Madrid, and methods of work were unchanged and unaffected by political theories except in Anarchist localities.

In some Anarchist villages, "libertarian" communes were set up, but these were exceptional. Some ultraorthodox Anarchists even abolished money and proclaimed their municipalities "republics." At best, money was considered a necessary evil to be used in dealing with the outside world. Churches were often turned into markets or hospitals.

In most places, wages were adjusted to needs. There was a genuine and instinctive desire to achieve equality, which is at the heart of any social revolution, but it was nowhere clearly formulated or followed through. There were silly manifestations of it, such as the disappearances of ties and hats, as being upper-class symbols. The Communist clenched fist salute became the universal gesture of all parties and classes, so much so that when Clement Attlee, then a Labor Member of Parliament, visited Madrid, he was photographed cheerfully giving the clenched fist salute. The good-bye was always *Salud!* and never the traditional *Adiós!*

The unevenness of the revolutionary manifestations was another reason why one cannot say that Republican Spain went through a genuine revolution. In the Basque country all the emphasis was on regional autonomy. The Basques had a long tradition of local autonomy and also of farm cooperatives, at least in the common use of tractors and shared work. All along the northern coast, fishing had long been collectivized; it was traditional to have cooperative ownership of boats. The Astorians, however, were really radical and thought in political terms. In many places, land was seized and collectivized and there was group marketing. In parts of the province, money was abolished for chits.

Many collective farms were set up in central and southern Spain by the Land Workers Federation of the Socialist UGT. There was no pattern, however, no planning, no overall direction. Something of the sort had happened in Spain during the Napoleonic invasion and again in the 1830's and in 1873.

One permanent revolutionary act was the taking over of the banks by the UGT in Madrid and by other groups in other cities. Millions of dollars in gold, jewelry, money, and securities were seized as booty and never returned. Much of it found its way to Mexico after the war and was used by the Spanish exiles.

Since it took the Madrid government several months to reassert its authority, the image of a great, popular social revolution stuck. It was a harmful image for the Second Republic, which was trying to encourage foreign businessmen and financiers. What were they supposed to think on learning that the Anarchist labor federation—the CNT—had taken over all the industries of Barcelona and turned the Catalan capital into a proletarian city?

An agrarian revolution was long overdue. The chance to own the land they tilled was not going to be missed by the Andalusian peasants.

All over the country, one saw the results of the Madrid government's loss of authority. Later in the United States, we saw what happened in the Watts district of Los Angeles or Harlem in New York when the lid of authority was lifted from a mass that felt itself oppressed, unjustly treated, and underprivileged.

On a wide scale, this was what happened in 1936. The racial flare-up in the United States and the revolutionary outburst in Spain were the result of generations of social injustice. Such manifestations show revolutionary potentials, but in Spain, as in the United States, the counterrevolutionary forces were strong enough to prevent the "complete change" of a social revolution.

Too many observers, then and later, equated the phenomenal rise of the Spanish Communist movement with the outburst of revolutionary manifestations around the country. In reality, the Communists did their best to discourage and quash such activities and, on the whole, successfully. George Orwell's shocked disgust and dismay when he discovered that the Spanish Communists were counterrevolutionary was revealed in his famous book *Homage to Catalonia.* The Central European sociologist Dr. Franz Borkenau is more philosophical in his work, *The Spanish Cockpit,* but clearly feels that an opportunity for a social revolution was being missed.

The unfortunate Premier Francisco Largo Caballero was the chief victim of the growth of Communism and its bourgeois moderation. He was in office from September 4, 1936, to May 16,

1937, during which time the Communist movement grew from 50,000 to perhaps as many as 300,000. Careful preparation, expert advice from the Comintern agents, skilled propaganda, the international fame of the Soviet Union among Liberals and Socialists, and the moderation of Communist policies within the Popular Front, all helped to lay the basis. Then in October 1936 came Russian military aid—the only aid from any country —and with it the fine performance of the Communist Fifth Regiment in the field and in the defense of Madrid early in November.

Men who were ambitious, or simply seeking a safe haven, joined the Communist party. Most of the new members who deserted the Socialist UGT and the Anarchist CNT were not peasants or workers. The Basques were never interested. In most cases, the attraction was not Marxism. The Army officers who joined were not interested in ideology, but in efficiency, discipline, and Russian weapons. The Communists formed an oasis of discipline and moderation in a generally disorderly, extremist environment. They disapproved of, even hated, the moral and revolutionary enthusiasm of the Anarchists and Left Socialists, which they loosely called Trotskyism. No other Spanish party had their dynamism, organizing ability, and training in modern military and political techniques.

All this was new to Spain. The Communists felt and acted superior and, not unexpectedly, they had an insatiable appetite for power. They were also utterly unscrupulous and opportunistic, but they were practical and pragmatic, and discouraged the typical Spanish impulsiveness and spontaneity. They were not, of course, a native movement; they were an importation, acting under foreign direction. So they never put down roots and never, by themselves, could have gained power in Spain. During the Civil War, the Russians and the Comintern agents had to remain in the background in civil affairs and, at most, could give orders only to the Spanish Communists.

Largo Caballero was far from being the "Spanish Lenin," for his chief difficulties were with the Communists who, finally, brought about his downfall. He had to back away from his revolutionary hopes; he could not prevent the Communists from taking over a good two-thirds of the commanding positions in the army; he could not deny that many of the best fighting troops—especially the Fifth Regiment—were Communist. He was frustrated when the Communists, with Álvarez del Vayo's connivance, named political commissars without getting his consent.

Largo Caballero's problem was that whatever his muddled revolutionary ideas, he saw that to prosecute the war there had to be a centralized political and military authority embracing the moderate Center Republicans, Socialists, Communists, and Anarchists. But he distrusted them all, even the right-wing Socialists headed by Indalecio Prieto.

The Communists, who joined his government in September 1936—apparently under orders from Moscow—hampered him at every step. The Anarchists, who took four cabinet posts in November, could not get over the fact that they were against all government, and anyway their principal interest was in trying to hold power in Catalonia. Prieto and Negrín, the ablest men in the Republic, felt frustrated by Largo Caballero's jealous, bumbling, slow, and narrowly bureaucratic way of working, and his insistence on exercising his power as Minister of National Defense as well as Prime Minister.

Largo not only had no military training but also had no military instinct. His failure to fortify and help Málaga (which fell on February 8, 1937, and where there were appalling Rebel atrocities) was inexcusable. When he reluctantly introduced conscription, he allowed Anarchists, Communists, and Socialists to join their own units despite the desperate need for political and military unity. He was jealous of the International Brigade. The first and one of the best commanders it had in the war, Emil Kléber, had to go because of Largo Caballero. He even quarreled with his own commander in Madrid, General Miaja.

The story of Largo Caballero is a sad one, for he was a man of complete honesty and integrity and much the most popular figure in Spain when he took office. Despite his great personal prestige, he could not control the bitter regional rivalries and the unending tensions and conflicts between the Anarchists, Socialists, and Communists. Largo Caballero was simply not big enough, in intellect or ability, for an almost superhuman task. Besides, he had made powerful enemies in the Communist and Anarchist camps. It is often said that he was forced out of office because he refused Communist demands to merge the Socialist and Communist parties. A similar refusal on the part of Juan Negrín, his successor, did not have the same result. The situation, as it developed by May 1937, would have forced Largo Caballero's resignation even if the Communists had not been determined to get him out.

Rioting in Barcelona, leading to a virtual uprising of the Anarchists, backed by the POUM, against the Valencia government, precipitated the crisis in the first two weeks of May. The Communists were ready. Largo Caballero was reluctant to act, but Prieto sent in 4,000 Assault Guards who restored order in Barcelona with help from the combined Catalan organization of the Socialists and Communists, the PSUC.

When Largo Caballero refused to dissolve the POUM, the two Communist ministers resigned, followed by all the others except the Anarchists. The famous old labor union leader was even deserted by his own Socialist party.

"The Spanish state has always been inferior to the Spanish people, from whom it has been deliberately cut off by high dividing walls," wrote Major Martín Blásquez. "The Caballero government was also inferior to the Spanish people, who were shedding their blood in defense of a democratic ideal."

The "May Crisis," as it was called, brought about a necessary clearing of the air. It ended any idea of a social revolution. The Anarchists could no longer go their revolutionary ways. Catalonia, which was not playing its proper role, was brought under control by moving the government from Valencia to Barcelona. The dissident and untrustworthy, if not dangerous, POUM was broken up and destroyed. The Spanish and foreign Communists gained greatly in power and influence. A new leader came on the scene, the only man in Republican Spain capable of holding the Loyalists together and waging a war for two more years.

Indalecio Prieto might have been an obvious choice, especially since he was cooperating with the Communists at that time and they with him, but his enmity toward Largo Caballero and the split in the Socialist ranks eliminated him. The only other possible choice was Dr. Juan Negrín, a Socialist, a moderate, a liberal, but also a man whom the Communists favored. He was, in fact, supported by all the parties except the left-wing Socialists and the Anarchists.

Hugh Thomas writes that Dr. Negrín demurred, pointing out that "he was unknown and unpopular" and, of course, not a Communist, all of which was true. He did not become Prime Minister just because the Communists picked him. He had been picked by the conjuncture of events, by the lack of any other choice, by the recognition of his abilities. There are times when it seems as if fate or destiny does the picking. Juan Negrín was Republican Spain's man of the hour.

Once he took office a new stage in the Spanish Civil War began. Dr. Negrín had no interest in the so-called revolution that had been sprouting like weeds all over the place. In fact, he was impatient with everything that interfered with the war effort. He was interested in the economy in order to bolster its contribution to the war, not in its role in distributing wealth or bringing equality or furthering some ideology.

Whether there had been a social revolution or not in Republican Spain before mid-May 1937, there was none after. The next two years were a grim, punishing and, of course, losing fight of Loyalist Spain against Nationalist Spain.

Yet, the issue was not decided by the combat of Spaniard against Spaniard. The Civil War was a world war before its time. It was Premier Negrín's tragedy, and Spain's, that world events—the Axis, appeasement, the Stalin purges, Japanese aggression against China, American isolationism, the worldwide economic crisis—would doom the Loyalist cause.

Put in its simplest terms, the decisive factors were a genuine intervention and a false "Non-Intervention."

6

INTERVENTION . . .

"IN THE SPANISH QUESTION," Goering told Mussolini during a conversation in Rome on January 23, 1937, "Germany intends to go only to the limits of what is possible, thus preventing a general war from developing from the complications in Spain."

The Duce, according to Count Ciano, who was present, said that Italy, on her part, had exactly the same idea. Mussolini added that "Léon Blum and his collaborators likewise wished to avoid war," and "England, too, fears a general conflict, and Russia will certainly not let things go beyond the limit."

This tacit understanding on all sides early in the war was a crucial factor in the Spanish conflict. The unspoken corollary was that if it ever became clear that nothing that happened in Spain would lead to a European war, one side or the other could decide the conflict. This is what occurred after Munich in September 1938, when Hitler realized that he could safely go the limit in aiding Franco, who then won the war.

Every European power had important, or even vital, interests in the Mediterranean, and hence in Spain. The Civil War was a great shock, even to Germany and Italy. A quick, old-fashioned *pronunciamiento* would not have caused much international concern, but a civil war was more than anyone had counted on. The rise of the German Nazis to aggressive power (Hitler had invaded the Rhineland on March 19, 1936), along with Mussolini's equally aggressive Italian Fascism (Italy finished the conquest of Abyssinia on April 5, 1936), were cast-

129

ing a menacing cloud over Europe. The Fascist powers were anti-democratic as well as anti-Communist. They soon learned that they could count on the timidity and fears of the democracies, but Stalin could not sit back and do nothing. Thus, forces were shaping up which were to lead, in three years' time, to world war. The trends were so obvious that in the spring of 1937, in Madrid, I could confidently entitle a book on the Abyssinian and Spanish wars *Two Wars and More to Come.*

In a speech to the Cortes in Valencia on November 1, 1936, Prime Minister Largo Caballero said: "It is, indeed, a European war which is occurring here, and all of us are being plunged into it. We see the hour coming when a frightful world catastrophe will be unleashed."

The decision to aid the Rebels seems to have been made personally by the Fuehrer and the Duce on the same day—July 26, nine days after the rebellion began. A Comintern meeting in Prague on the same July 26 decided to raise an international volunteer force, but no decision was made there or in Moscow about Russian military aid. Stalin was not ready.

The intricacies and minutiae of the so-called Non-Intervention policy and the story of the Committee set up to carry it out, have long been of interest only to professional historians. It is enough to recapitulate the simple facts about the way the policy worked to bring victory to the Nationalist cause. Germany, Italy, the Soviet Union, and the United States were the main actors in the drama of deception.

There were two themes in the plot. One was intervention, which was real, and the other non-intervention, which was a sham. On both counts, the Republican government suffered. "Non-intervention" prevented the Loyalist government from buying the arms which it needed to defend itself and which it was legally entitled to buy. At the same time, the policy could not prevent the Nationalists from getting German and Italian aid without interruption. Russian aid for the Loyalists was inadequate and reached Spain with difficulty, when it was not blocked entirely. It was, anyway, cut down and stopped by Stalin long before the war ended.

The nineteenth-century English poet Walter Savage Landor wrote a curiously prophetic poem about a conquering ruler, which Alvah Bessie of the Abraham Lincoln Battalion quoted. The second stanza reads:

> He swears he will have no contention,
> And sets all nations by the ears;
> He shouts aloud, "No intervention!"
> Invades, and drowns them all in tears.

The theory of non-intervention was understandable and apparently sensible: to see to it that no foreign powers furnished or sold arms or war materials to *either* side in the Civil War. In that respect, it was a complete and obvious failure. The argument that was always given in favor of the policy is that with all its falsity and its unneutral effect of assuring victory to Franco and the Insurgents, it had stopped a civil war from becoming a European war. This is a doubtful argument, because the European war was merely postponed. In fact, the success of Hitler's and Mussolini's policy in Spain encouraged them to believe that there was no limit to Franco-British appeasement. A firm stand by the democracies in Spain might well have given the Fascist powers pause. Moreover, Germany —not Britain and France—learned valuable military lessons in Spain which were used in the great war. The time Hitler gained through the appeasement policy was used effectively by him to rearm.

Intervention on the Insurgent side began with a bang; on the Republican side it began with a whimper. France was the obvious and only place for the Madrid government to get help quickly. Prime Minister Giral telegraphed to his French Popular Front opposite number Léon Blum, "to help us immediately with arms and airplanes." His representative in Paris asked for twenty Potez bombers and a small consignment of arms—on purchase, of course. This required a French government license. Blum was willing and his Air Minister, Pierre Cot, eager. Most of the other members of the cabinet were against any intervention. More than fifty obsolete planes were sent early in

August, but on the second, the cabinet voted to appeal urgently to the "interested governments" to sign a non-intervention pact. As early as July 22 Blum was invited to London, where his Socialist ardor was dampened by Prime Minister Stanley Baldwin and Foreign Secretary Anthony Eden.

The men who flew the French planes in Spain were, with a few exceptions like André Malraux, mercenaries. Their activity had little effect, whereas the German and Italian planes that helped Franco at the same time played a decisive role. The Franco-Spanish frontier was anyway closed on August 9 as a result of a menacing *démarche* from London.

André Malraux was a veteran of the Chinese Nationalist struggle against Japan, from which came his novel published in English as *Man's Fate*. At the beginning of the Spanish War Malraux bought arms, tanks, and planes with Loyalist money in Czechoslovakia, Belgium, and France. He was not, himself, a pilot; he acted as a machine-gunner on a bomber. He also recruited a foreign "Legion of the Air" in August, using the old planes he had bought, and he organized an air squadron for the International Brigade. Some Spanish pilots were trained in France until the Non-Intervention Committee stopped the practice on March 8, 1937. Shortly before August 1, 1936, small amounts of Swiss, Czech, and Belgian arms were allowed to pass through France.

This was all the foreign aid that the Republican government could get in the first stage of the war. French aid throughout the conflict was insignificant and poor in quality. There was only one period when French help saved the Republic, temporarily. This was in the spring of 1938, after the Insurgent forces had cut Loyalist Spain in two by a drive through Aragon to the sea. At this critical moment, France opened her frontier to allow the passage of Russian and Comintern arms which had reached the country months before. It was a negative gesture, but it permitted the Loyalists to go on fighting. The border was closed again in a few weeks and remained closed until so near the end of the war that the material released never reached the front.

Paris, incidentally, also applied "non-intervention" to Spanish gold reserves of about $30 million on deposit in the Bank of France—money that was needed to buy arms. Most of it was held and turned over to the Franco regime after the war.

France was the most bitterly and deeply divided of the countries involved. There was an overwhelming popular majority for the Loyalists, but the minority contained many high military officers and politicians, and important businessmen and financiers. Add the fear of Hitler and dependence on the British, who warned Premier Blum that they would not consider themselves obliged to come to France's defense if her actions in Spain brought on a European war, and the reasons for French policy are understandable. French military and naval officers were frightened by the Italian occupation of the Balearics, and the Italian air and naval bases in Majorca. This was a threat to French lifelines from Africa and to all of the western Mediterranean.

The refusal of the French to do more than provide a minimal amount of help to the Republican government was at all times a bitter and tragic development for the Loyalists. The French could have made all the difference at the beginning of the conflict. There was an open frontier with adequate railway and road connections; the nearby great port of Marseilles; a Popular Front government under a Socialist leader, Léon Blum; and a powerful, strategic motive to help a democratic government to remain in office and prevent a right-wing military dictatorship allied to Nazi Germany and Fascist Italy from gaining power in Spain. There was even a secret clause in a December 1935 commercial treaty giving Spain the right to buy arms and munitions from France.

These apparently cogent reasons were not enough. Léon Blum, who had been Premier only since June 5, 1936, was timid and unsure of his political position at the head of a weak and divided government. Powerful political leaders like Daladier, Chautemps, Herriot, and Delbos were against France's intervention in Spain. President Albert Lebrun told Blum on July 25 that arms for Spain "may lead to war or to a revolution in France."

Moreover, Blum did not believe that France could act without the support of Great Britain, which was firmly opposed to any involvement in the Spanish war. French policy toward Spain was dictated by London. Toward the end of October 1936, Anthony Eden denied in the House of Commons "that Britain had exerted any influence on French policy"—which was a false statement. It was a fact of life that Blum dared not risk any act that might lead to war, since without Great Britain's active support France could not defend herself. This situation resulted in one of the crowning ironies of the Spanish Civil War: that the suggestion for a "Non-Intervention Committee" came from Léon Blum.

The French government formally proposed non-intervention on August 8, 1936, through Yvon Delbos, the Radical Foreign Minister, acting for Blum. Germany and Italy stalled until the end of August, by which time they had conveyed Franco's Army of Africa over to the mainland. Count Dino Grandi, who was Italy's ambassador in London and her representative on the Non-Intervention Committee (NIC), had secret instructions "to give the Committee's entire activity a purely platonic character," which he did brilliantly.

The Committee first met in London on September 9, more than a month before any Russian arms reached Spain. Twenty-six nations were represented. The initial proposal was for supervision of the Spanish frontiers and control of ships carrying war materials to Spain. Proceedings were interminable, as each representative had to consult his government and then both sides in Spain had to be brought in. Every proposal took several weeks.

By the time NIC started operating, the Madrid government had ample proofs of German, Italian, and Portuguese intervention but it was not allowed to present them to the Committee. The League of Nations General Assembly, which convened on September 21, 1936, refused to place Spain on its agenda. The chairman, Carlos Saavedra Lamas of Argentina, was notoriously pro-Franco. Spanish Foreign Minister Álvarez del Vayo was persuaded by the British to be circumspect, but on September 30 many of the facts about intervention were published in Madrid. The three Fascist powers—counting Portugal—blandly denied the charges to the Non-Intervention Committee and no democratic member dared, or cared, to note that they lied, although the facts were known.

Russia had joined the NIC because Stalin had good reasons to hope that the proposed policy would work. Up to that time only food and medical supplies had been sent from the Soviet Union. Ivan M. Maisky, the Russian representative on the Committee, brought Italian and German intervention up in precise detail, but to accept his facts would have meant that "non-intervention" had failed from the beginning. Anyway, all of the European countries were expecting the Insurgents to win quickly.

Stalin, however, began issuing warnings that the Soviet Union would be no more bound by non-intervention than the others. When the Russian arms shipments started in October, they were naturally observed. This time, the London Committee had no hesitation in making a fuss. Eden even spoke of "a country guiltier than Germany or Italy."

The treatment was blatantly unequal for reasons of power politics. The Non-Intervention Committee was never to be a receptacle or source of truth, facts, or international justice. It was a crudely effective instrument to permit intervention in the name of non-intervention, thus avoiding a confrontation for which no country was yet ready. The powers excused and justified the cynicism and immorality under the shield of what they considered to be a higher morality—the maintenance of European peace. In the process, of course, each foreign country put its own national interests above any other consideration. People, everywhere, became emotional about the Spanish Civil War, but there was no sentimentality about the way any government or any leader, least of all Hitler, Mussolini, and Stalin, acted.

The possibility of foreign troops fighting in Spain had not been envisaged in the original agreement, which only embargoed the sale of arms. A ban on volunteers was not passed by the NIC until February 1937, but it meant nothing. There were long meetings and endless discussions about it, all of them fruitless, theoretical, and unreal. Germany and Italy made some verbal concessions about their "volunteers" but went on sending them. Russian and Comintern advisers and technicians, and International Brigaders—the only real volunteers—continued to enter Spain.

The term "volunteers" was used by the NIC indiscriminately. League of Nations resolutions used a cagey phrase: "Non-Spanish combatants." No military officers or advisers were sent by any democratic nation to Spain. Except for Russian and European Communist advisers, technicians, and specialists, all the foreigners fighting for the Spanish Republic were volunteers whose governments had nothing to do with their presence. On the Franco side, except for very small contingents of Irish and French volunteers, and the mercenaries from Morocco, all foreign soldiers, advisers, and technicians were sent to Spain by the German, Italian, and Portuguese governments, and were fighting for their countries as well as for the Insurgents. This was one of the extraordinary features of the Spanish Civil War. It was probably unique in history.

The most important single reason for the victory of Generalissimo Franco and the Nationalists was German intervention. Throughout the war, German equipment gave the Insurgents a greatly superior arms balance in virtually every battle. The German Condor Legion, formed in mid-November 1936, with its bombers, fighters, tanks, artillery, and technical advisers, was the best and most effective unit—foreign or Spanish—on either side.

The *Luftwaffe* had only recently been formed and was still ill-provided and untried. The Junkers 52 sent to Spain, for instance, were the first ones to be used in combat.

"Franco ought to erect a monument to the glory of the Junkers 52," the Fuehrer is quoted by his confidential secretary, Martin Bormann, as saying in *Hitler's Table Talk*. "It is this aircraft that the Spanish revolution has to thank for its victory."

The decision to help Franco was made by Hitler and his Nazi party leaders. The German Foreign, War, and Economic ministers were all opposed to intervention. The Fuehrer was making his first big international move and was following his uncanny flair for adventure and for what he could get away with. The professional German civil servants, diplomats, and regular military officers were still swayed by international conventions.

Hermann Goering, chief of the *Luftwaffe,* advised Hitler to go ahead, "firstly, to prevent the further spread of Communism; secondly, to test my young *Luftwaffe* in this or that technical respect," as he said at his Nuremberg trial in 1946. Most of the pilots whom Goering sent to Spain were young Nazis.

The first vital intervention in the war by any power was by the twenty Junkers 52 transport planes which ferried 15,000 troops of the Army of Africa from Tetuán to Seville between July 28 and August 5. Italy, starting on July 30, furnished a dozen bombers. A few of them were forced down en route in French Morocco. Their logbooks indicated that they had been assigned to the mission on July 15, two days before the uprising began, but this must have been a mistaken notation.

Both German and Italian bombers attacked and drove off the amateurishly handled Republican warships and, on August 6, Franco began sending troops in ships across the Strait. By August 29, he had thirty Junkers 52 and Italian Savoia Marchetti bombers. He cabled Mola: "We are masters of the Strait; we dominate the situation."

The German officers and specialists of the Condor Legion were secretly recruited or chosen, although the existence of the organization was never hidden. It was at all times under German command, and the soldiers' wages were paid by Germany until November 1938. The Condor Legion was so effective because of the experience of its officers and the fighting qualities and discipline of its members, and not because of especially good or new equipment. None of the intervening powers, except, perhaps, the Russians, used their best planes, tanks, and artillery in Spain except when experimenting with certain arms. Captain B. H. Liddell Hart, the British military expert, pointed out that Franco's superiority in the crucial item of artillery, mainly thanks to the Germans, exceeded the other side three to one.

There were no official figures, but it is safe to say that the Germans sent at least 16,000 specialists—not infantry—to Spain, keeping 6,000 to 6,500 of them there at a time. There were bomber and fighter squadrons (Junkers, Heinkels, and Messerschmitts), gun batteries, and tank companies. These were in addition to the arms furnished to the Spanish Insurgent army for use by Spaniards. The main Nazi contribution was heavy equipment and the organizing, supplying, and manning of the air, tank, and artillery services. German engineers designed and built field fortifications. Germans set up and ran training schools for Spanish officers and noncoms. German naval vessels played a key role in keeping the sea lanes open for war material and troop shipments and in paralyzing the activities of the Loyalist navy.

As was mentioned before, the Germans organized the Nationalist intelligence service and maintained a secret police corps in the Insurgent zone.

Advice was one thing the stubborn, cautious, complacent, and self-assured Caudillo would not accept from the Germans. As a result, the war lasted a longer time than was militarily necessary. It is arguable that the Republican zone was thereby saved some of the destruction and slaughter that a German-type *blitzkrieg* would have imposed.

The importance of German aid was not fully realized until the Reich's documentation became available after World War II. There were also some revealing confessions at the Nuremberg trials. Research by historians completed the picture. During the Civil War, the Germans took great pains to conceal the extent of their aid, unlike the Duce and Count Ciano, who boasted openly about Italian intervention and permitted the Italian press to publish gloating accounts of the Fascist deeds in Spain. Only on June 9, 1939, after, the Civil War was over, did Hitler permit the Condor Legion to show itself and accept a popular tribute. Fourteen thousand of its members paraded in triumph in Berlin. A Spanish Nationalist historian wrote that 300 had been killed in combat.

Hitler gave different reasons at different times for helping the Nationalists, but his dominant motive was probably economic. The Germans needed wolfram, mercury, zinc, copper, and iron ore to build up their armaments—and Spain had them all. After the Insurgents conquered the north, Franco controlled all the important mines of Spain and Morocco, as well as Bilbao's heavy industries. The Germans succeeded in supplanting British and French interests until well into World War II. A few months after the Civil War began, Franco confiscated the output of the British-owned Río Tinto copper mine and resold the minerals to Germany. Heavy shipments of iron ore and pyrites were exported to Germany in 1937 and 1938.

On November 19, 1938, in exchange for enough armaments to win the war, Franco made his biggest deal with the Nazis, permitting a high German participation in Spanish mines and virtual control of the mines in Spanish Morocco. Thanks to Spain, Germany had an important stockpile of minerals by 1939 with which to start the World War. The final deal between Franco and Hitler came at a time—six weeks after Munich—when Stalin had obviously decided to write Spain off as a mildly regrettable defeat. It was clear to him that there was no hope of an effective collective agreement with the democracies against the Axis. Besides, as I mentioned, Stalin was well advanced in his idea of making a deal with Hitler.

No figures were ever published to cover the extent or the details of the aid which Hitler sent in war matériel. Thomas gives the cost figures, which were ascertained when the German diplomatic documents were published after World War II. The total was slightly under $200 million (500 million Reichsmarks, of which Franco repaid 378 million).

The Italians, unlike the Germans and Russians, built up a true expeditionary force in Nationalist Spain, called the *Corpo di Truppe Volontarie* (Corps of Voluntary Soldiers). It began to take shape at the end of November 1936. Mussolini had already sent planes, tanks, war material, and naval vessels, as well as groups of specialists. Then he offered, through Ciano, to send a whole division of Black Shirts (Fascist party troops) and more if required. When Franco accepted, the Italians organized a division and sent it off, well equipped, to Spain. Before the end of January 1937, there were 14,000 Italian soldiers and pilots in Spain. In the disastrous—for Italy—battle of Guadalajara in March, there were four Italian divisions with supporting air force and artillery units: a total of about 45,000 men. By October, there were more than 50,000 Italian troops in the CTV.

There had been a few prewar arrangements which made it seem, deceptively, as if Mussolini had long plotted to help a generals' revolt. In 1932, some Spanish Army officers made an agreement for aid with Air Marshal Italo Balbo, but it was not formal and not followed up. Two years later, the Monarchist leader Antonio Goicoechea and some Carlists visited Mussolini in Rome. The Duce paid them 1,500,000 pesetas and promised to send machine guns and grenades when the uprising started. The Carlists used the money for paramilitary training; they were not the ones who started the rebellion.

Luis Bolín, correspondent for the Monarchist daily *ABC*, flew to Rome on July 21, 1936, to ask Mussolini on Franco's behalf for bombers and fighters. He saw Ciano, who later said that the dozen or so planes asked for would be enough to win the war in a few days. The Duce was not as enthusiastic as his son-in-law, and withheld his consent until July 26. Twelve Savoia Marchettis left Sardinia for Spanish Morocco on July 30.

The rebellion in Spain came at a moment that seemed ideal to the vainglorious megalomaniac who was Fascist dictator of Italy. Mussolini had just completed the conquest of Abyssinia, the one great triumph of his career. Like a make-believe Alexander, he was looking for more worlds to conquer. He dreamed of turning the Mediterranean into what it was in the Roman Empire—*Mare Nostrum* (Our Sea). A right-wing, fascistoid ally in Spain, put into power with his help, would secure the western end of the Mediterranean Sea and form a hostile barrier between metropolitan France and her African colonies.

The Duce's vain effort to turn his peaceful, civilized, easygoing people into tough and disciplined Roman warriors was one of the tragicomedies of modern history. Much to Mussolini's despair and frustration (but be it said in their favor) Italians could not behave like Germans. Nevertheless, the Italian contribution to the Insurgent cause was vital, combined with German help.

The Italian dictator was once again playing his phony game of anti-Communism. He had used it to great effect in his domestic conquest of power in 1919–1922, although there was no real Communist threat at that time. Now, in 1936, as he said, he was "not prepared to see the establishment of a Communist state in Spain." Throughout the Civil War, this was his publicly proclaimed reason for intervention. When Russian aid began reaching the Loyalists, Mussolini's feigned fear of Communism must have become real.

"In Spain, Italians and Germans have together dug the first trench against Bolshevism," Ciano wrote of a conversation with Hitler on October 24, 1936. In this same talk, the Fuehrer prophetically told Ciano: "In three years Germany will be ready."

All the same, Mussolini was reluctant to intervene when first asked. Ciano, like the Duce, was vain and power-mad and, as mentioned, bitterly anti-British. Appeasement and Chamberlain's groveling policy of making an alliance with Rome at any price simply made Ciano despise the British all the more, as his *Hidden Diary* and *Diplomatic Papers* show.

Once involved, the prestige of the Fascist regime was at stake. The humiliating defeat at Guadalajara in March 1937 made it all the more necessary to ensure a Franco victory and redeem the damaged reputation of Italian arms. The Duce never had the slightest intention of abiding by the non-intervention agreement, and he made this clear to the British and French.

Had Italy been operating alone, all Mussolini's ambitions

concerning Spain would have been in vain. One of the international tragedies of the Spanish Civil War was that it brought Italy and Germany together and cemented the "Rome-Berlin Axis," which was to play such a fateful role in the coming years. In 1936, when the Civil War began, the relations of Rome to Berlin were still uncertain, suspicious, and worried. The Germans were never anything but tolerantly contemptuous of the Italians. Yet, Hitler's National Socialism was a straightforward copy of the Fascism which Mussolini had created in the 1920's. The Fuehrer simply added racism and anti-Semitism. The Italian people learned to hate the Germans, but Mussolini admired them, although he may well have hated Hitler personally. The Germans, with their discipline and fighting qualities, were ideal material for Nazism. The course which the Spanish Civil War took understandably led the Duce to believe that Nazi Germany was invincible and the democracies weak and contemptible. In Spain, the two dictators found a common task, and it was natural for the Duce to hitch his rickety Roman chariot to the bright Nazi star. (It was also during the Spanish Civil War that Japan became linked to Germany and Italy through the Anti-Comintern Pact.)

Italy was too weak to move in Spain without Germany and, when the Civil War ended, she was so exhausted that Mussolini could not join Hitler in World War II until the infamous "stab in the back" of France when he thought the war was all but over and that Italy could feast on the carcass killed by the lion, Germany.

The base of operations for Italy's naval and air forces throughout the war, as I have written, was Majorca. The island, in fact, was a temporary Italian colony, much to the dismay of the British. The main street of Palma de Mallorca, the capital, was even renamed Via Roma. Naval operations were launched from the Bay of Pollensa. War material was transshipped through Majorca. Nearly all the incessant Italian bombing raids on Spanish cities and on ships in Spanish ports or en route to Spain started from Majorca. The fortifications were strengthened and the waters around the island mined.

This was all open knowledge, and was even mentioned in the British Parliament, but the Non-Intervention Committee resolutely ignored what was happening. The existence and size of the Italian force, however, was obscured for the general public by censorship and emotions. When, for instance, I cabled to *The New York Times* a detailed, first-hand account about the Italian divisions from the battlefield at Guadalajara, it was disbelieved.

Mussolini's humiliation in that battle could not have been greater. It was the first military defeat of a Fascist army, coming less than a year after the Duce's triumph in Ethiopia and Hitler's bloodless victory in the Rhineland. The hapless Italians were laughed at everywhere in the world. A large quantity of Italian arms and about 300 prisoners were captured, thus giving the Republican government massive proof of the Italian violation of the Non-Intervention Pact, but the London Committee refused to accept the information on the technicality that Spain was not a member of the NIC. The best that Álvarez del Vayo could do was to present his proofs to an indifferent League of Nations. Count Ciano, in fact, bluntly told the Non-Intervention Committee that Italy would not withdraw any of her "volunteers" until Franco's victory had been clinched.

Mussolini openly vowed revenge, which was, in a fashion, given to him by Generalissimo Franco, who permitted the Italians an easy victory at Santander on the northern coast, in August 1937. There was an exchange of messages between Franco and Mussolini afterward.

"I am particularly glad that during ten days of hard fighting the Italian legionary troops have made a valiant contribution to the splendid victory of Santander," the Duce replied to the Caudillo, adding that "this comradeship of arms—now so close —is a guarantee of final victory."

"The Italian government has never concealed the existence in Spain of a legionary air force," Ciano told Sir Noel Charles, the British *chargé d'affaires* in Rome on August 8, 1938, "and frequent bulletins are published by us to provide evidence of the activity of the Italian Air Force in Spain."

The Italians were never on good terms with the Spaniards, who looked down on them as fighters and resented their arrogance. Franco quarreled frequently with Italian commanders and diplomats. It was well known, even in Madrid, that the Insurgents were gleeful when the Italians took their terrible drubbing at Guadalajara.

"The Italian defeats," the British ambassador to Madrid, Sir Samuel Hoare, wrote in 1940 of Italy's setbacks in Greece and Africa, "were delighting the Spanish public, and Italian buildings in Madrid were being placarded with anti-Italian insults. . . . This showed that Guadalajara was all that most Spaniards remembered of Italian help during the Civil War."

There was an anecdote that went the rounds of Madrid cafés during World War II and which was not forgotten afterward. An Italian officer tries hard to woo a Spanish girl, using every passionate appeal he can think of. As a last plea he begs her for "one word!"— *"Una palabra, señorita, una palabra!"* She turns to him contemptuously and spits out one word: "Guadalajara!"

There were a few exceptions to the generally unfortunate or mediocre fighting record of the Italians. I witnessed one from the receiving end in the first stage of Franco's Catalan offensive at the end of 1938. The Italians fought hard and bravely, and took high casualties to break through Colonel Lister's defenses at Borjas Blancas. Italians are capable of great bravery, as they proved in Ethiopia and in the Resistance during World War II, and as the Garibaldini of the International Brigade demonstrated in the Spanish Civil War, but they must have their hearts in the cause for which they are fighting, and they had little or no heart for Mussolini's Spanish adventure.

One of the landmarks in the sordid history of British appeasement was Neville Chamberlain's negotiations to achieve an Anglo-Italian pact. The Second Spanish Republic, as well as Czechoslovakia, was a victim of this folly, as both also were of Munich. Chamberlain would have preferred an alliance with

Germany, and tried to make one, but there was no possibility of that. He then turned to Rome in the vain hope of driving a wedge between Italy and Germany. In the process, Anthony Eden had to be sacrificed. Eden was far more intelligent and experienced than Chamberlain, and he still bitterly resented Britain's humiliation over Mussolini's triumph in Ethiopia. He reached the end of his patience on February 20, 1938, when he resigned as Foreign Secretary, much to Chamberlain's satisfaction.

Lord Halifax, who succeeded Eden, shared Chamberlain's hopes and illusions. So did Britain's inept, obsequious ambassador in Rome, Sir Eric Drummond (later Lord Perth). None of them was a match for Count Ciano or Ambassador Grandi in London.

"Only a base, vile, insignificant country can be democratic," Ciano wrote loftily in his diary after the Anglo-Italian agreement was initialed on April 16, 1938. "A strong and heroic people tends to aristocracy."

"The Italian pact is, of course, a complete victory for Mussolini, who gains our cordial acceptance for his fortification of the Mediterranean against us; for his conquest of Abyssinia; and for his victories in Spain," said Winston Churchill. Harold Nicolson's scathing judgment when Chamberlain called the agreement "a splendid piece of give and take" was, "So it is. We give and they take."

The pact was ratified in November on the basis of Mussolini's promise to withdraw some troops from Spain, but an Italian force was to stay. Actually, the Duce was pulling out 10,000 battle-weary and demoralized soldiers, leaving some 12,000 crack troops, artillerymen and officers, and thousands of rearguard support. Lord Halifax admitted in the House of Lords that Mussolini was not prepared to see Franco defeated, whatever the British thought. Britain and the Non-Intervention Committee cynically equated the Italian withdrawal with Negrín's decision to withdraw *all* the foreign volunteers of the International Brigade.

"Mussolini has always been right," Ciano wrote in his diary, "and this time, in the bargain, he is associated with the conquerors on every front: Spain, China [which the Japanese were attacking], Africa."

Once during the war—in Rome on October 29, 1937—Count Ciano almost acquired some doubts about the Spanish adventure. "In the morning," he wrote, "there was a presentation of medals to widows of those who have fallen in Spain. The ceremony was a success. But as I watched these men and women in mourning file by and looked into their eyes red with weeping, I examined my conscience and asked myself whether this blood has been shed in a good cause. Yes, the answer is Yes. At Málaga, at Guadalajara, at Santander, we were fighting in defense of our civilization and our Revolution. And sacrifices are necessary in order to forge the bold and strong spirit of the nation."

The full extent of Italian aid to the Nationalists came as a surprise to the outside world when the official news agency, Stefani, published the figures on February 27, 1941. The Italian government was asking Madrid for 7.5 billion lire (the lira was then worth a little more than five cents) as payment for Italian aid. Among the long list of items were 763 planes, 7,668 motor vehicles, 1,930 cannon, 240,747 small arms, and hundreds of millions of rounds of ammunition. Stefani also claimed that 91 Italian warships took part in the Spanish conflict as well as 92 cargo vessels to carry Italian material. Italian submarines, it said, sank 72,800 tons of "hostile" shipping.

To this formidable list which, without counting German aid, far exceeded the total aid received by the Republican government from Russia, France, and Mexico, some uncharged items should be added. The Italians often used air force bombers from Sardinia. Transport planes went up and back from Italy. A large part of the upkeep of the Italian expeditionary force was borne by Rome.

Franco settled after the war for five billion lire in Spanish treasury bonds. It was hard to believe at the time, but Mussolini, unlike Hitler and Stalin, was not demanding his pound of Spanish flesh. His chief interest was the aggrandizement of Italy, the control of the *Mare Nostrum,* and the image of Rome as the feared scourge of the Communists and the terror of the timid democracies. He saw glory for his soldiers, power and greatness for himself. There was a high degree of irrationality in it, a true megalomania, vainglory and meanness, cynicism and shameless deceit. It was a sordid page in Italy's history.

Count Ciano wrote in his *Diplomatic Papers* that he told Lord Perth on May 18, 1938: "The British Government . . . must make Paris understand that on the question of Spain the Duce does not intend to modify in any way the attitude assumed from the beginning of the [Anglo-Italian pact] conversations," which was that Italy would not withdraw from Spain until Franco had been assured of victory. The British government dutifully complied, and the French "understood."

In his memoirs, referring to August 1, 1938, Léon Blum wrote: "In the case of Spain, the initiatives have been coming from London for more than a year, and it is the positions London takes which, in the last resort, have determined or carried with them the position taken by Paris."

Viscount Cranborne, Under Secretary for Foreign Affairs, speaking for the Chamberlain government in the House of Commons debate of December 14, 1938, frankly said in a burst of honesty: "The last word in French policy is always said in London."

"As many at the time foresaw," wrote Gerald Brenan, "the war would be won or lost in London." Such statements could be multiplied.

Chamberlain took office as Prime Minister on May 17, 1937, and immediately began his notorious appeasement policy. The role of Great Britain in the Spanish Civil War was ignominious, cynical, and short-sighted. The policy was dictated by one overriding aim: not to let the Spanish conflict spark a European war. The mistake that Britain made—one of the worst in her history—was not to realize that by appeasing Hitler and Mussolini, first in Spain and later in Austria and Czechoslovakia, she was encouraging the Fuehrer to believe there was nothing he could not get away with. The great war came anyway, with Spain in the hands of a dictator friendly to the Axis and with Nazi Germany stronger than she should have been.

The recently available British Foreign Office papers for 1937 to 1939 confirm in almost incredible detail the obtuse, ignorant, misguided career of Neville Chamberlain in the field of foreign affairs. No single British statesman of modern times did his nation such harm, and he did it with a fatuous assurance of righteousness. It was tragic that his authority could not be challenged. When Anthony Eden tried it, he was forced to resign.

The British wanted to keep Italy and Germany apart, and could not see that it was the Spanish conflict that brought the Axis into being. They tried to isolate the Soviet Union—only to drive Stalin into an alliance with Hitler. They were the dominant power in the League of Nations, but their own cynicism, immorality, and timidity contributed as much as anything to the League's collapse. They disarmed while Hitler armed.

Presiding over all these follies were the great British appeasers: the dim Stanley Baldwin, who could not get interested in foreign affairs; Neville Chamberlain, "feebly brandishing his umbrella in the faces of Hitler and Mussolini"; and the Foreign Secretaries, the well-meaning, overly diplomatic Anthony Eden who woke up too late, and the Uriah Heep of Britain's Foreign Office, Lord Halifax, whose intense religiosity never kept him from utterances on Spain which even so restrained and balanced a historian as Hugh Thomas (who once served in the Foreign Office) labeled as "contemptible." Over in Berlin was the pro-Nazi British ambassador, Sir Nevile Henderson, and in Rome the pro-Fascist Lord Perth.

Something about the information reaching London from Spain must have been confusing or misleading. Winston Churchill never achieved an understanding of what happened in Spain, not even when writing his memoirs after World War II. He always called the Republican government "the Communist regime." He referred to the Nationalists as "the patriotic, religious and bourgeois forces." However, toward the end of the

Civil War he realized that a Franco victory "could be a threat to British interests, and the others not."

"From the early months of 1937," wrote Anthony Eden long afterward in the first volume of his memoirs, "if I had to choose, I would have preferred a [Republican] Government victory." But he felt that he had no choice.

The situation in England made it particularly difficult for Britons to take sides. Popular sympathies, on the whole, were with the Loyalists, but not even the Laborites wanted to get actively involved in the Spanish conflict. The Tories were naturally inclined to favor the Nationalists, as were the business and financial interests. They were all alarmed by the revolutionary manifestations on the Loyalist side. Both political parties, and the Liberals too, of course, feared and detested the Nazi and Fascist regimes, but appeasement, like isolationism in the United States, was popular. Here is a typical example of the way "non-intervention" was applied by the London Committee under Eden's guidance: in April 1937 the powers agreed to a naval patrol whereby Britain and France guarded the Nationalist zone, Italy and Germany the Loyalist, with international supervision of the French frontier and British "observers" on the Portuguese border. The result was an effective naval blockade of the Republican zone, an ineffective watch on the Rebel zone, a tightly closed French frontier, and a wide-open Portuguese border. The cynicism could hardly have been more flagrant.

In Ciano's *Diplomatic Papers* there is a revealing "conversation with the British *chargé d' affaires"* in Rome on August 23, 1937. Counsellor Edward M. Ingram "after stating that what he was about to say did not represent a formal approach, wished to call my attention to events which have lately occurred in the Mediterranean and are still occurring," Ciano wrote. The events included "the air attack on a British steamship" and "repeated cases of torpedo attacks and shelling aimed at ships of various nationalities.

"Mr. Ingram was anxious to inform me that the British government did not wish to make the least protest through his communication," Ciano continued. "It merely wished to inform us of its earnest desire that the atmosphere between Great Britain and Italy, which had so fortunately been cleared, should not be troubled by unforeseeable and deplorable complications."

Count Ciano, as always, was sly, evasive, and bland. In the end, Ingram said that he was "fully satisfied," but during the thirty-nine days—July 27 to September 3—eighteen ships were attacked by the Italians, some of them British and French.

The only time the British government was stirred to take action to stop the brazen attacks by Italian submarines and bombers against British and other ships in the Mediterranean —at Franco's request, incidentally—came in September 1937. The Chamberlain government was reluctant to act, but Eden forced the cabinet to take a determined position. French Foreign Minister Yvon Delbos suggested a conference, which was held at Nyon, Switzerland. It was decided that the British and French fleets should patrol the Mediterranean and sink any suspicious-looking submarines. Germany and Italy refused to attend, but the Duce saw that he had to do something. Since he could not "lick 'em" he joined them, and privately told Hitler that he would not stop torpedoing ships. The Soviet Union was not allowed to take part in the patrolling of the Mediterranean, but Italy was invited later to join the sea patrol. So the Non-Intervention Committee was asking Mussolini to hunt and sink his own submarines!

As Ciano wrote in his diary for September 21, 1937: "Nyon is a fine victory. From suspected pirates to policemen of the Mediterranean—and the Russians, whose ships we are sinking, excluded!" The Duce, he added, "showed that he is very pleased."

By the spring of 1938, the Italian bombers were busier than ever. Twenty-two British-registered ships were attacked, of which eleven were sunk or badly damaged. British sailors were killed. Never in their once-proud history had Britain accepted supinely what Winston Churchill, in the House of Commons called "humiliation" and "this abjection." Chamberlain was still afraid to annoy the Italians who, in fact, only ceased their attacks when they were warned that if the raids continued, the

Chamberlain government might fall. That was the last thing Italy or Germany wanted. Chamberlain was wooing Mussolini at the time and he had no intention of implementing the Nyon decisions against Italy in any effective way.

For Neville Chamberlain, the Spanish Civil War was an intense annoyance. He did not consider it at all important. He just wanted to see it over with and out of the way. The last of the many bitter and futile debates on the Spanish Civil War in the House of Commons took place on February 22, 1939. Chamberlain solemnly read out a telegram from Franco which pledged "his patriotism, honor as a gentleman and his generosity" as guarantees that peace in Spain would be just and merciful. This was acceptable to the British Prime Minister as a basis for diplomatic recognition of the Franco regime. Clement Attlee, leader of the Opposition and of the Labor party, called it "a gross betrayal of democracy, the consummation of two and a half years of the hypocritical pretence of non-intervention and a connivance all the time at aggression."

Chamberlain was, of course, unshaken. The Generalissimo's massive reprisals after the Civil War ended showed that the Caudillo had his own conception of a "just peace."

"No foreign issue since the French Revolution," commented Hugh Thomas, "had so occupied the House of Commons." But in the French Revolution, the British did something.

One of the most tragic aspects of the German and Italian intervention in Spain was that it introduced the merciless bombing of open cities which now characterizes modern warfare. Germany's famous World War II ace, General Adolf Galland, who began his career as a fighter pilot in the Condor Legion, boasts in his autobiography that he and his mechanics even developed and used an early version of the napalm bomb in Spain. All the bombers flown for the Insurgents were either German or Italian, with German or Italian crews in nearly all cases. The crews, who were rotated fairly quickly, received training that must have proved invaluable in the great war that followed.

The Loyalists used their bombers to attack cities on the Insurgent side only a few times, and then against the desires and orders of the Republican government. The Loyalist leaders did not consider it either right or politic to bomb Spanish civilians and destroy Spanish property. This would have gone counter to what they were fighting for and to the image they were presenting to the world. The Russian commander, "Duglas," was forced by Prieto to leave Spain because he ordered Seville and Valladolid to be bombed.

It is known that Generalissimo Franco was sometimes unhappy over specific excesses, such as the German bombing of Guernica and the merciless Italian bombings of Barcelona, but there is no evidence that he asked his allies to stop the practice generally. Moreover, it was General Franco who gave the orders for the bombing of Madrid in late October and early November 1936, when the Insurgent forces thought they would capture the capital. He told a group of Portuguese journalists that he would rather destroy Madrid than "leave it to the Marxists." This was the first "blitz" of a modern city, but not the worst in the war.

The palm for the worst goes to the Italian bombers that came over from Majorca and Sardinia in seventeen raids against Barcelona, every three hours from March 16 to 18, 1938. I was there and could testify in dispatches to *The New York Times* to the terrifying effects on the population, the extent of the destruction, and the heavy loss of civilian lives. When Lord Perth told Count Ciano a few days later that the air raids on Barcelona might arouse a hostile public opinion in Britain, the Italian Minister was not at a loss for an answer.

"I replied," Ciano wrote in his diary for March 20, "that operations are initiated by Franco, not by us—we might, therefore, exercise a moderating influence, but we could make no promises. . . . The truth about the air raids on Barcelona is that the orders for them were given to Valle [head of the Italian Air Force] by Mussolini in the Chamber a few minutes before he made his speech on Austria. Franco knew nothing about them, and asked yesterday that they should be suspended for fear of complications abroad. Mussolini believes that these air raids are an admirable way of weakening the morale of the Reds, while the troops are advancing in Aragon. He is right. He wasn't very worried when I informed him of Perth's *démarche.* In fact he said he was delighted that the Italians should be horrifying the world by their aggressiveness for a change, instead of charming it by their skill at playing the guitar."

There was no special military objective in Barcelona; the idea was to strike terror. The reaction of the Catalans—as with all such raids from World War II to Vietnam—was the opposite of what the military expected. The attacks, of course, struck terror, but far from breaking the spirit of the population they engendered a bitterness and fury which hardened the will to resist. Moreover, the world was not impressed in the way Mussolini expected. There was nothing but condemnation. Even the cautious Secretary of State Cordell Hull expressed horror on behalf of the people of the United States.

Enough has been said about Guernica, the most famous, and infamous, of all the air raids in the Spanish Civil War. It was a systematic job of destruction by the German Condor Legion of the defenseless medieval capital of the Basques on April 26, 1937. It lives in history as a symbol of the often wanton character of the death and destruction to which Spain was subjected —in this case by foreign intervention.

7

... AND NON-INTERVENTION

THE ROLE OF STALIN AND THE Soviet Union has been one of the most misunderstood features of the Spanish Civil War. Contrary to the popular image, the Russian dictator was at first opposed, then reluctant, and at all times full of misgivings on the question of aiding the Republican government. He was determined, as I have said, that Russian intervention should never reach proportions that might lead to a European war. While he sent some military advisers, pilots, and tank drivers to Spain, they were few in number and always worked as secretly and as isolatedly as possible. Almost all the Communists in the International Brigades, secret police, intelligence organizations, and government affairs were non-Russian.

The evidence indicates that while Stalin did not want to see the Republicans lose, he did not feel it worthwhile or safe to help them enough to win. He wanted to prolong the war, but at no risk to the Soviet Union. Whether his aid was entirely paid for by Spanish gold is still in dispute. In any event, the amount owed one way or the other would be small and would not obviate the fact that Stalin was handsomely reimbursed for the help he provided.

The Russian dictator was one of the most secretive and enigmatic figures of history, but it is not difficult to understand how he felt about Spain and why he did what he did. His policies were not, of course, guided by idealism, morality, or any love for Spain. He sought to do what best suited Russian Communist

154

policy at the time. It was important for him to sustain the Soviet Union's image as the leader of world revolution and the champion of anti-Fascism. With good reason, he feared the fast-rising, aggressive, and anti-Communist Nazi regime. He was determined not to provoke Hitler to the point where the Fuehrer would strike back at Russia. And he sought a *détente* with Britain and France.

The German and Italian dictators realized soon enough that there was a limit to Stalin's interventionism. In his *Diplomatic Papers* Count Ciano quotes the Duce as saying to Goering in Rome on January 23, 1937:

" 'Russia has sent no cadre of volunteers, but only commanders and material, and would certainly adapt herself even to accepting a defeat of the Reds. It must be borne in mind that the aid to the Reds from the Communist side was intensified at the moment when the Spanish Reds had in any case stopped Franco in front of Madrid. . . .

" 'Count Ciano observed that the Italian Ambassador to Moscow, who is at present in Rome, had informed him that the Bolsheviks are slowly preparing for a Red defeat in Spain. . . .' "

"Franco and Company can consider themselves very lucky to have received the help of Fascist Italy and National Socialist Germany in their first civil war," Hitler says in *Table Talk*. "For, as the Red Spaniards never cease explaining, they had not entered into cooperation with the Soviets on ideological grounds, but had rather been forced into it—and thence dragged into a political current not of their own choosing—simply through lack of other support."

A Communist government in Spain during the Popular Front period of the Comintern (1935–1939) would not have fitted into Stalin's policies. Spain was too far away from the Soviet Union to be safely controlled or to be so strengthened as to be able to stand alone in Western Europe. Britain and France would have been frightened by a Communist Spain at a time when Stalin was seeking friendly relations with them as a counterweight against the rise of Nazi Germany. On the other hand, if the democracies and the Fascist powers tangled with each other over Spain, Russia would be the gainer. So long as the war continued, Stalin would have a free hand. He intended to have his cake and eat it, and not be left out of any of the great power moves. This is why he, as cynically as the other dictators, joined the Non-Intervention Agreement and even, on August 28, 1936, issued a decree banning the export of war materials to Spain.

When he saw that Hitler and Mussolini continued to send men and materials to Franco, he finally organized the Russian shipments. They were always arranged clandestinely through foreign, seedy, and sordid agents, who were more like characters in an Eric Ambler thriller than serious businessmen or revolutionaries. An elaborate, clumsy, and inefficient network was set up. First, Stalin had to be sure that Spain paid for everything to be sent. Before a single Russian plane or tank saw action in the Loyalist zone, more than half the gold reserves of the Bank of Spain was en route to the Russian port of Odessa. With this money, Russian agents, always including a representative from the NKVD, set up "export firms" in the capitals of Britain, France, Czechoslovakia, Poland, Switzerland, Denmark, Holland, and Belgium. Through these companies, arms of all sorts were bought—often obsolete, sometimes faulty, always exorbitantly expensive. Bribery, trickery, cheating, and secretiveness were usually involved. Dr. Negrín confirmed to me that some arms were even bought from Nazi Germany in 1938.

Stalin did not send a great deal of Russian matériel, but what he did send from October 1936 into the first half of 1937, and again in the spring of 1938, was of crucial importance, especially tanks and fighter and bomber planes. However, the depredations of the Italian bombers from Majorca and submarines from Italy made it too costly for Stalin to ship military goods from Russia to Spain by sea. He was not willing to give his freighters naval protection. That would have been risky, and he was careful never to take risks when it came to Spain.

Thereafter, Russian aid that reached the Loyalists had to pass through France when the French opened their frontier into Spain. Such matériel, for the most part, was bought by the

Russians in other European countries, although in April and May 1938, about 300 airplanes and some 25,000 tons of war material, some of it Russian, were allowed by the Daladier government to be transported across France into Spain. The British became alarmed, remonstrated to Premier Daladier and, on June 13, the French frontier was closed down again. Only once more, early in 1939, as the Insurgents were sweeping through Catalonia, was the border opened, but it was too late and the material never reached the front.

There were at least two occasions when the Republican government could—or at least might—have avoided the necessity of appealing to Moscow for aid. The first was at the beginning of the rebellion when German and Italian aid for the Rebels could have been matched or surpassed if the democracies had sold arms to the Second Republic which was, after all, the legitimate government of Spain. The second occasion was in mid-1937, when Andrés Nín was tortured and killed. The highhanded police terror of the Russian and Spanish Communists so incensed Premier Negrín and his associates that a breakaway from dependence on the Soviet Union must have been tempting. A bitterly angry and frustrated Negrín was left by the democracies with no alternative except to depend on Russian help.

Stalin may well have had no more intention of conforming to the Non-Intervention Agreement than Hitler and Mussolini. However, he was playing a losing game and he must have known it. He could not compete with the Germans and Italians, especially while Britain and France showed that they would do nothing to prevent the Fascist dictators from intervening as much as they pleased in Spain. The inability to ship arms freely through France was an insurmountable handicap under the rules that Stalin had set for himself.

After the grand climax of appeasement at Munich in September 1938, Stalin had nothing to gain by a policy of *détente* with the British and French. Only one road then remained open to him, or so he must have thought: an alliance with Hitler. Such being the case, he had to cut his losses and back out of Spain, leaving himself free to move quickly in any direction. He had started reducing his commitment in Spain as early as mid-1937, and virtually ended it after Munich. A few military advisers remained to the end, but no pilots or other technicians. There had never been any Russian troops.

"The Russian advisory staff," as Professor Payne wrote, "was never large enough to provide the sort of supervision given by German instructors." He could have added: "Nor were they as good."

In January 1938, U.S. Ambassador William Bullitt cabled Secretary of State Cordell Hull from Paris that, "Communist influence had diminished enormously and, at the moment, the Spanish government, while radical, was by no means Communist and was definitely hostile to Moscow." This was an impressive judgment coming, as it did, from an envoy who was inclined to be sympathetic to the Nationalists during the war. Ambassador to the Republican government Claude G. Bowers never had any doubts about the independence of the Loyalist government and continually denied to Washington that Moscow dictated or dominated in Spain. However, Bowers was well known to be sympathetic to the Republican cause and his reports were discounted by Secretary of State Hull and Assistant Secretary James Dunn. In fact, Bowers told me after the war that during the latter part of the conflict he always sent copies of his dispatches directly to the White House to be sure that they were available to President Roosevelt.

A guiding factor in Soviet foreign policies in the 1930's was a deep-seated fear of war, which the new and belligerent Fascist powers did not share to anything like the same degree. Russia had had her own devastating Civil War after World War I. It was logical of the Kremlin to seek peace through collective instruments like the League of Nations and alliances with the democracies. The Popular Front policy was one result of this search for security in the face of the aggressiveness of the Germans and Italians and—on the eastern flank—the Japanese.

The Non-Intervention Committee, in theory, fit into the

Soviet designs, ironically very much more so than was the case with Germany and Italy. Stalin could be imagined asking himself: "What price Spain?" Clearly, it was worthwhile paying some price to help the Republicans, but it was never going to matter greatly to the Russians if the Loyalists lost. It is, in fact, possible that Stalin did not want the democratic, bourgeois Republicans to win.

At the Nuremberg trials Hitler was quoted as having said on November 5, 1937, that "from the German point of view a 100 per cent Franco victory is not desirable. Our chief interest is in the war continuing." Stalin was taking much the same position at the same time, although his reason was that a continuing war in Spain would tie Hitler down and—a vain hope!—keep him from greater adventures.

It is one of the ironies of the history of the Spanish Civil War that none of us realized at the time how carefully intervention was being manipulated until near the end of the war so as not to achieve victory for either side. Mussolini alone among the ruling statesmen of Europe, really did want to see the Nationalists win as quickly as possible. However, his troops were not good enough, and he could not supply the necessary war matériel. In any event, he could not act alone against the wishes of the Fuehrer.

The dangerous contest in which all these European statesmen were engaged had too many unknown factors for any of them to be sure of what would happen. Meanwhile, the Spaniards were fighting a *civil* war in which foreign intervention was an extraneous factor, even though it was this intervention that decided the outcome.

Hitler's rearmament, the occupation of the Rhineland, and the anti-Communism of Nazi Germany, Fascist Italy, and militaristic Japan, were forcing Russia to spend all available resources on armaments. Stalin wanted to keep what arms he possessed for the Soviet Union, which is one of the reasons why nearly all the military material sent by Russia to Spain was bought by Comintern agents in third countries.

The Russian people were genuinely and naturally sympathetic to the Republicans. There were spontaneous collections in factories and collective farms, amounting to a few million dollars, but this money was used for food and medicines. Russian memories and emotions were stirred. Lenin had seen Spain as the European country best suited for a Russian-style revolution. The Asturian revolt of 1934 resulted in about 600 Spaniards going to Russia for military training. Perhaps Spaniards could do what the Hungarian, German, Austrian, and even, at that time, Chinese Communist movements had failed to do. But there were no dreamers in the Kremlin. It was surely clear to the sophisticated men in the Russian government that a Communist Spain was, at best, a distant goal. Present realism demanded support for a moderate, non-revolutionary "bourgeois democracy" whose primary objective was to win the war, not foment a revolution.

This paradoxical, but understandable, policy was to bewilder millions of observers, combatants, partisans, and some later historians. It was nevertheless vital, in the overall strategy, for the Spanish Communists to strengthen themselves as much as possible; to gain a maximum degree of power; and to follow Stalinist policies. As one could see later, there was a crystal simplicity and consistency to Communist activities, which made them the best soldiers, the firmest supporters of the bourgeois Republic, and the ugliest and most ruthless enemies of those Spaniards on the Loyalist side who did not conform to their ideas.

The Spanish Communists kept for themselves and for the Army units they could trust most of the arms which the Russians sent in; they supported political leaders, especially Juan Negrín, who recognized their value and the validity of their policies; they attracted to their ranks ambitious, brave, intelligent young men who saw in Communist policies the only hope for a victory and their own advancement. And the Communists were the ones who created and ran the International Brigade.

Stalin played his cards cleverly and well, and in the process got far more credit for helping Republican Spain than he and the Communists deserved. History has only gradually been setting the record straight.

Official and diplomatic relations between the Soviet Union and the Second Spanish Republic were virtually nonexistent until August 1936. An ambassador, Marcel Rosenberg, arrived on the twenty-seventh, and with him an embassy staff which expanded in time to include trade and intelligence agents. Russia's representation in Spain can best be called an extensive military mission. There was no infantry such as Italy sent, nor anything comparable to Germany's Condor Legion. The International Brigades were commanded by Communists, but always Eastern European and Spanish. There were some Russian advisers.

The best estimate for the total number of Russians—military and civilian—is 3,000. The hostile Indalecio Prieto wrote after the war: "I am sure that at no [one] time did the Russians in our territory total more than 500, including aviators, industrial technicians, military advisers, interpreters and secret agents." Louis Fischer's figure was 700 at most at one time. The largest numbers were aviators, who had a high turnover rate. They stayed a short time, as much for training as to help Spain. The same was true of the Russian tank crews, the next most numerous. There were about fifty instructors.

Moscow's authority and influence were not through personnel so much as through being the only important source of war material. The air force was the most strongly dominated by Russians, partly because the Soviet Union was furnishing the planes, and partly because the Spanish commander, General Ignacio Hidalgo de Cisneros, was inexperienced and a new (January 1937) convert to Communism. It is generally agreed that for at least the first half of the war, the Loyalist air force was directed by a Russian general called "Duglas" or "Douglas." His real name was Jacob Schmutchkievich. In the early stages, half the pilots were Russian, but the proportion gradually dwindled to nothing as Spanish pilots were trained. The same was true of the tank units, at first commanded by General G. D. Pavlov.

From the beginning, in Dr. Borkenau's words, the Russians were kept "in monastic seclusion and absolute separation from the rest of the government troops, though the fact of their existence was not kept secret." Burnett Bolloten wrote of "the minatory and imperious behavior of the Russian officers" and even of civilians like Mikhail Koltzov, the *Pravda* correspondent, who seemed to have the equivalent of a "hot line" to Stalin. If so, this was behind the scenes and it never reached the stage of being high-handed with men like Premiers Largo Caballero and Juan Negrín, who would not have stood for "imperious behavior." Negrín's contacts with the Russian officers were slight and formal.

Even in 1936, and certainly during the Great Purge of 1937–1938, Stalin could not, or would not, trust many of his Russian officers out of the country. He used as many non-Russian and Comintern officers as possible. Most of them were exiles living in Russia. Real Russian "volunteers" would, in some cases, have defected, as did Orlov.

The Insurgents took a few Soviet merchant seamen prisoner, but never any military personnel. Stalin's orders, General Walter Krivitsky (another defector) wrote, were: "Keep out of the range of artillery fire."

The Comintern has been called "that worldwide conspiratorial organization for the fostering of revolution which was as much feared as it was grossly overrated." It, and the Profintern (the Communist international federation of trade unions) as well as the various national Communist parties, were as anxious to minimize their aid to Republican Spain during the war as they were to exaggerate its importance afterward. A great many organizations were established in Europe and the United States to provide food, medical supplies and services, and other kinds of nonmilitary aid. In many cases sponsors with distinguished names did not know of the Communists behind the scenes, nor did contributors.

The period of Soviet history through August and September 1936 is an obscure one in the field of foreign affairs. Stalin, having embarked on his murderous purge, must have found Spain a nuisance. The year 1937 saw an appalling slaughter in the Soviet Union. Nearly all of the Russians sent to Spain were also to become victims of the Stalinist purges. It was not a time when Stalin wanted to become too heavily committed to a foreign venture like the Spanish Civil War. However, urgent messages came to the Kremlin during July and August 1936 that the Spanish Republican cause would be lost if help did not arrive and, what mattered much more, a Nazi and Fascist triumph was being gained.

No one knows the exact day on which Stalin made up his mind to send arms and technicians to Spain, nor just what finally decided him. Maurice Thorez, the French Communist leader, was in Moscow on September 21, 1936, and Hugh Thomas believes that he is the one who persuaded Stalin to act. The Comintern did get busy around that time, setting up purchasing agencies in various European capitals.

And, finally, on October 14, 1936, Soviet arms began arriving in Spain. Russian military advisers had begun joining Ambassador Rosenberg's staff in September. The first Russian bombers, tanks, and artillery went into combat on October 24, and the first Russian "Mosca" fighter planes on November 2. By that time—probably not accidentally—the shipments of Spanish gold were well on their way to Odessa.

In those days, bomber planes did not have the long range they developed during World War II. Military planes could not fly directly from the Soviet Union to Spain. The Germans, who flew from Stuttgart, and the Italians, who sometimes used Sardinia as well as Majorca, had the advantage. After the Italians sank some Soviet freighters in the spring of 1937, the Russians notified the Valencia government that it would have to furnish its own transportation. At that time there was a great deal of war matériel in France, partly Russian, for which the Spanish government had paid, but the frontier was closed.

Russian aid was always strictly on a commercial basis, but this did not mean that Stalin or the Spanish Communists let the Republican governments dispose of the material as they pleased. When, for instance, the first big plane shipment—fifty pursuit planes bought from an Eastern European country—was arriving on a Norwegian ship, Stalin would not allow it to be disembarked in Anarchist Barcelona. The ship had to go to Alicante, running the Franco blockade.

Some figures on the grand total of Soviet aid to the Loyalists between October 1936 and March 1938 were given by the German military attaché in Burgos, and quoted in Thomas's *The Spanish Civil War*. Among them were 242 planes, 703 guns, 500 howitzer guns, 1,386 trucks, 187 tractors, 100 rifle-machine guns. The Russians used only 34 of their own vessels to transport matériel. The German attaché also listed "920 officers and men" who were Russian. This was not a source likely to minimize the extent of Stalin's aid.

The contrast between the way Moscow dealt with Spain and the way it dealt with Egypt in recent years is striking. Stalin gave up Spain as a bad job because it meant little to him. When Egypt lost nearly all her Russian war materials in June 1967, the Russians poured new armaments in until Egypt was armed with the most powerful air defense system outside of NATO. The Kremlin lavished well over $5 billion on Egypt up to 1972. Stalin spent virtually nothing on Spain.

Almost all historians are now agreed that Russian aid arrived late, was too limited in scope, and was stopped too soon to be decisive. Nevertheless, it has to be conceded that Russian help did save the Republic in November 1936, when Madrid was in dire peril, and the help that arrived throughout the war was vital. After all, the Republican government had no other source of aid.

The Loyalists fought Spaniards, Italians, Portuguese, and Germans; the Insurgents fought Spaniards, plus a small and rapidly dwindling International Brigade, which was withdrawn six months before the war ended. Russian and Comintern support did not alter the essentially Spanish character of the Republic's conduct of the war.

For Stalin, Republican Spain had been a pawn in a deadly power game which he was playing with Hitler and Mussolini. When the moves went against him, he surrendered his pieces without a qualm.

With the exception of some Portuguese soldiers from the Salazar dictatorship and a few small groups from Eire and France, all the genuine volunteers in the Civil War fought for the Loyalists. The crusading emotion that moved men everywhere in the free world in the 1930's was anti-Fascism, not anti-Communism.

The assiduous Hugh Thomas dug up the names of only two Americans on the Insurgent side, one a pilot. F. J. Taylor, in his book *The United States and the Spanish Civil War,* notes that "a study of State Department files did not reveal a single reference to Americans serving in the armies of Generalissimo Franco."

A semi-Fascist group of Irish nationalists, called Blue Shirts, formed a battalion under its leader, General Eoin O'Duffy, who once worked for De Valera. It totaled 600 or 700 men, but half of them were adventurers and mercenaries who did not belong to O'Duffy's Blue Shirts. After some training at Cáceres in the Nationalist zone, they were sent to the Jarama River front. Their first encounter, on February 16, 1937, in which they suffered their heaviest losses—four killed—was a mistaken exchange of fire with a Spanish Insurgent detachment. They saw real action, briefly, in March 1937. After that, they were not heard from until O'Duffy and another Irish volunteer wrote books about their experiences.

There were some Irishmen in the International Brigades. On two occasions, the British battalion was led by Irish Communists, Peter Daly and Paddy O'Daire. An American of Irish birth, Hans Amlie, who once belonged to the Irish Republican Army, commanded the Abraham Lincoln Battalion for a while.

There was a small French rightist group of volunteers called the Jeanne d'Arc Battalion, who fought for Franco and evidently fought well.

There was, finally, an even smaller White Russian group which came from France. Its commander, General Anton Fock, was killed in action.

These were all the volunteers that the Insurgent cause attracted and none of them gave the Nationalists significant military or moral aid. They were so few and so ineffective that they simply served to underline the fact that the idealists of the world were with the Loyalists, not the Nationalists.

. The right-wing clerical dictatorship of Premier Antonio Salazar de Oliveira was a natural and very helpful ally of the generals. Before the war, Portugal was a refuge where the Spanish military men could and did plot. Later, she provided a permanently open channel for German arms and other materials. In the critical period when Franco's Army of Africa was divided from Mola's northern army, Portugal provided exactly the service which the Ho Chi Minh trail through Laos gave to the North Vietnamese.

Portuguese guards almost always turned back hapless men, women, and children of Loyalist persuasion seeking escape and a refuge from the savage behavior of the Moors and Legionaries as they moved northward. It was a cruel practice, since the men and some of the women who were turned over to the Insurgents were shot. Like Spain, Portugal was a once-great imperial power in decay. Like Spain she also had lost her New World possession, Brazil, as a result of the defeat and degradation caused by foreign occupation in the Revolutionary and Napoleonic Wars, at the beginning of the nineteenth century. Proud, reactionary, and church-ridden, Portugal was ruled in the 1930's by one of the narrowest and most bigoted of modern dictators—Dr. Salazar—who naturally was horrified by the liberal, revolutionary, anticlerical upheaval taking place in Republican Spain.

Dr. Salazar never made any bones about helping the Insurgents, to use his own words, "with all available means." There had been times in the history of the Iberian peninsula—the latest in 1808 during the Napoleonic campaigns—when Portugal was taken over by the much larger and stronger Spanish neighbor. A leftist government in Madrid would have seemed like a dangerous threat to the Portuguese.

Portugal was not only a friendly base and a wide-open door for the Nationalists; she sent a fighting force of about 20,000 men, some of them volunteers, called the *Legión de Viriato.* They saw hard front-line service and about 8,000 of them were killed. This very high proportion of deaths is evidence of their bravery and spirit.

Mexico has been the only Western country to champion the Spanish Republic openly, fearlessly, and generously from the beginning of the Civil War to this day. The Mexican government, alone in the West, still recognizes the Republican government as the legitimate government of Spain. Yugoslavia is the only Communist country still maintaining its old diplomatic link.

Mexico is a Spanish-Indian country with a revolutionary background. From 1934 to 1940, she had a left-wing, anti-Yankee President, General Lázaro Cárdenas. The other Latin American countries were covertly or openly pro-Franco. The Mexicans saw what a fraud non-intervention was and refused to have anything to do with it. While the Basque port of Bilbao was open, for instance, Mexico sent $1,500,000 worth of arms to the anti-Franco forces. Cárdenas wanted to send more, but Washington blocked him.

Mexico helped the Loyalists as much as possible during the war, but she could not do much. After the war she opened her shores magnanimously to the Republican refugees. Many a valued Mexican citizen today is a former exile, or the child of an exile, from the Spanish Civil War. Moral support was at all times unstinting and—unlike the Russians—the Mexicans did not ask for advance payment in gold for what they could send.

The League of Nations needs an inglorious mention in any account of the "Non-Intervention" policy. By the time the Civil War started in July 1936 the League had become worse than ineffectual. It had been unable even to hamper Mussolini's conquest of Ethiopia, which was completed in April of that year. In 1931 Japan, with impunity, had staged the first of its aggressions—in Manchuria. The United States had earlier crippled the infant world organization by refusing to join when it was formed after World War I. The League became an institution dominated by the victors in that war, especially by Great Britain. The years of the Spanish conflict saw the climax of the democracies' appeasement, the Fascist and Nazi dictators' aggressions, and a war between China and Japan, while the United States stood aloof in neutral isolationism.

Until the Abyssinian War of 1935–1936, the League had at least served as a forum and symbol of aspirations for world peace, and it had helped to end two minor conflicts. In the Spanish Civil War period, the League's behavior was an exercise in cynicism, futility, and duplicity. Manchuria, the Rhineland, Ethiopia, Austria, Spain, Czechoslovakia—these were the mileposts along which the League of Nations went to its ignoble death. Perhaps the world organization was premature and its weakness inevitable, but it was a pity for the historic record that it should have been allowed to go out with a whimper and in dishonor.

In the Spanish conflict, the League followed Britain's example of paying pious tribute to the doctrine of Non-Intervention, turning a blind eye to the violations and a deaf ear to the protests of the Spanish government, which was a member of the League Council and which had incorporated the Covenant of the League into its Constitution. The world organization performed some minor functions, such as reluctantly allowing Álvarez del Vayo a forum from which to plead (vainly, as it happened) for justice. It is ironical that even Maximo Litvinov, representing the Soviet Union, tried to prevent Vayo from speaking. Although considered, with much justice, as a fellow traveler working with Moscow, Vayo would not be muzzled, nor would Negrín. But they spoke to deaf ears.

Toward the end of the Civil War, the League provided an

impartial commission to verify the withdrawal of the International Brigades, after ascertaining their numbers and nationalities.

The Nationalists had no official relations with Geneva, but they had good friends and frightened enemies. The negative process by which Republican Spain was allowed to lose and Nationalist Spain to win was mirrored in the League of Nations, as it was elsewhere. The League had helped the Nationalists to win the Civil War, but Generalissimo Franco was so contemptuous of it that he withdrew Spain soon after his victory. Japan, Germany, and Italy had previously withdrawn.

Economics, international finance, and Spanish gold played important roles in the murky picture of "non-intervention."

It was the Second Republic's misfortune that business and financial interests everywhere saw their cause best served by a Franco victory. This meant powerful lobbies in Paris, London, and Washington operating against the Loyalists. Credits extended to the Franco regime were as helpful as soldiers. American oil shipments to the Nationalists were invaluable. In such ways, "non-intervention" served the Nationalist cause.

Although the Republicans had possession of the entire gold reserve of the Bank of Spain—the sixth largest in the world—the Insurgent peseta was worth double the Republican on the international exchanges. The great asset on the Nationalist side was the expectation of victory which, in practical terms, meant credit.

The German trade and finance organization set up in Seville, HISMA, and the complementary Berlin firm, ROWAK, using the mineral exports of Spain and Morocco and the agricultural exports of the Canary Islands and Andalusia, were able to stabilize the Nationalist peseta at a relatively high level. When the northern zone was conquered, the industries of Bilbao and the coal of the Asturias were added to the Nationalist economy. Food was always adequate, for Franco held the meat and wheat producing regions, while the Loyalist zone had to import food for the cities. There was much hunger although no starvation on the government side. The Republican government worked hard to protect foreign investments in its zone and to comply rigorously with its international financial obligations.

"Then and until the end of the war," Álvarez del Vayo wrote in his book, *The Last Optimist,* "the Spanish Republic paid the interest on the external gold debt. It observed scrupulously the convention governing the international mercury monopoly, and later prolonged it, out of respect for its obligations, on conditions favorable to Italy even when Mussolini was fighting on the side of the Rebels. Years later I heard British authorities praise this behavior as something almost unique. The Republic gave facilities for clearing operations, at times to the detriment of its own war economy, and was willing to give foreign interests in Spain all guarantees compatible with national sovereignty."

This is an accurate statement. However, there was no confidence abroad because of the revolutionary activities of the Spanish left-wing and distrust of the Soviet Union. It was a vicious circle for the Republic. The Soviet Union was the only country which helped and could be trusted by the Loyalists, but the dependence on Moscow repelled foreign bankers and businessmen.

France held 60 per cent of the entire foreign capital investment in Spanish industry in 1936. Britain held much of the rest. These facts of economic life greatly influenced the policies of both countries.

The Republic had to fall back on gold as its one great asset, and that gold could not be left in Madrid, which was always threatened with capture, nor anywhere in the Loyalist zone since the revolutionaries were also a threat in the early months. Neither France nor Britain could be trusted. In fact, as I have mentioned, some Bank of Spain gold was impounded in Paris, held until the end of the war, and turned over to Franco.

Meanwhile, Stalin was demanding his pound—in fact, many pounds—of flesh in payment for whatever arms and food were sent to Spain. Dr. Juan Negrín, then Minister of Finance, with the agreement of Prime Minister Largo Caballero and President Azaña, arranged to send more than half of Spain's gold reserves to Moscow.

Negrín told Louis Fischer in October 1936 that the Republic had about $1 billion in gold and silver when the war began. Some of it remained in Madrid until the end of the war. There is no agreement on the value of the gold sent to Russia. I have seen figures ranging from more than $400 million (Hugh Thomas) to more than $700 million (Stanley G. Payne). My information puts the total at about $575 million. The shipment for Odessa, the Russian port, was sent secretly to Cartagena on the east coast of Spain and embarked between October 22 and 25, 1936, on four Soviet freighters. Dr. Negrín told me in 1954 that the purchases from the Soviet Union did not use up the full amount of the gold sent, and that Moscow therefore owed Spain a sum that had to be calculated, partly because the Russians, without asking permission, had melted down the more valuable English gold sovereign coins into bars, and partly because Spanish raw materials were shipped to Russia in partial payment for purchases. Dr. Negrín bequeathed the receipt for the gold and other pertinent documents to the Franco government on his death in 1956.

After his defection to the United States, Alexander Orlov wrote that when the treasure arrived in Russia, Stalin said, "The Spaniards will never see their gold again, as they don't see their own ears."

Both sides in the Spanish Civil War retained their economic independence, although it seemed toward the end as if the Franco regime had pawned the Spanish and Moroccan mineral resources to Germany. In 1943, when the Axis started losing the war, the Caudillo was in a position, with British help, to start taking back from the Germans what he had given them in the Civil War.

Aside from any consideration of the much greater economic resources that the Nationalists controlled during the Civil War, there was a clear superiority in management and expertise. The Insurgents' finances were cleverly handled, and they traded profitably as well. The Loyalists were always bogged down in a partially revolutionary, partisan, and amateurish economy.

The support that the Nationalists received in foreign financial and commercial circles naturally made it much easier for them to sustain a viable economy. In that regard, American interests deserved and got a special vote of thanks from Generalissimo Franco.

8

THE UNITED STATES

IN THE FIRST YEAR OF THE Spanish Civil War, American public opinion presented a baffling picture. No event in the outside world, before or since, aroused Americans in time to such religious controversy and such burning emotions. Yet the Gallup Polls, even through much of 1937, showed that a great majority of Americans were indifferent to, and ignorant of, what was going on. Two-thirds of the population, according to the polls, were unconcerned. Only 20 per cent favored the Loyalists, and that seemed to be because of the intervention by Hitler and Mussolini. Because of their feelings, religious or ideological, about Communism, 10 per cent favored the Insurgents.

The solution to the puzzle, no doubt, lies in the fact that most people do not interest themselves in foreign affairs except when their own country is directly involved, as is the case with Vietnam. This was especially true in the United States in the 1930's. The impact of the Spanish Civil War, nevertheless, was very great because the minority who were interested, whether they were well- or ill-informed, felt strongly about what was happening in Spain. The entire Roman Catholic community of the United States was intensely moved, stirring up a Protestant and liberal reaction. American Jews were deeply disturbed by Hitler's intervention.

As the war went on and people read about the ever-greater involvement of the Nazis and Italian Fascists, and about the ruthless bombings of civilians and open cities by the Franco forces, the public picture changed. Before the end of 1938, only 40 per cent expressed neutrality in Gallup Polls, and only 14 per cent were for the Insurgents. Among those expressing a preference for one side or the other, three-quarters favored the Loyalists.

It is therefore fair to make the statement—as historians of the war do—that a large majority of those expressing public opinion in the United States, or having ideas about Spain, supported the Republicans. It cannot be said, however, that what President Nixon later called the silent majority of Americans ever wanted to become actively embroiled in the Spanish conflict.

It was the height of the United States period of isolationism. Uncle Sam sat like King Canute and ordered the tide of world affairs not to come in. In the countries that intervened in Spain —Germany, Italy, Portugal, and the Soviet Union—the people were not asked which side they favored. In the democracies, where the majority of informed opinion favored the Loyalists, there was no direct intervention except a little, fitfully, by France.

Yet, of all the non-domestic problems facing the Roosevelt administrations, none was so important or fateful as whether or not to sell arms to the Spanish government. Because it meant so much to the course of the Civil War, and because Americans were so divided on the subject of the conflict, Washington's arms embargo and "neutrality" became the subject of violent controversy.

It is difficult for Americans in the 1970's to understand or imagine the fervor that the Spanish Civil War aroused as the conflict continued. The intensity of feeling for the Loyalists and against Franco by American writers, artists, actors, students, teachers, liberals, workers, and radicals of all shades, had to be experienced to be realized. And it must be emphasized again that the Roman Catholic community was aroused to a religious passion unique in American history.

"In the United States the Spanish Civil War was one of this generation's most impassioned political and religious controversies," F. Jay Taylor wrote in *The United States and the*

Spanish Civil War. "Catholics and Protestants, liberals and conservatives, rightists and leftists—all expressed clashing views, championing either one or the other of the protagonists in Spain. American opinion became inflamed in an almost unprecedented manner. The issue was hotly debated—from the pulpit, in the halls of Congress, on college campuses, in the editorial columns of the press, and through every agency designed to influence public opinion."

The great service which the United States performed for Generalissimo Franco and the Nationalist cause (and it was a crucial one) was to impose an arms embargo and keep it in effect from the beginning to the end of the Civil War. In the name of "neutrality," the Republican government was barred from purchasing arms in the United States. It was one of those bitter ironies that doomed the Loyalists for the same reason that official "non-intervention" served to doom the Republic in Europe.

Secretary of State Hull noted in his *Memoirs* that the State Department realized, as early as three weeks after the conflict started, that the "British and French governments believed that a European agreement strictly abstaining from intervening in Spanish affairs was the best means to prevent the spread of the conflict" and he felt that "the initiative in dealing with the Spanish problem lay with the European nations." Hull, throughout, let Britain call the tune to which the United States danced. He even doubted German and Italian intervention as late as December 1936, although his ambassadors in Europe were accurately informing him.

(*New York Times* editorials, incidentally, were consistently and wholeheartedly in favor of the non-intervention policy.)

On August 7, 1936, an official statement of United States policy made the neutrality position clear: "In conformity with its well-established policy of non-intervention with internal affairs in other countries, either in the time of peace or in the event of civil strife, this Government will, of course, scrupulously refrain from any interference whatsoever in the unfortunate Spanish situation."

President Roosevelt let his cautious, ill-informed, and narrow-minded Secretary of State make the policy on Spain. There is no evidence that the President ever sought to interfere in what Hull was doing. The difference between them was that Cordell Hull, handicapped by the limitations of his experience and knowledge, was sincere in believing that he was doing what was morally, as well as practically right. Roosevelt was too intelligent and experienced to fool himself about the moral issues involved. He put them aside, as statesmen and rulers have always done. His overriding consideration was not what was right or wrong, but what was best for the United States and, incidentally, for himself and the Democratic party.

When the Civil War started in 1936 the United States was in the throes of a presidential campaign. Franklin D. Roosevelt was elected to his second term in November. Foreign affairs were not an issue, although Europe was rearming, Hitler was on a rampage, and the Spanish conflict had taken on a dangerous aspect. Both major parties were isolationist, dreaming naïvely of an America attending to its recovery from the devastating financial crisis which began in the fall of 1929, and "neutral" so far as the troubles of the Far East and Europe were concerned.

The year before, during the Abyssinian War, a Neutrality Act had been passed which prohibited the sale of arms to belligerents in a foreign war. Those who drew up the text of the act had ignored the possibility of civil wars or even rebellions against legally constituted governments. Nevertheless, it was generally accepted that the United States should remain "neutral" in the Spanish conflict, although a number of the leading figures in government and politics—including President Roosevelt himself—were sympathetic to the Spanish Republicans.

Washington started with admonitions and efforts at moral persuasion to prevent exports of arms and supplies to either side in Spain. However, since the administration had no legal grounds to prevent the export of arms to Spain, it arranged for Congress to impose an arms embargo against the Spanish gov-

THE UNITED STATES 177

ernment. Thus, "moral" persuasion was given the force of law seven months after the war started.

The United States had never before denied to a legitimate government, with whom, incidentally, it had a "Treaty of Friendship and General Relations," the right to buy arms. However, as Secretary Hull pointed out, the question of controlling arms exports was a domestic issue to be decided by the United States government. Since that government had induced Congress to enact a law preventing export of arms "to warring nations," Spain's legal right to buy arms did not apply to the United States.

"We are taking a stand against a democratic government, the parliamentary government of Spain," Representative Maury Maverick, Democrat of Texas, pointed out during the debate on the arms embargo in the House, "and we are not indulging in neutrality, because this is the opposite. . . . It has always been the practice of our Government to send munitions to the legal government, irrespective of its merits." Maverick was not alone in his protest, but when it came to voting on the measure on January 8, 1937, it passed unanimously in the Senate while only one Representative, John Bernard, Farmer-Laborite of Minnesota, voted against it in the House.

"President Roosevelt behaved in the manner of a true gentleman," said General Franco. "His neutrality legislation . . . is a gesture we Nationalists shall never forget." The Germans and Italians also had reason to be pleased. For the Republican government, the American embargo was a crushing blow, perhaps a decisive one.

The result was paradoxical. The embargo was the most effective piece of American intervention—on the Nationalist side—which could have been devised. Whatever the United States did or did not do was bound to help one side or the other. The arms embargo helped the Insurgents, and in the process helped Nazi Germany and Fascist Italy. Hitler was therefore better prepared for the great conflict that was coming, into which the United States was going to be drawn.

American policy was, of course, well-intentioned. The nation was isolationist and President Roosevelt could not easily have taken steps that would have appeared to embroil the country in a European quarrel which seemed to have no relation to American affairs. The mistake of the Roosevelt administration was to believe that the Spanish conflict need not, as well as should not, affect the United States. It was bound to do so, because by January 1937 the war clearly held within itself the seeds of a much greater conflict. The arguments for neutrality seemed strong, but the United States could not be neutral in the Spanish Civil War, no matter how many resolutions or laws Congress passed.

The United States had the equivalent of two Spanish ambassadors in Washington during the war, one legitimate, the other pseudo. Madrid sent Fernando de los Ríos, a distinguished intellectual who served faithfully throughout the war. Franco sent a career diplomat, Juan F. de Cárdenas, who was an unsympathetic ambassador of the Republic in Paris when the rebellion began. In theory, he was simply a Nationalist agent in Washington, but he was received regularly at the State Department by the pro-Franco, Roman Catholic Under Secretary, James C. Dunn. As the months passed and the tide of war favored the Insurgents, Cárdenas's position was virtually that of an envoy. (Dunn, by coincidence, was ambassador to Madrid in 1953 when the naval and air bases agreement with Franco was concluded.)

The double relationship—one with the legal ambassador and one with Franco's agent—was another way of twisting American "neutrality." However, the fact that the United States continued to have formal diplomatic relations with the Republican government until the end of the war at least showed that the Second Republic was recognized as the legitimate government of Spain. Nevertheless, in August 1936, when the Glenn L. Martin Company asked for an advisory opinion on whether it could sell planes to the Spanish government, the State Department replied that this would be contrary to "the spirit" of American policy. This attitude never changed for arms shipments.

However, when it came to oil, one of the most important of

all war materials, an exception was made, although it was stipulated that sales could be made only on a "cash-and-carry basis." Neither Germany nor Italy could supply the Insurgents with oil. The United States could and did from the beginning. Standard Oil, the American-owned Vacuum Oil Company in Tangier and, especially, the Texas Oil Company (Texaco) provided Franco throughout the war with all the oil he needed and, it can be argued, they did so illegally. They granted the Nationalist government credit, although the Neutrality Act banned private loans and credits to belligerents. No oil was sold by American companies to the Republicans, ostensibly on the theory that Loyalist ports were unsafe, whereas the Insurgent harbors were open and protected.

(History was repeating itself. Mussolini got his vitally needed oil from the United States during his conquest of Abyssinia in 1935–1936.)

Charles Foltz, Associated Press correspondent in Madrid, was told by a high Franco official in 1945: "Without American petrol, American trucks and American credits, we could never have won the war." Herbert Feis, economic adviser to the United States Embassy in Madrid during World War II, wrote that Franco was supplied with 1,866,000 metric tons of oil and 12,800 trucks from the United States in the years 1936 to 1939 —on credit. At the very least, as the State Department warned the Glenn L. Martin Company, this should have been contrary to "the spirit" of American policy.

American Roman Catholics reacted to the belief, sedulously fostered by their hierarchy, that the Republican government represented, at worst, an atheistic and communistic force and, at best, a weak democratic element under the domination of Moscow and the Spanish Communist party. Pope Pius XI at the beginning of the war and Pius XII at the end, openly sympathized with the Nationalists. A majority of the American Catholic community accepted their hierarchy's belief that the Loyalists were out to destroy the church in Spain. The killings of priests, monks, and nuns and the burning of churches in the first mad, uncontrollable weeks of the rebellion, reinforced these fears. An indelible stamp of antireligion and anticlericalism was put upon the Republicans from the earliest days. At all times, the Catholic hierarchy in the United States used intensive propaganda methods in their publications and in pressures on federal, state, and local administrations, on the press, in schools and universities and, of course, in sermons and pastoral letters.

There was evidence, however, that a great many American Roman Catholics sympathized with the Loyalists, while in practice they accepted faithfully the strong pro-Franco policies of the bishops and cardinals. Gallup Polls taken toward the end of the war indicated that only 39 per cent of American Catholics sympathized with the Nationalists and as many as 30 per cent were pro-Loyalist. The rest were neutral or had no opinion.

British and French Catholics were, on the whole, favorable to the Republicans. The Spanish Basque Catholics fought for the government. It was also awkward for the church that Nazis, Fascists, and Moslem Moors were winning the war for Franco.

Many Catholics must have known that the Caudillo was not a champion of the social principles enunciated before the war by Popes Leo XIII and Pius XI. (Nor was he ready in the 1960's to accept the progressive encyclicals of Pope John XXIII.) The Generalissimo never pretended to be a democrat. Americans who thought and felt in terms of what was called the "American heritage" could hardly find these principles in the Franco cause, unless they were misled or deluded.

The American Roman Catholic antagonism to the Loyalists was based on anti-Communism, an identification of the Republican cause with "atheistic Marxism," a fear that a victorious Republic would go Communist, an acceptance of the slashing label of "Reds" for all who embraced the Loyalist position.

One American Catholic who did not use the "Red" label was John F. Kennedy. He visited Spain during a tour of Europe in the summer of 1937 and went from there to Rome where, to be sure, he admired the Fascist corporate system, "as everyone seemed to like it in Italy." James MacGregor Burns, in his biography of the late President, cites a letter from Spain which young Kennedy wrote to his father, Joseph P. Kennedy, then ambassador in London and a powerful advocate of the Franco cause. Jack Kennedy remarked on "the almost complete ignorance 95 per cent of the people in the United States have about situations as a whole here. For example, most people in the United States are for Franco, and while I felt that perhaps it would be far better for Spain if Franco should win—as he would strengthen and unite Spain—yet at the beginning the Government was in the right, morally speaking, as its program was similar to the New Deal. . . . Their attitude toward the Church *was* just a reaction to the strength of the Jesuits who had become much too powerful—the affiliation between Church and state being much too close."

The future President was then only twenty and attending Harvard. Back home in the United States there was no such open-mindedness among Roman Catholics. In 1938, when there seemed to be a good chance of lifting the arms embargo, Secretary of the Interior Harold Ickes wrote in his diary that President Roosevelt said frankly it "would mean the loss of every Catholic vote next fall and that the Democratic members of Congress were jittery about it and didn't want it done." In cities like New York, Boston, and Chicago, the Catholic vote would have been decisive—and it was traditionally Democrat.

As I have remarked, despite their fervent support for the Nationalists, not a single young American Roman Catholic is on record as fighting for the Insurgents, while several thousand Protestant and Jewish Americans went to fight—and many of them to die—for Republican Spain. American Protestants could not see the Spanish Civil War as a religious struggle. They saw it in political terms as a conflict of democracy against Fascism, or in nationalistic terms as a fight in which Germany and Italy opposed the Soviet Union while the democracies tried to be neutral. American Jews were aroused by Hitler's support of Franco, as well as by the same political and humane motives which impelled the Protestant majority.

One unfortunate result of these different attitudes in the

United States was that there was much criticism of the Roman Catholic minority by the Protestant community. The Spanish war divided Americans along religious, as well as political lines for the first, and thus far only time in American history. This is one reason why the Spanish conflict is still an emotional subject in the United States.

Many Americans were becoming conscience-stricken. The pressures on President Roosevelt to lift the arms embargo became stronger and stronger. Prominent Americans from all walks of life were signing statements, publishing advertisements, and lobbying in Washington. It was estimated that congressmen received as many as a quarter of a million letters urging repeal. Helen Keller, for instance, deaf, dumb, and blind from childhood to her death in old age, showed her sympathy by attending a meeting "to commemorate the American dead in Spain."

By 1938 the public clamor against the embargo resembled the Vietnam moratoria of recent years except that there was no violence. Thousands of university students, educators, Protestant and Jewish clergymen, lawyers, scientists (Albert Einstein was one), trade unionists, and many newspapers and magazines demanded an end to the arms embargo. These were liberal elements. The Communists, Socialists, and other left-wing organizations were, of course, even more emphatic.

After mentioning the "college presidents, professors, Protestant bishops and ministers, governors and congressmen who signed petitions or worked on committees" to help the Spanish Loyalists, Allen Guttmann, in *The Wound in the Heart,* makes the point that "most Americans who supported the Spanish Republic did not do so because they were Marxists; they did so because they believed in liberal democracy and were willing to join other anti-Fascists in a fight for their faith."

The chief factor in influencing American opinion and stirring the public conscience was the bombing of open cities and the killing of hundreds of civilians. Virtually all such raids were made by Insurgent planes, which even the least informed

THE UNITED STATES 183

knew were German and Italian. The bombing of Guernica was a watershed for many Americans, senators included. Later, President Roosevelt was only the most prominent among those who expressed horror over the bombings of Barcelona on March 16–18, 1938.

This was not a radical American response. It was a traditional protest against man's inhumanity to man, much stronger than we know today, in the 1970's, because Americans were not hardened to modern cruelty as they have become to the slaughter of Vietnamese civilians by—the irony of it!—American bombers. My Lai would not have been conceivable.

A few months after the Barcelona bombings, Sumner Welles, then Acting Secretary of State, issued a statement denouncing the continuing raids. "When the methods used," he said, "take the form of ruthless bombing of unfortified localities with the resultant slaughter of civilian population and in particular women and children, public opinion in the United States regards such methods as barbarous. . . . This Government, while scrupulously adhering to the policy of non-intervention, reiterates this nation's emphatic reprobation of such methods and acts."

The Barcelona raids also elicited an open letter from sixty-one Protestant Episcopal and Methodist Episcopal bishops asking the Roman Catholic hierarchy "to disavow any tacit approval of these appalling tactics. We realize," the letter went on, "that the Catholic hierarchy in this country has for reasons which seem good to it, chosen to defend the Franco cause. It is for this reason, knowing that word from you would carry weight and force, that we call upon you to act."

There was no reply from the Catholic hierarchy. Their most fervent Franco apologist at the time, and since, the Jesuit Father Joseph Thorning, was, in fact, outraged. He demanded a "dignified apology" from the Protestant bishops. Generalissimo Franco, he said, was "the highest type of Christian gentleman and Spanish officer, who is leading his hosts to victory in a triumph that will have its impact on the civilized world."

The nation—in fact, the world—was too divided, too frightened of war, too anxious to appease. One of the paradoxes of the period was the failure of the working-class organizations in the democracies to help the Republican government. The British Labor party, the Trades Union Congress (TUC) and its affiliates; the French Socialists and the *Confédération Générale du Travail* (CGT); similar labor organizations in Belgium, the Netherlands, and the Scandinavian countries—not one would do more than express sympathy and raise money for humanitarian purposes. All of them backed or accepted the counterfeit non-intervention policy. Only the Communist parties gave active help and this, of course, was another reason why the Spanish Communist party, the Comintern, and the Russians gained such power and influence in Spain.

The situation in the United States was no better than in Europe. The Roosevelt regime's policy of "neutrality" and the arms embargo met no opposition from the American Federation of Labor and the Congress for Industrial Organizations. Aside from the Communists, the most effective friends of the Spanish Republic in the United States were the liberals and those workers who had to go through Communist channels (sometimes unknowingly) to join the Abraham Lincoln Battalion in Spain.

The problems and the arguments always got back to reasons of state. Protests against the policy could have no effect so long as the reasons for making the policy continued to exist. This is why all the efforts of Loyalist sympathizers in the United States were bound to fail. We can say this now because we are looking back at what happened. At the time, there were hopes.

Americans who favored the Loyalists realized belatedly in the spring of 1938 that the Nationalists would win unless the Republican government got arms. Public pressure was so great that the United States came close to repealing the embargo in May 1938, when the State Department shifted ground and agreed to support a resolution introduced by Senator Gerald P. Nye of North Dakota. Nye told the Senate that he was prompted by "a desire to right an injustice," because American policy was "partial to one side [the Nationalists] and against the side of a friendly, recognized government."

However, such a storm was raised in Catholic circles that President Roosevelt ordered the matter to be dropped. Ambassador Kennedy had cabled from London that repeal would endanger the European non-intervention policy. Among other things, the ambassador was an intimate friend of James Farley and an important member of the Democratic National Committee. Roosevelt, once again, lost courage, shifted back to "neutrality," and the arms embargo remained in effect until the Civil War ended. As F. Jay Taylor wrote: "Kennedy's influence on American Spanish policy during the whole era of appeasement cannot be overestimated."

As the course of the war was to prove, it would not have been too late to take action in May 1938. The Republicans made their startling drive across the Ebro River in July. In the autumn of 1938, as I have told, Franco received a new flow of matériel from Germany to replace his depleted stock of arms after his long and costly counteroffensive. With those fresh arms, he launched the decisive campaign which was to roll over Catalonia and sweep the Loyalists back to the French frontier. That offensive, by all indications, could have been stopped if the Republicans had also received fresh supplies to replenish their even more depleted stocks, but none were forthcoming.

On January 24, 1939, *The New York Times* published a very long and now historic letter to the editor from former Secretary of State Henry L. Stimson. It is one of the most important American documents on the Spanish Civil War. Some brief passages from the letter will provide one of the weightiest judgments to be found on the American policy.

> The basic reasons which govern my views consist of simple and longstanding principles of American international conduct . . . [Stimson wrote]
> First. The Republican government of Spain (commonly termed the Loyalist government) has been recognized as the true government of Spain by our government. . . .

Second. One of the most important [conventional] rights which a state like Spain is entitled to expect from another government, which has recognized it as a friendly neighbor in the family of nations, is the right of self-defense against any future rebellions which may challenge its authority. . . . Such a nation has the exclusive right to the friendly assistance of its neighbors by being permitted to purchase in their markets the necessary supplies and munitions for the purpose of putting down the rebellion: and, further, that no similar assistance shall be given to the rebels who have challenged its authority. . . .

Third. No nation has gone further than the United States in sustaining this general right of a nation against which civil strife or rebellion has broken out. . . .

Sixth. . . . The first thing to be said about this [non-intervention] agreement was that it was a complete abandonment of a code of practice which the international world had adopted through preceding ages as the best hope of achieving the same purpose and minimizing the spread of disorder. International law is the product of the efforts and experience of the nations aimed to promote peace and stability. In the second place, however well intentioned it may have been, an experiment based upon the promises of the totalitarian states was more wishful than sensible. Those states had already progressed too far along the primrose path of treaty violation and the non-intervention agreement at once became a mockery and a failure. . . .

Thus the non-intervention agreement has simply resulted in closing to the recognized government of Spain those world markets for supplies and munitions which under the law of nations she had a right to depend upon to have open to her purchases. It has not prevented supplies from going to the rebels who, under international law, have no right to them. . . .

Eighth. The results have shown how futile as well as dangerous novel experiments in international law can be. The United States on its part has abandoned a traditional policy to which for a century and a half it had carefully adhered as a means of protecting the peace and stability of nations, which like itself, preferred to live not armed to the teeth. It is likely sorely to rue the day when that principle was abandoned and when it consented to a new precedent which may hereafter weight the scale in favor of a militaristic and thoroughly armed nation. . . .

To an extent which probably few anticipated, the Loyalist Government has succeeded in defending itself not only against a surprise attack by its own rebellious army but against a powerful combination of aggressive interveners by land and sea and air. By so doing it has furnished strong evidence of its vitality and of the fact that it must be supported by the great mass of the people within its territory. Starting without an army of its own, forced to organize and train its raw militia, conspicuously lacking in the powerful modern guns, planes, and other munitions which have been available to its opponents, it has for many months been putting up a most surprising and gallant defense against opponents who have had every advantage in the way of land and naval organization and who are illegally aided both on land and on sea by powerful organized forces from Italy and Germany.

If this Loyalist government is overthrown, it is evident now that its defeat will be solely due to the fact that it has been deprived of its right to buy from us and other friendly nations the munitions necessary for its defense. I cannot believe that our government or our country would wish to assume such a responsibility.

Ninth. In short, I have come to the conclusion that the [arms] embargo imposed under the resolution of May 1, 1937, should be at once lifted by the President. . . .

It was too late. The Insurgent forces were sweeping through Catalonia. Stimson's letter was answered by a prominent Catholic layman and lawyer, Martin Conboy who, in turn, was answered by legal authorities upholding and elaborating on the Stimson arguments. The correspondence was read into the *Congressional Record.* Roosevelt, of course, did nothing. The Stimson letter stands as a monument to the American tradition.

The reasons put forward by Stimson probably explain why Sumner Welles, who had been Roosevelt's Under Secretary of State, wrote in his book, *The Time for Decision* (1944), that "of all our blind isolationist policies, the most disastrous was our attitude on the Spanish Civil War. . . . In the long history of the foreign policy of the Roosevelt administration, there has been, I think, no more cardinal error than the policy adopted in the Civil War in Spain."

This was wisdom after the event. There is no evidence that Welles tried to get Roosevelt or Hull to change their policies during the conflict. He may have expressed dissent privately, but all his public statements conformed to the administration's policies.

The historic burden for the American refusal to treat the Republican government as the legitimate ruler of Spain and the Nationalists as rebels must be placed on President Roosevelt. Often, he was following Secretary of State Hull's advice but the authority was always in the President's hands.

"Franklin frequently refrained from supporting causes in which he believed because of political realities," Mrs. Eleanor Roosevelt wrote in her book, *This I Remember,* published in 1949. "There were times when this annoyed me very much. In the case of the Spanish Civil War, for instance, we had to remain neutral though Franklin knew quite well he wanted the democratic government to be successful. But he also knew that he could not get Congress to go along with him. . . . By trying to convince me that our course was correct, though he knew I thought we were doing the wrong thing, he was simply trying to salve his own conscience, because he himself was uncertain."

President Roosevelt never needed to be enlightened on the legal, moral, or traditional reasons for lifting the arms embargo. He had to be convinced that it was politically desirable to do so, and that American security was being endangered. He realized, too late, the strategic mistake which had been made. According to Harold Ickes, his Secretary of the Interior, there was a cabinet meeting on January 27, 1939, at which the President conceded that the embargo had been "a grave mistake," and that it "controverted all American principles and invalidated established international law."

Roosevelt's political philosophy placed him in the American tradition of liberal democracy. He went against his own convictions in the Spanish Civil War. Like so many aspects of that conflict, the historic record does justice to the Republican cause, but this is like rehabilitating the character of an accused person after he has been executed. At the time, the President persuaded himself that he had no choice but to follow the deceptive path of "neutrality."

The experience through which Americans went in the Spanish Civil War is hardly likely to be repeated in the same form, but there has been a long spillover as the many American books and university theses on the Spanish war attest. The subject is still very much alive. Nearly all of the published works portray sympathy for the Republicans and antagonism toward Generalissimo Franco and the Nationalists. The presumption is that unpublished academic papers would have had the same bias. This is in part due to the fact that Spain has had a fascistic-type dictatorship under the Caudillo ever since the Civil War ended. A notable exception in the American academic world is Stanley Payne, whose diligent inquiries and impressively documented books are impregnated with a mild but noticeable pro-Nationalist, anti-Loyalist bias. Burnett Bolloten's *The Grand Camouflage* is an extraordinary and massive work of scholarship which took twenty years to compile. It is a study with a thesis into which all the immense, but chosen, documentation is made to fit, as into a Procrustes bed: that the Republican government was merely a façade for Russian and Spanish Communism. In my opinion Bolloten reaches false conclusions.

In general, American academic opinion at all times has a distinctly liberal slant. It would be hard for a present-day liberal, however objective he tried to be, to espouse the cause of the Nationalists against the Loyalists in writing about the Spanish Civil War. An earlier generation of American students and scholars, during and immediately after the Civil War, had been fervently pro-Republican.

By a curious loophole, it was not a violation of the neutrality laws for an American to volunteer to fight in a foreign army so long as he volunteered abroad. The State Department tried vainly to circumvent this by making American passports "Not valid for Spain." Americans who wanted to volunteer had no difficulties. They were helped along to Paris and, once there, the International Brigade organization took care of the rest and, incidentally, took care of the passports which the volunteers never saw again. They were invaluable to the Comintern and NKVD, who used them as passports for Communist agents.

American policy in the Spanish Civil War was not successful. A war in Europe was not prevented; Hitler was encouraged in his aggression, both by the Axis victory in Spain and by his belief, which the American policy fostered, that the United States would at all costs stay out of a European war. Washington's policies strengthened the British and French appeasers, which was also an encouragement for the Fuehrer.

In the world war that soon followed, the Allies were faced with a Spain friendly to the Axis, where they would otherwise have had an ally in Republican Spain. The negotiations between Japan and a Germany apparently winning the European war obviously presented to the Japanese a picture of an isolated United States, weakened on its Atlantic front by a crumbling Europe. All through 1942 and much of 1943, the American armed forces were handicapped by a Spain friendly to the enemies of the United States and trying to help the Axis win the war.

The Franco victory, no doubt, gratified millions of American Catholics. Other millions were unhappy. For many, the dismal historic record of the United States in the Spanish Civil War was saved, to a degree, by the 3,000 or so young Americans who offered—and in a great many cases, gave—their lives for the Republican cause. It was not, however, a contribution that was appreciated at the time, and certainly not by the United States government, nor has it yet been properly understood. The history of the International Brigade is still controversial, and for Americans no facet of it is more so than the story of the Abraham Lincoln Battalion.

9

THE INTERNATIONALS

THE INTERNATIONAL BRIGADE WAS UNIQUE
in the history of warfare. It was a response to two different, but
not contradictory, motives. The concept, organization, and
leadership were basically Communist, but the men who volunteered, served, and died in an appalling proportion were, with
few exceptions, idealists.

Of those who joined, a fair guess would be that some 40 per
cent were not Communists, but many of these, perhaps half,
became Communists while in Spain. All but a handful of
professional, Stalinist, Communist party members were genuine volunteers. It would have been of no use for the individual
Communist parties or the Third Communist International (Comintern) to send men to Spain who were not prepared to die
and, at the very least, to suffer great hardships and danger.
Such men are rare in any society at any time. As the English
poet, W. H. Auden wrote: "They came to present their lives."

Many books and parts of books have been written about the
Brigaders. The accounts are conflicting; the official records
few; much of the documentation is still held by the Franco
government. During the war, the Republican government
rarely interfered directly in the affairs of the International Brigades, and did not try to keep fully informed about them.

One author confusingly lists "unemployed men, adventurers,
mercenaries, scientists, intellectuals, writers, poets, idealists,
Communists, sailors, soldiers and thousands of ordinary working men." Actually, with the exception of the American

Abraham Lincoln Battalion, where the volunteers were mostly students, the majority were workmen. But there were many professional men who were exiles from Fascist Italy and Nazi Germany. There is no use trying to pin a class, trade, economic, or even ideological label on the Internationals. Such tags do not explain the only meaningful factors—the motives that impelled civilians from all walks of life and fifty-four nations to go to Spain to fight with such bravery under the worst conditions and the greatest possible dangers. I have always felt that to understand the phenomenon which they embodied, it was necessary to know them, see them in action and talk to them before and after battles. By and large, as human beings, they were an enormously impressive lot.

It stood to reason that the International Brigade had some men from the dregs of society, some gangsters and adventurers, some *lumpenproletariat,* some who were weak and cowardly, but these were a minority to begin with, and they soon deserted or were weeded out. It is no explanation to say, as I have indicated, that a majority went to Spain because they were Communists and were ordered to go. It does help to say that they went to defeat Fascism, because this was a compulsive emotion in the 1930's, but the concept of "Fascism" embraced more than the movements of Mussolini and Hitler. The great majority of young men who went, like today's restless youth, were discontented with their generation, rebellious against what we now call the Establishment, alienated (a Marxist word not used so generally then).

In Spain they found an outlet, a cause so compelling that they offered their lives to it. It was both a rejection of their childhood and working-class or bourgeois environment, and an affirmation of ideals of social justice and, in many cases, of liberal democracy. Just as for the Nationalists there was a sense of crusading against the godless atheism of Marxism, so on the Republican side there was the conviction of a crusade of good against evil. For nearly all men in the International Brigade, there was also a deep feeling of comradeship, of shared dangers in a great cause which, for the survivors, was to leave them with some of the most precious and proudest memories of their lives.

Foreigners began fighting for the Loyalists from the outbreak of the war. These were men and women who happened to be in Barcelona at the time, some for the "Workers' Olympiad" which was due to start on July 20, others on holiday. There were German anti-Nazi and Italian anti-Fascist refugees, a handful of English Communists, a British Medical Aid unit. The Italians formed a Gastone-Sozzi Battalion, the Germans a *Centuria* (a hundred men). Some Frenchmen and Belgians formed a Paris Battalion. There were small groups of Poles, Hungarians, Austrians, Czechs. They saw action on the Aragon front and south of Madrid. The first foreign volunteer to be killed was an Englishwoman—Felicia Browne, a painter and Communist who had been living on the east coast.

By the time they left Aragon in October for the chosen headquarters of Albacete, they made up a full battalion, with a splendid fighting record. There were several Americans, according to P. A. M. van der Esch, a Dutchwoman who wrote a doctoral dissertation in 1951 called *Prelude to War.*

Practically speaking, the inspiration, creation, and direction of the International Brigade came from the Comintern. It is not clear who thought up the idea of raising a foreign corps of volunteers to fight for Republican Spain. Recruitment was to be open to non-Communists as well as Communists. Maurice Thorez of France, the Englishman Tom Wintringham, and Palmiro Togliatti, the Italian exile in charge of the Latin European section of the Comintern, are among the Communists credited with getting the idea first. Gustav Regler, in *The Owl of Minerva,* says that Koltzov, the *Pravda* correspondent in Spain, showed him a telegram from Moscow stating that the Comintern had decided to form an International Brigade, but Regler is not a reliable witness. It does not seem as if the concept originated in the Kremlin.

Before the Comintern moved in, Randolfo Pacciardi, a non-Communist lawyer living as an exile in Paris, had suggested an

Italian anti-Fascist "Legion," but Premier Largo Caballero turned it down. Like all Spaniards (Franco was the exception in this regard) Largo Caballero recoiled against the idea of using foreign troops in Spain. Wellington had learned in the Peninsular War that the men who made up his army were, as he put it, "disliked and even despised" by the Spaniards, although they had come in to fight the French invaders. For the Iron Duke, this was normal Spanish behavior. In fact, the Internationals were generally popular with the Spanish people—the Americans most of all, but also the anti-Fascist Italians and the British. They supported homes for children orphaned by the war, gave fiestas, and handed out toys and gifts and set up hospitals.

Had Largo Caballero been imaginative enough to accept Pacciardi's original proposal, the International Brigade might not have developed into an overwhelmingly Communist-dominated force. With the war going disastrously and Madrid threatened, the Premier finally agreed, but by that time Georgi Dimitrov, the Bulgarian head of the Comintern, and other Communist leaders had moved in.

When the Third International got into the picture Togliatti, who was one of their most brilliant and durable officials, was chosen as the chief organizer in Paris, which was geographically and politically the most convenient center. He was ably supported by the Yugoslav Communist, Josip Broz—later so famous as Marshal Tito.

Stalin was as slow and obtuse as Largo Caballero, but he finally saw the great propaganda value of such an international force. It was also a means of occupying a number of anti-Fascist refugees in Russia whom he did not know what to do with. And, finally, it would bolster the Spanish Communist party and provide a channel through which to direct Russian military aid to Communist-dominated units like the Fifth Regiment. Once he gave consent, the formation of the International Brigade became the chief occupation of the Comintern for the next two years.

Recruiting began in earnest in the latter part of September 1936. A "secret railway" was organized out of Paris. Many volunteers in the first months did not know that the International Brigade recruiting was being handled by Communists. Prime Minister Largo Caballero chose Albacete, known as "the saffron center of the world" and also famous for producing knives, as the headquarters. It began functioning in mid-October, by which time Madrid was already under siege.

Eight to ten thousand volunteers had crossed the French border. They were now sent to Albacete. Largo Caballero named Diego Martínez Barrio, President of the Cortes and moderate head of the Republican Union party, as director of the base. The idea was to keep the volunteers under Spanish government control. This did not work, except in a general sense as the Internationals were in time merged into the Republican army. The International Brigade was inescapably dependent on the Comintern and on the Russian government for arms.

The effective leaders from the beginning were Togliatti ("Ercolì," as he called himself in Spain) who went up and back from Paris; and in Albacete, the brutal, half-mad French Communist, André Marty. During the last ten days of October 1936, thirty Red Army instructors and some Russian and Eastern European staff officers arrived to help in the organization of the Brigade and the defense of Madrid. Among them was the Pole, Karol Swierczewski who, under the name of General Walter, commanded the Fifteenth Brigade in which Americans fought. He was one of the ablest Communist officers sent in. He became Minister of Defense in Poland after World War II, but his chief claim to fame is that he was the "General Goltz" of Ernest Hemingway's novel, *For Whom the Bell Tolls.*

The then General (later Marshal) Kulik, a veteran of the Russian Civil War, was probably the comander of all the Russians in Spain. Louis Fischer and others rated "Goriev" as the most important commander in the beginning. Fischer calls him "the savior of Madrid." He was never surely identified. General Emil Kléber was the outstanding battlefield commander of the International Brigade at Madrid.

Among the Russians who moved in and out of Spain were a number of generals, four future marshals of the Red Army and one future admiral. Nearly all of the Russian group—military and civilian—were liquidated by Stalin in his Great Purge. Since they all went under *noms de guerre*—Walter, Duglas, Julio, Paulito, Manolito, Kléber, Grishin, Gál, et cetera—and in nearly all cases kept discreetly in the background, their true names did not emerge until after the war, and even then some could not be identified. Hugh Thomas, as in other respects, was the most diligent of the scholars in digging up their identities and fate. Many of the Eastern Europeans and Italians became important figures in their own countries after World War II.

André Marty, who was the International Brigade headquarters commander until the volunteers were withdrawn, had two Italian assistants: Luigi Longo ("Gallo"), who was Inspector General, and Giuseppe di Vittorio ("Nicoletti"), Chief Political Commissar. Both men were as humane as they were able. Longo, until 1972, was President of the Italian Communist party in succession to the deceased Palmiro Togliatti. Di Vittorio was, for many years until his death in 1958, the efficient leader of Italy's greatest labor confederation.

Many threads ran from the International Brigade in Spain into the history of later decades. None was more curious than the story of Ramón Mercader, a Catalan, whose mother, Caridad, was a Communist. She became the mistress of a Russian intelligence agent, who started trusting Ramón with secret tasks. After the war, Mercader was given a Canadian passport by the NKVD. The young Catalan managed to win the trust of Leon Trotsky, then an exile living in a villa outside of Mexico City. On August 20, 1940, Ramón Mercader killed Trotsky with an ice pick.

It is, and always will be, impossible to estimate the proportion of Communist party members in the International Brigades. Party membership in nearly all countries was secret. "The majority of volunteers were Communists, but it is impossible to say how much of a majority," writes the American Verle B. Johnston in *Legions of Babel*. According to Gabriel Jackson most of the European volunteers were not Communists; most of the Americans were.

"Let not posterity impugn the sincerity of these men," Hugh
Thomas writes. "Many of the leaders were time-serving Stalinists. But the majority were not." Thomas thus makes a distinction between "time-serving Stalinists" and ordinary Communists.

My estimate during the war (inescapably a guess) was that
a large majority of the Brigaders were Communists, but "a
goodly proportion" were democrats, liberals, and Socialists. I
gave the proportion for the Lincoln Battalion as 80 per cent,
but a number of these had joined the party after reaching
Spain, and left it after the war. John Gates, Commissar for
the Lincoln in 1938, who left the party many years later,
also estimated the American Communists at 75 to 80 per
cent. Even as Commissar he did not know precisely. The
Americans undoubtedly had the highest percentage of Communists in any Brigade outfit.

Once in Spain, there was a great deal of pressure to turn
Communist, although the Comintern organizers of the International Brigade would have preferred a greater proportion of
non-Communists below the leadership level. The Republican
government would have preferred fewer Communists at every
level. On the whole, there was no problem of double loyalty or
of placing Communism above the cause of prosecuting the
Civil War. The Communists were the Republican government's
most loyal and effective supporters—and this was also the case
for the International Brigade. Yet, it was an embarrassment to
the government that the Internationals should be identified
with Communism. The fact that a great many of the Brigaders
were not Communist, that many joined the party only after
arriving in Spain, and that Communist or not, the guiding motives were anti-Fascism and a genuine idealism—all these facts
could be acknowledged only by the open-minded and sophisticated. To call a man a Communist was to blacken his name.
The Communist label stuck and has permanently distorted the
truth about the composition, motives, and ideals of the men
who served in the International Brigade.

The first International Brigade group—nearly all French—reached the base at Albacete, which is halfway between Madrid and Valencia, on October 14, 1936, three months after the war began. (It was on this same day that the first Russian arms arrived.) The volunteers traveled by train or ship and, when France closed the frontier, many made the exhausting trek over the Pyrenees on foot. Some were arrested before they could get over the border and were thrown into French jails; some were drowned when the Italians sank the ship they were on. The first arrivals were joined by the foreign volunteers who had already been fighting in Spain.

It can never be known how many volunteers there were in the International Brigade. There is general agreement that the total number was between 35,000 and 40,000, of whom no more than 17,000 or 18,000 could have been in Spain at any given time. The maximum who could have been used in any battle or campaign would have been between 7,000 and 8,000. Since the Spanish Loyalist army reached a total of about 700,000, the Internationals were never more than a tiny proportion of the Republican armed forces. Their importance was in their quality as shock troops, not in their numbers.

As André Malraux wrote in his novel about the Spanish Civil War, *Man's Hope:* "The Brigade was made up of men who could fight, not extras from a film studio." Incidentally, they faced more than danger; there were lice, dysentery, fierce heat in summer, bitter cold in winter. Casualties were naturally very high. The French were always the most numerous, with about 10,000, of whom 3,000 were killed. German and Austrian exiles totaled about 5,000, of whom 2,000 died. Of the 3,350 Italian exiles, 600 to 700 were killed. The American volunteers numbered between 2,800 and 3,200, of whom 900 are estimated to have been killed, according to Edwin Rolfe. (The Veterans of the Abraham Lincoln Brigade gave 1,800 as killed; Professor Eby says 1,500.) And so it went for the Eastern Europeans, Scandinavians, Canadians, British (500 dead out of about 2,000), and other national groups. (These figures were mostly gathered by Hugh Thomas.)

The wounded, of course, greatly outnumbered the killed. In fact, casualties on the average ran at about 15 per cent a month, or 180 per cent a year, indicating that a volunteer's chances of coming through unscathed were slim. The Brigade casualties at Madrid, the Jarama River, and Brunete in the first nine months of the war were appalling, but the men were fighting as hard and as bravely in the Ebro battle a year later as they had at the beginning.

Discipline often had to be harsh—"strong" as Luigi Longo (Gallo) put it. The French were the most unruly. There was a higher percentage of adventurers, unemployed, and riffraff among them than for any other nationality. At times, some of their units were mutinous, and there were many deserters. The nearness to their home country was a temptation. General Walter, who commanded the Franco-Belgian Battalion as part of the Fourteenth Brigade, called them "dear bandits." Gustav Regler, a commissar until he was severely wounded, wrote of "the eternally grumbling French." There were mutinous feelings among their rank and file even before Madrid, but they always calmed down to fight again. One reason was that they had one of the best and most popular commanders in the International Brigade, the Alsatian Colonel Putz, a cultured, ex-regular army officer, who was a Socialist, not a Communist. He survived, only to be killed in December 1944, fighting in the French Army.

It was calculated that nearly 10 per cent of the volunteers—more than 3,000—were Jewish. Hitler's intervention was a major reason for that, but the fact that the Jewish element in all countries contained a high proportion of liberals and, relatively, of Communists, also counted. The Jewish percentage in the Lincoln-Washington Battalion was probably higher than average. I remember, on occasions, hearing their comrades say that the Jews in the battalion agreed among themselves that they had to fight with exceptional bravery to disprove the historic slander that Jews were not good fighters, this being before the Israelis came on the scene.

Before any Americans arrived, all available Internationals

were thrown into the battle for Madrid on November 8, 1936. They numbered at most 2,000, with another 1,500 moving in four days later—very few, but they went into the critical sector of University City. The Spanish populace and militiamen, as I wrote earlier, had held back the best troops General Varela could throw into the battle, but the defenders were taking terrible punishment, as were the attacking Moors, Legionaries, and Spanish Insurgents.

The Internationals now took the same punishment. The Eleventh Brigade suffered more than 900 fatalities and many more wounded in its first three weeks of action, while the Twelfth (both were then a mixture of nationalities) lost more than 700 killed. The Brigaders thus had a terrible baptism of fire, but no scholar has since come along crying bitter tears—as Professor Cecil Eby does for the Americans—that they were betrayed by their Communist leaders because they were sent in without proper training or arms.

Of course, morale was low after—not during—such experiences, of which Madrid was only the first, but it never interfered with combat effectiveness, nor did it in the case of the Lincoln Battalion, which was at all times one of the best in the Loyalist army.

As I have written, there can be no certainty, ever, as to whether the Internationals "saved" Madrid. They certainly *helped* to save Madrid, probably more by their "spirit, courage and faith" (as the Franco regime's historian, Manuel Aznar, put it) than by their small numbers and miserable arms. As General Kléber said: "No doubt we set an example, but it was eagerly followed." "The victory was that of the populace of Madrid," Hugh Thomas writes. Historians agree that the Insurgent forces had been stopped on the edge of the capital before the volunteers arrived. Even Mussolini noted that fact. The question is whether the lines at University City could have been held by the Spanish militiamen without the Brigade reinforcements and that, of course, is unanswerable.

By the spring of 1937, about 70 per cent of the Internationals who started in Madrid were either dead or hospitalized. On April 20, the International Brigade battalions began to be incorporated into the Spanish Republican army and from that time on ever-increasing numbers of replacements were Spanish.

After some juggling around, five permanent Brigades had been formed, whenever possible of single-language volunteers or of men from groups of Central or Eastern European countries. Each Brigade had four battalions of about 700 infantrymen—foreign and Spanish. In May and June 1937, they were grouped into two largely Spanish divisions: the Thirty-fifth and Forty-fifth. The Eleventh Brigade (mainly German, partly Central European), the Thirteenth (mostly Polish with some Balkans), and the Fifteenth (American, British, and Canadian), went into the Thirty-fifth Division. The Twelfth (mainly Italian) and Fourteenth (French and Belgian) were part of the Forty-fifth Division, which was commanded by one of the outstanding Internationals, a Prussian World War I officer, Hans Kahle, an exile and a Communist, who served until the Brigaders were withdrawn.

Each Brigade had one or two Russian technical advisers. All the Brigades and Battalions had Communist commissars of their own nationalities. The Twelfth and Fourteenth were the only Brigades under non-Communist command during most of the war. The Italian Garibaldini were headed by Randolfo Pacciardi and Carlo Penchienati. (Pietro Nenni, the most famous of the Italians, who started as a company commander and became a leading commissar, was—as he is today—a Socialist.) I have already mentioned Putz, the Franco-Belgian Brigade commander, who was also a Socialist.

In addition to the Lincoln and Washington Battalions (merged into one after the heavy losses at Brunete), there were two other American military units: the antitank John Brown Artillery Battery and the First Transport Regiment. A number of Americans also served with the Canadian Mac Pap (Mackenzie Papineau) Battalion, which was, in fact, two-thirds American. To conclude for the Americans: there were twenty-five hospital units, with doctors and surgeons, nurses and ambulance drivers, stretcher bearers and first-aid men. The head was Dr. Irving Busch. The one who was to become best known, because of his accepting imprisonment after a sensational post-World War II anti-Communist trial, was a distinguished New York surgeon, Dr. Edward Barsky.

The volunteers were at all times asked to accept almost unbearable tasks and hardships. Professor Cecil Eby, in what is evidently intended as an exposé of the ill-treatment, dangers, privations, and bungling leadership which the Lincoln-Washington Battalion faced *(Between the Bullet and the Lie)*, overlooks the fact that every international unit and all Brigaders, whatever their nationality, suffered exactly the same fate. It was a condition of being a volunteer in the International Brigade. The extraordinary feature was not the grumbling, sporadic mutinies, and desertions, but that the overwhelming majority stuck it out, usually in the expectation of death or wounds. Moreover, there was no deterioration in the fighting quality of any of the units, except for the sometimes erratic French. The Lincoln Battalion never fought better than in its last battle across the Ebro River in 1938.

The Americans always hated André Marty, the International Brigade commander who, incidentally, seemed to hate them. Despite this, the Veterans of the Abraham Lincoln Brigade later jumped to Marty's defense and vilified their staunchest friend, Ernest Hemingway, for his truthful picture of Marty as a stupid paranoid in *For Whom the Bell Tolls*. The "Butcher of Albacete" was a source of bitterness and division in the whole International Brigade, but he must have had powerful friends in Moscow, for he was left in command until the very end. He was finally expelled from the French Communist party, but that was after World War II.

There was a story I heard about André Marty in the panicky Aragon retreat of 1938 which I have never seen printed in the many accounts of the International Brigade. There had been a disastrous weakening of discipline and spirit on the part of the then "mixed brigades" of Spaniards and foreigners in which the Internationals served. In order to set an example for the

Spanish soldiers, Marty lined up a Battalion of Internationals (I believe it was from the Fourteenth Brigade, which contained French and Belgian and some Eastern European volunteers) and asked for volunteers to step forward who were willing to give their lives before execution squads to show how brave men die. There were some volunteers—I do not know how many—and they died. The incident was typical both of the mad courage of so many Internationals and the callous insanity of André Marty. It didn't do any good and the affair must have been hushed up.

There were executions in the International Brigade during the war for cowardice and treachery. They were always secret at the time, but there is no later evidence to indicate that the number could have been large. There was only one execution in the Lincoln Battalion, as John Gates, the Commissar, told Verle Johnston. It occurred after the disastrous Aragon retreats. The man (I believe his name was White) had deserted three times under fire. He was court-martialed, found guilty, and shot. The next day an order came through commuting the sentence.

There had always been a fair amount of trouble among the Brigaders. Such individualistic types could not be expected to conform easily to the discipline and hierarchy of a professional army. It was hardest to maintain discipline during lulls between battles, especially after the always high casualties and often inept leadership in those battles. Nearly all the desertions or attempted desertions occurred during those rests, and not during the fighting.

Of a hopeless attack, ordered with no artillery preparation early in the war, the Hungarian Communist Commander of the Twelfth Brigade, General Paul Lukacz, told Gustav Regler, Commissar of the Brigade: "If it had happened in Russia, I should have called it sabotage, but here it seems to have been nothing more than stupidity." (Lukacz—Máté Zalka was his real name—was a distinguished critic and writer and was one of the most popular commanders in the International Brigade. He was killed late in 1937.)

One of the worst-bungled attacks ever made by the Internationals was the baptism of fire for the Canadian Mac Paps. It was at Fuentes de Ebro in mid-September 1937. One out of three of the Canadians and Americans were casualties: 60 killed, 100 wounded. Many such stories could be told, but so could many more of an opposite kind. The picture of the International Brigade cannot be painted all one color.

News of the terrible Stalinist purges taking place in the Soviet Union seeped through the censorship and brought disillusionment with their Communist leaders among the new or younger Communists and, of course, among all liberals in the International Brigade. It was made hard at times to remember that the cause for which they were all fighting was for *their* ideals of Communism or for democracy, however much Communism was mixed in it.

The Spanish Insurgents were told by their officers in the first year or so of the war that the *Internacionales* killed their prisoners and therefore that they were to kill Brigaders when they captured them. Until the spring of 1938 when the breakthrough to the coast took place, this was what happened. Internationals taken prisoner were usually executed as "outlaws." They were not considered prisoners of war. The Fascist Italians, however, took prisoners when they could in order to try to exchange them for Italian prisoners in Loyalist hands.

The one time that the Insurgents captured a large number of Brigaders was during the drive to the coast when the Loyalist army was routed. Among them were seventy Americans. There were nearly 500 International Brigade prisoners when the war ended. The State Department could have obtained the release of the Americans for Italian prisoners held by the Republicans during the war, but it would not do so. Because of the Roosevelt administration's policy of refusing to accept responsibility for the American prisoners, they were held by the Franco regime afterward much longer than any other Brigade prisoners. All but eight were finally released in two batches in April and August 1939. The last eight did not leave Spain until March 1940.

The Americans had been late in arriving. The only major group of foreigners to reach Spain after them was the Canadian. The presumption is that the ability to get men from the United States to Spain did not exist until the Communist Party of the United States (CPUSA) was able to organize and finance an "underground railway." It was necessary to get around the obstructions that Washington placed in the way with its Neutrality Act, passport ban on travel to Spain after January 11, 1937, and the standing law against Americans enlisting in a foreign army. Until the CPUSA provided the facilities, there was no way for a young American to reach Spain.

This was a major reason why the Lincoln Battalion had such a high proportion of Communists. There must have been hundreds of prospective volunteers who did not learn how to get to Spain, as the Communists naturally could not act openly and, anyway, they wanted to attract as many non-Communists as possible. Many liberal and Socialist-minded Americans must have balked on learning that they would have to put themselves in the hands of the Communist party.

The fact that the two American battalions were named for Abraham Lincoln and George Washington did not seem to upset anyone at the time, but some later writers felt that it was effrontery. Allen Guttmann in *The Wound in the Heart* calls it "a lie, a conscious attempt to persuade people that Communism was, indeed, '20th Century Americanism.'" This is an unduly harsh judgment, for it overlooks the sincere idealism of the great bulk of American volunteers who did not fight for Stalin simply because Fascism was the enemy of Communism. Besides, there were plenty of non-Communists among the Americans. It was natural for young Americans—the majority of them students—to identify with their past history, whatever their ideology. They sincerely considered themselves to be patriotic, and millions of Americans agreed with them at the time. The symbols and examples for all the young, history-conscious volunteers were the American Revolution, Valley Forge, Washington, Tom Paine, Jefferson, Lincoln, and the like. Franco was Benedict Arnold;

the Insurgents were Hessians; and Brigaders Lafayette's men.

"The level of political development among the men of the Lincoln Battalion was probably higher than that of any other American military group in history," Edwin Rolfe wrote in *The Lincoln Battalion.* They did not need political commissars for indoctrination. Eby's picture of virtually all the men treating Communist party propaganda and pep talks as "superloyal drivel" and "this treacle of propaganda" was exaggerated. Rolfe, a member of the Battalion, sensibly wrote that "since [the commissars] were the ones whose job (among other things) it was to give the pep talks, they came in for more criticism than any other officers." The unpopular ones were called "the comic stars."

The Americans, on the whole, were many years younger than the volunteers from the European continent, although probably not younger than the British. And they were more nationality conscious. The Germans, Italians, and some other Europeans were refugees from Fascist, Nazi, or right-wing dictatorships who, after disbandment, were "men without countries." Many were veterans of World War I. Even the young Europeans had had conscript training. The great majority of the Americans from the CPUSA were *young* Communists, not hardened, Stalinist revolutionaries.

It was, incidentally, more difficult for the Americans to adjust to the hardships of Spain, having come from a country with a much higher standard of living than most. Not that they were pampered in Spain, as United States soldiers were in World War II, Korea, and Vietnam. The conditions they found in Spain were a terrible let-down, which contributed to the loss of morale in the trying lulls between battles, leading to some desertions. Although the five weeks' training they got was ridiculously insufficient, it was more than the Brigaders received who fought at Madrid. Moreover, they were better armed than the first Internationals.

"The simple act of going to Spain was not enough," as Rolfe wrote. "Only in actual battle, under fiercest fire, under danger of death, could a man's convictions and true mettle be really, finally tested." (Edwin Rolfe, as his writing may indicate, was a poet of considerable merit.)

"I was the first American to enroll in the International Brigade," Louis Fischer wrote in *Men and Politics*. This was true for Albacete early in November 1936. He became Chief Quartermaster under André Marty, but he soon quarreled with Marty and for much of the war acted as Premier Negrín's purchasing agent in Paris. Negrín spoke highly to me of Fischer's work and scrupulous honesty.

The first detachment of ninety-six (perhaps fewer; there is no agreement on the figure) Americans sailed from New York on the *Normandie* on December 26, 1936. They arrived in Albacete on January 5, 1937. By the time they went into action in the Jarama River battle in February there were 487 men in the Lincoln Battalion. Many American volunteers thought they had enlisted for six months. There seem to have been some verbal commitments back in the United States to that effect, but this understanding was never accepted by the International Brigade command or the Republican government. When six months had passed, some Americans thought they had a right to quit, and deserted, or tried to.

I discussed in my first chapter the battles in which the Americans fought. They began at the Jarama River, southeast of Madrid where a powerful Rebel force, with Moors and *Tercios* as shock troops, tried to break through and cut the Madrid-Valencia highway.

The Abraham Lincoln Battalion was still training in the Albacete area when the battle began. It was the 600-man British Battalion (which contained a small number of Americans) who took the first thrust of the Rebel attack on February 12, suffering very high casualties. Two-thirds of the men and nearly all their officers were killed. The Lincolns reached the front on February 16 and went into battle on February 23 and 27, commanded by the University of California lecturer, Robert Merriman, who was not a Communist party member. (Eby believes he was the Robert Jordan of Ernest Hemingway's *For Whom the Bell Tolls.* I do not think so.)

The Americans were very young, very green but, as Hugh Thomas rightly states, "they fought with great gallantry." Of about 450 who went into the Jarama battle, at least 125 were killed and 175 wounded. It was an awful baptism of fire (Merriman aptly called the February 27 attack on Pingarron Hill "murder"), but the International Brigade and the Spaniards—Lister was there with his former Fifth Regiment, now incorporated into the Republican army—stopped the Insurgents so decisively that the battle lines did not change for the rest of the war. The Moors and Legionaries were so decimated that they never regained their early effectiveness.

The next great battle (in some ways the greatest battle of the war) was at Brunete, northwest of the capital, in July 1937. There were enough American volunteers by then to make up two battalions, the now veteran Abraham Lincoln and a new George Washington Battalion. The offensive bogged down in a week (July 6 to 13) with, once more, appallingly high casualties for all concerned. One half of each of the American battalions were casualties before the battle ended. They were combined into one Lincoln-Washington Battalion which, as the war progressed, came to be called simply the Lincoln Battalion.

There was no battle in the war—although Professor Cecil Eby seems to give that impression in his book—where the Americans were asked to do any more than other battalions and nationalities of the International Brigade.

When the International Brigade was formally incorporated into the Republican army in January 1938, the battalions had come to have many more Spaniards than foreigners in them. The Lincoln Battalion's ratio in the Ebro battle was three and a half Spaniards to one American. The supply of fresh volunteers never quite stopped. Three hundred and fifty new British volunteers arrived toward the end of 1937 and small numbers of Americans kept dribbling in until the Internationals were withdrawn, but recruiting was naturally falling off. The European exiles had been drained of recruits long before; the first blaze of worldwide fervor had died down; and the Republican government was placing more and more emphasis on the *Spanish* character of its army.

The Internationals, including the Lincoln Battalion, were called upon for the defense of Teruel, which had been taken in December 1937 by a Spanish force. They went into action on January 19, 1938, under General Walter, and retreated with the Spanish troops a month later when Teruel fell. As always, the International Brigade casualties were high but, of course, so were the Spanish Loyalists', who lost 10,000 killed in the final stage of the battle. It had been fought in cruelly cold weather. Paul Robeson sang Christmas carols to the Americans, standing in the snow at their camp behind Teruel while they were in reserve.

On March 9, 1938, along the Aragon front, Franco launched what was to prove to be one of the two decisive campaigns of the Civil War. The Republican troops were weary after Teruel and, as always, pitifully short of war materials. There were not even half enough rifles to go around. The Nationalists—also as usual—had been well supplied by the Germans and Italians with artillery and military planes. The air superiority was enough in itself to guarantee a Franco victory. The tactic was an exact forerunner of that often used by the Americans in Vietnam and Laos. In this case, the Germans and Italians bombed, strafed, and broke up the Loyalist forces, after which the Insurgent troops moved in, usually simply to mop up. Where brave stands were made, units would be flanked and have to fall back.

The Americans were driven out of their hard-won town of Belchite on March 10. The International Brigade was then concentrated at Caspe to make a stand, which it did on March 15 and 16: two days of truly superb fighting. For the small number of survivors of the Lincoln Battalion, "this was their finest hour" of the war. It would not have occurred without the leadership of the much-maligned Commissar Dave Doran, who was killed a few weeks later. At the time, the men reviled him, for he was a hard taskmaster, a martinet with too much Communism in him for most of the men.

The Fifteenth Brigade was commanded then, and for most of the war, by an incompetent Yugoslav Communist, Lieutenant-Colonel Vladimir Copic. He had been an able commissar, but was too inexperienced for field leadership. In Spain he had a talent for survival, but he was recalled to Russia in June 1938, after the Aragon retreat, and was presumably liquidated.

The Republican army was in rout, but the Fifteenth Brigade, with the Americans, made one more gallant stand at Gandesa. It was here that 140 Americans and British were taken prisoner when the town was overrun.

"It is a tribute—a tragic tribute—to the youth and spirit and sincerity of the volunteers who fought for Spain," wrote Edwin Rolfe, "that their officers not only directed their men, but led them personally in battle; that the proportion of officers and commissars killed and wounded among Americans was greater even than that among the men in the ranks."

The Aragon retreat was a heartbreaker for the International Brigade. "The men were demoralized almost to tears," to cite Rolfe again. " 'If we could only meet them face to face,' they repeated; 'if we could only fight them head on, not this running, this being surrounded and flanked.' " It was not to be. The Lincoln, which had 550 men at Belchite, had only 150 men left, armed with rifles. Franco broadcast news of "the complete annihilation of the Americans."

The disaster, which did wipe out three-quarters of the soldiers in the Fifteenth Brigade, came while the line was near Batea, west of the Ebro River in Aragon. It was the beginning of April 1938. The Brigade was encircled and scattered. Merriman and Doran were killed. When it was all over, the Lincoln Battalion started up again, as men straggled in one by one, with forty Americans and thirty-five Spaniards. More than 400 were gone: killed, wounded, ill, prisoners, or deserters. Those who survived had had to swim the Ebro River.

"The scenes that occurred as the men returned were emotional to a degree never before known among the Americans," wrote Rolfe. . . . "Of the 2,800 Americans who had reached Spain, there were now fewer than 200 in the Lincoln Battalion, about fifty or sixty in the Canadian Mac Paps, a dozen in the British and Spanish Battalions and perhaps two dozen more in the Brigade staff. In addition there were about 200 Americans in the transport, medical and other services, and about 150 scattered through Central Spain."

This makes roughly 650. There must have been about 200 more in other units. Of the remaining 2,000 or so, a large number had been repatriated; the rest were dead or wounded or had deserted, and there were seventy prisoners.

The Fifteenth Brigade now got its best commander of the war, an Asturian, a veteran of the 1934 uprising, Major José Antonio Valledor. He had a splendid Civil War record. The Fifteenth's commissar who succeeded Dave Doran was John Gates, who had one of the best records of the Lincoln Battalion: tough, hard, and a fervent Communist while in Spain.

The Lincoln Battalion also got a new commander, Captain (later Major) Milton Wolff, who had fought through every battle starting with Brunete, where he was a machine-gunner. He was then twenty-two years old, Brooklyn-born, six feet two inches tall. Wolff denied that he was a member of the Communist party. Rolfe wrote of him: "He was intelligent, egalitarian, blunt and fearless. Most of the men admired him enormously. To the Spaniards of the Brigade he was always *El Lobo* (The Wolf.)" Hemingway and I thought him the best commander the Battalion had in the war. He served until the very end.

After the rout in Aragon there were a number of American desertions. Cecil Eby listed forty-eight men who successfully reached the United States between April and July 1938. "French frontier guards estimated that six hundred Internationals had crossed into France immediately following the Aragon retreat," he writes. It took stout hearts to *want* to stay and keep on fighting, but a surprising number did. Eby called them "a sixth column . . . not defeatist but defeated." In a sense, they were not "defeated"; they were still fighting hard when they were withdrawn.

Five hundred young Spanish draftees were added to the Fifteenth Brigade. They were of poor quality, not like the early militia, mostly bewildered peasants. There were four completely quiet months in which to train them. The waiting was like the lull after the Jarama River battle for the Americans—long, dull, and tedious.

Then came what I called in my first chapter the most dramatic offensive of the Civil War. Generalissimo Franco's troops had turned toward Valencia after reaching the Mediterranean coast. It seemed like an easy objective, but it was not. Then, an hour after midnight on July 25, 1938, the Army of the Ebro went quietly into action. The dismayed Caudillo had to halt his drive on Valencia.

The Republican offensive gained 500 square miles of territory along a ninety-mile front across the Ebro River. The Loyalists took 4,000 prisoners and tied up the Insurgent armies on that sector for four months. The offensive stunned the world as well as the Rebels, for almost everyone not in touch with the Republicans had thought that the Civil War was all but over.

The Fifteenth Brigade was in the second wave, after Lister's Spaniards. Captain Leonard Lamb, Brigade Commissar (who was wounded in the battle), stood up in the prow of the boat being rowed across the Ebro and struck the pose of Washington crossing the Delaware. The terrain was familiar to the survivors of the Aragon retreat—full of vividly remembered landmarks, a sweet, if temporary revenge. And, of course, there were many more casualties. "Death walked always by your side," Major Wolff remarked.

The Ebro was a heroic, bloody, costly battle, a truly magnificent example of human courage. The defense by the Americans of Hill 666 above Gandesa against just about the heaviest artillery barrage, bombing, and strafing of the war and against Franco's crack Moorish troops, was a proud achievement.

While they were fighting, the House Un-American Activities

Committee claimed to have evidence that the Lincoln Battalion was "a subsidiary of the Red Army."

In two months, three-fourths of the International Brigade were dead or wounded, for all the Brigaders and Spaniards had fought with equal valor. Of the 70,000 Spanish Republican casualties, about 30,000 were deaths. The Germans estimated the Nationalist casualties at 33,000.

The saga of the International Brigade was nearing its end. The Abraham Lincoln Battalion got its last recruits: five men who reached the front less than a week before the withdrawal. One was killed and two were wounded.

One of the late recruits was James Lardner, son of the American author, Ring Lardner. He had come as a war correspondent and was deeply stirred by the same motives that had brought so many foreigners to Spain to fight for the Loyalist cause. Lardner was a symbol of the Brigade ideal—young, brave, idealistic, self-sacrificing. He was a graduate of Andover and Harvard; students, as I said, made up the largest group in the Lincoln Battalion. It was not a hasty decision. He had thought long and hard before enlisting in early May 1938. Soon after midnight on September 22, Lardner was given his first task at the front—to lead a patrol of three behind the Insurgent lines. He never came back. He was not, as Vincent Sheehan wrote in *Not Peace but a Sword,* the last American to be killed. The final day, September 23, 1938, was a cruel one. The bombing and shelling by German planes and artillery were incessant.

"Each death," as Edwin Rolfe, who was there, wrote, "was the more bitter, since the men knew that relief was on the way, that this was the last action."

Relief came soon after midnight of September 24, 1938, and the survivors stumbled across the wooden pontoon bridge over the Ebro River just before dawn. The Spanish Civil War was over for them. Of the 280 Americans who went into the battle of the Ebro—perhaps the bloodiest of the whole war—sixty-one were left.

A dispatch I sent to *The New York Times* during the Ebro

battle, which was published August 14, 1938, told of my talking to some American soldiers on leave from the front. The story as cabled contained the following passage which, however, was killed by the cable desk and not printed:

> Peasants in the neighborhood of Corbera have told them a terrible story of the time the Lincoln Washington Brigade was broken up early in April, and many Americans and English captured. Every night, they said, two or three of the Internationals would be taken out and shot. Many of them were forced to dig their own graves. This went on for many nights, it appears, until more than 100 were killed. The soldiers have no means of checking this story but they believe it because they read Carney's dispatch about his visiting American prisoners and there should have been more than eighty.

(William P. Carney, *New York Times* correspondent, had talked to the American prisoners and given many names, a dispatch that may have saved their lives.) The story the soldiers heard may explain why there were so few American prisoners.

On September 21, 1938, Premier Negrín addressed the Assembly of the League of Nations. "In her desire to contribute to the pacification and restraint which we all seek," he said, "and in order to eliminate all pretexts and possible doubts about the genuinely national character of the cause for which the Republican Army is fighting, the Spanish Government has decided to withdraw immediately and completely all the non-Spanish combatants who are participating in the fight in Spain on the side of the Government. . . .

"It is not necessary for us to provoke catastrophe to solve our problems. It would have been sufficient, and it will be sufficient, to recognize our rights and re-establish our international rights which have been violated, to assure a rapid solution of the Spanish problem."

He called on the General Assembly to set up an international commission to verify and guarantee that the decision would be "carried out in its totality." The British tried hard to have the issue placed under the jurisdiction of the Non-Intervention

Committee but, for the Spaniards, this was an insult, and they refused. The Committee had not met since July 1938. (It was dissolved on April 20, 1939.)

The decision, as Premier Negrín said to the Cortes back in Spain, was *"muy española"*—very Spanish. Negrín expressed "the debt of gratitude that Spain had contracted toward these authentic volunteers." Hugh Thomas, normally careful and accurate, is one of the historians who mistakenly writes that the decision to withdraw the Internationals was made by Stalin, who was preparing the ground for his pact with Hitler and wanted to have his hands free. As I have said, the decision to pull out the volunteers was Dr. Juan Negrín's, and his only. Thomas is especially wrong in saying, as nearly all historians do, that the Brigaders could be withdrawn "without risk," since their role was ended.

Those Internationals were still sorely needed. Dr. Negrín told me years later that he considered his decision to withdraw the volunteers to have been the worst mistake he made as Prime Minister. The one possibility left to him and Republican Spain was to hang on in the hope that the threatened wider European conflict would break out while the Second Republic was still fighting. The Internationals were few, but they were precious. Their withdrawal, for one thing, hastened the end of the Ebro battle. They might have made a crucial difference at the central front and Madrid later, where there was so much defeatism.

Theoretically, a promise that the Republican government made earlier remains in force. Volunteers with a year's service had been given the right to eventual Spanish citizenship, if desired.

After Negrín's announcement, Mussolini told Chamberlain —always so eager for the Anglo-Italian pact—that he would withdraw 10,000 Italian "volunteers." Franco was still left with some 30,000 Italians, including the Littoria Division, and all the Italian aviators, tank crews, artillerymen, and specialists, as well as officers and noncoms for four mixed Italian and Spanish divisions.

The Brigaders had a farewell parade in Barcelona on October 28, 1938. It was a proud occasion and, in some curious way for those who watched them, a triumphal procession.

"The Internationals did not march like automatons," I cabled *The New York Times.* "There was no goose step or Roman step. Those men had learned to fight before they had learned to parade. They were not clad in spick-and-span uniforms; they had no arms, and they could not seem to keep in step or in line. But everyone who saw them—and above all those who fought against them—knew that they were true soldiers."

In judging the American volunteers, it is misleading to proclaim, as Professor Eby does, that they were caught "between the bullet and the lie"; were betrayed, and suffered nothing but costly defeats. After all, the Spanish Republicans lost the war in a series of costly defeats. Their story as a whole is one of defeat—inevitable defeat. What happened to the Internationals happened to the Spanish Loyalists, but the Brigaders helped to delay that defeat on many a battlefield and they wrote pages of courage and idealism which no carping critic can expunge. In that history, the Americans played a brave and honorable role.

Ernest Hemingway's tribute to the Lincoln Battalion two years after the Jarama River battle (which appeared in *The New Masses* of February 14, 1939) has become a classic.

> The dead sleep cold in Spain tonight and they will sleep cold all this winter as the earth sleeps with them [it reads in part]. But in the spring the rain will come to make the earth kind again. . . .
> The dead do not need to rise. They are a part of the earth now and the earth can never be conquered. For the earth endureth forever. It will outlive all systems of tyranny.
> Those who have entered it honorably, and no men ever entered earth more honorably than those who died in Spain, already have achieved immortality.

The Spanish Civil War brought out an idealism that has not been equaled for American youth since, because there has been no such cause to draw volunteers to sacrifice themselves to an idea and not only to patriotism.

In all, 875 Americans were left in Spain at the time of the withdrawal, a higher figure than Rolfe had given six months before. A first batch of 327 left Ripoll on December 2, 1938. Insurgent planes bombed the railway tracks of Puiqcerdá when it was thought that the train with the Americans would cross. More went in January, and a final batch in early February. The French demanded that the costs of transportation through the country to the port of embarkation be paid in advance. The Spanish Republic, not the American government, defrayed all the expenses.

The International Military Commission appointed by the League of Nations to check on the withdrawal of all foreigners at Dr. Negrín's request, made a report on January 16, 1939, after three months' investigation in Spain. It certified that there had been six International Brigades, belonging to two divisions. (Actually there were only five Brigades officially, but some International groups were divided.) The investigators found 12,-673 foreigners in all Loyalist services, plus 488 prisoners. The Commission stated that there were no Russian infantrymen, nor were any Russian pilots or technicians left at the time they began their investigations in October 1938.

Of the total, only 4,640 had left the Catalan zone by January 14, 1939, but the Commission acknowledged that this was "owing to the length of the diplomatic negotiations and consular formalities." The French were making the greatest difficulties. The Canadian government refused at first to repatriate their nationals, and 110 Canadian Brigaders were left stranded in Ripoll until it was almost too late to get them out.

The main body of Internationals, about 750, withdrew into Le Perthus, France, on February 6 and 7, 1939, "with flags flying, songs on their lips and fists raised in the Popular Front salute," as I wrote to my newspaper. Among them was a mixed contingent of 170, containing Americans, Canadians, and British. There were also Poles, Germans, Austrians, Yugoslavs and, at the end, a group of about 250 Hungarians, Czechs, and Balkans. Another 1,500 came over the mountain passes or through Port Bou in groups during the next few days.

They met a brutal and hostile reception from the French authorities, as did all the Spanish civilian refugees—so many thousands of men, women, and children who had fled wearily before the Insurgent advance, some of them since the first days of the war. They were nearly all herded into two "camps" which were really open fields with no facilities, and no shelter against the wintry weather. The women and children were soon moved to slightly better camps. It was a heartbreaking stop for the Spaniards on a still bitter and weary journey.

The mood of the Republican soldiers had to be captured directly from them at the time. A historian would find it hard to believe. I cabled a news dispatch that appeared in *The Times* of February 7, 1939, but with this passage of my copy eliminated:

> I spoke to a few [Spanish] officers who said that they are going to the Franco side because they expect that there will soon be a war against France and they would rather fight France than the Rebels. Let no one suppose that the feeling they expressed is unusual among the Loyalists. Your correspondent has called attention frequently to the resentment against France, and it has now reached its culmination as they see how their people and government are being treated by the French.

About 300,000 refugees were to return to Spain under amnesty after World War II. Most of the men, including many Internationals, were first used like slave labor by the French, building fortifications. Then, after the German occupation of France, the Nazis, certainly with Franco's agreement, perhaps at his desire, worked the Spaniards to death or let them die in Dachau, Mauthausen, and Buchenwald.

Their story is painstakingly and painfully told in a recent book by a Spanish exile, Antonio Vilanova, called *Los Olvidados (The Forgotten Ones)*. To have been what the Germans called a *Spanischer Kämpfer,* he writes, qualified them for the gas chambers.

Some of those who escaped to England were sent back to France. Others joined the British Army and served as commandos or infantry with the British in North Africa and Norway.

Some, of course, fought in the Russian Army. A large number joined the French *maquis*. They sabotaged railways, destroyed locomotives, bridges, factories, and coal mines. In southwest France, after the Allied invasion, they liberated seventeen towns. A group of them entered Paris with General Leclerc in Spanish tanks flying the Spanish Republican flag. Three tanks had names painted on them: Madrid, Guadalajara, Belchite. Of course they thought, as so many people did, that the overthrow of Hitler and Mussolini would be followed by the overthrow of Franco.

Their story was also that of hundreds of Internationals, scattered among them or in other units. Many, like Tito, fought in the underground in their own countries and afterward became important figures in postwar politics.

The surviving Americans of the Abraham Lincoln Battalion had a rough time of it after the Civil War. To be sure, none of them was persecuted for volunteering or for giving up his passport. About 600 fought in World War II, but they were so distrusted that they were not allowed to serve abroad until late in the war. They were not given officer rank or permitted posts of trust.

The House Un-American Committee (HUAC) set out to establish a relationship between the International Brigade and the Comintern, which was easy since there actually was a relationship. However, it did not follow that Lincoln Battalion veterans deserved to have their service records marked S.O.D. (Suspected of Disloyalty). They had never been disloyal, at least not in Spain, and they could have offered the American armed forces a unique record of fighting experience and proven courage. To have fought in Spain was almost made to seem as if they had fought against the United States. It was acceptable in World War II to be a fervent anti-Fascist, but they had been what one of them ironically termed "*premature* anti-Fascists."

The Veterans of the Abraham Lincoln Brigade (VALB) was ordered to register as a Communist-front organization after the war. In 1947, nine veterans working in Hollywood, including Alvah Bessie whose *Men in War* was, in my opinion, the best novel written about the Spanish conflict, were investigated by HUAC for "subversive" writings and sentenced to six months to a year in prison for contempt of Congress when they refused to talk. As screen writers they were blacklisted by the motion picture industry for years. Dr. Edward K. Barsky, whom I have mentioned, and who worked in the medical service of the Lincoln Battalion, was also imprisoned. In 1955, some veterans at least received a grudging acknowledgment from the Subversive Activities Board in a report branding the VALB once again as a Communist front.

"This report," the Board concluded, "and the findings herein, relate to the VALB as an organization and should not be considered as embracing all veterans of the war in Spain. The record shows that some Americans fought there on behalf of the Republic out of motivations completely alien to Communist purposes. Further, it is clear that many veterans of the Spanish war are not members of the respondent [the VALB] or in any way represented by it."

On April 26, 1965, the Supreme Court vacated the order requiring the VALB to register as a Communist-front organization. And there the record stands and presumably always will stand. Whatever else they may have been, the men who fought in the Abraham Lincoln Battalion in Spain were Americans; there is no need to think of them as anything else.

So we leave the International Brigaders now, scattered around the world, some in high posts, all with stirring memories of "battles long ago." Together, the Internationals made one of the truly grand gestures of modern times. They will live in history for this, more than for the heroic, but vain, military contribution which they made to the Spanish Republican cause.

10

THE FIGHTING STOPS

TWO MEN WERE RESPONSIBLE FOR the pro-
tracted duration of the Civil War. Premier Negrín sought a
compromise solution a year before the war ended, but he was
unwilling to surrender unconditionally; Generalissimo Franco
was determined to win total victory, whatever the cost and
however long the war lasted. Both men did what they thought
was best and honorable for their country. Both were being *muy
español.*

A group of Republican leaders, including Negrín, Álvarez del
Vayo, Lister, and Modesto, flew from Toulouse on February 9
and 11, 1939, to the central zone. The Premier planned to organize a resistance, in the hope either of holding out until a European conflict started, or of inducing Franco to give a guarantee
against reprisals. Plans were drawn up to make a last stand in
a moderately well-fortified and well-armed semicircle around
the naval base of Cartagena.

It was clearly probable that sooner or later, as events were
moving, there would be a European war. Negrín's self-imposed
task—and his only chance—was, as he said, "to resist, resist,
resist." With wars, as with individuals, while there is life there
is hope.

One can only speculate on what could have happened if Dr.
Negrín and those Spaniards (mostly Communists) who were
willing to fight on had had their way. There were troops enough
in the central zone—more than 300,000 men in the Armies of
the Center, Estremadura, Andalusia, and the Levant—and al-

though poorly armed they could have held out for some weeks, perhaps for months. Hitler's occupation of Prague on March 15, 1939, and Mussolini's invasion of Albania on April 6 aroused the British and French to some realization of their danger and the futility of appeasement. That one can speculate in this manner at least demonstrates that Premier Negrín was not being perverse or foolish in trying so desperately to avoid unconditional surrender. He fell short only by four months. Besides, it is arguable that he and all the Republican leaders owed it to the tens of thousands who had supported them and who now faced death or imprisonment, to fight to the very end rather than to doom them to die before firing squads or to rot in jail for years.

Disintegration, defeatism, war weariness, and treachery were to make a theoretical possibility into a practical impossibility. Only the Communists, as a group, were willing to keep on fighting; only Juan Negrín, among the non-Communist military and civilian leaders, had the determination to make the effort, but he faced insuperable opposition.

President Manuel Azaña, who had been completely defeatist and devoid of courage for many months, refused to go to the central zone and resigned in Paris on February 27, 1939. Azaña was an intellectual, as unfit for war as Don Quixote, whose creator Cervantes was born, like Azaña, in Alcalá de Henares, and he was poles removed from the hard-bitten Russian police who set up their headquarters in the same town.

Azaña's successor by constitutional authority, Diego Martínez Barrio, would not take office at that time. For most nations, the Second Spanish Republic had ceased to exist. On that same February 27, Britain and France recognized the Franco regime as the legitimate government of Spain.

The last events in the Madrid zone are shrouded in a certain amount of confusion and mystery which will never be dissipated.

The Army of the Center had been under the command of a former regular army officer, Colonel Segismundo Casado, always a lukewarm Republican, who had been plotting against Negrín for months. He shared the now widespread antagonism toward the Communists and knew how weary and disheartened the people were. Casado believed that he could get more lenient terms than Negrín could. No doubt he thought that he was being patriotic and humane and, anyway, he could see no point in carrying on a hopeless struggle. In terms of the Second Republic he was a traitor, whose treachery did not save any of the lives of those who had fought for, or served, the government. He saved his own life and the lives of those leaders who had joined him by deserting the Loyalist cause. The key figure among them was the one outstanding Anarchist commander of the Civil War, Cipriano Mera of the Fourth Army Corps. Thus Anarchists, Socialists, and Communists fought each other to the very end.

Dr. Negrín's last gamble was therefore ill-advised. It was a fatal mistake to deal with Colonel Casado, promoting him to general and naming him commanding officer of the Madrid forces. At the same time, Negrín promoted the Communist military commanders. Modesto was given the rank of general to replace the demoralized General Miaja. Lister became a colonel. The remaining ports of Valencia, Alicante, Cartagena, and Murcia were placed under Communist commanders.

The effect was deplorable, since it turned over all military power outside of Madrid to the Spanish Communists, causing resentment and disaffection among Negrín's non-Communist followers and military commanders, and convincing world opinion that the rump Republican government was simply a Communist regime. Negrín's one thought was that only the Communists would and could keep on fighting—and he was right—but they would have backed him in any circumstances for they had no choice. At that, the Premier was not being straightforward in his dealings with the Communists. In promoting Casado and striving to hold what moderate Republican support he could, he gave the appearance, which his confusing actions fortified, of fumbling and hesitation.

The ironical result was to earn severe criticism from the

Communist leaders, especially Dolores Ibarruri, who had been in the central zone for some time. "While Negrín has frequently been accused of being the tool of the Communists," *La Pasionaria* wrote in her autobiography, "in reality it was we who were *his* victims, because of our blind loyalty to our responsibilities and our unconditional support of the resistance policy, which was the only just one at the moment."

For the first time, Dr. Negrín seemed unable to act decisively, perhaps from physical and nervous exhaustion. This was not the man who had been such a tower of strength in 1937, whose courage and determination had rallied the Republicans against all belief when the Loyalist zone was cut in two in April 1938, who had inspired the incredible offensive across the Ebro River. No doubt he was asking almost the impossible in the central zone in March 1939, but he was not asking it in the commanding tones of faith and authority which had been normal to him. A vital spark had gone, and with it the ability to inspire his people.

Juan Negrín was a great man with a great heart, but he had driven himself beyond endurance. Faced with treachery, personal feuds, and an atmosphere of black despair in which every man was for himself, he acted as if he were dazed, almost paralyzed. He needed much more help than the Communists could give, but it was not forthcoming. Civilian morale had long since crumbled. None of the Republican or Socialist leaders had the requisite drive, boldness, dedication, faith, willpower, and ruthlessness. Negrín had them all, but he was too exhausted to draw upon his own resources.

Dr. Negrín, Spain's greatest physiologist of the time, could never turn himself into a typical politician. His Socialism was a conventional label and his admiration for the Communists had nothing to do with ideology or Marxism, of which he was even rather contemptuous. Everything about his character, his very virtues, isolated him as a human being and a leader. In the final crisis he stood alone and—for the first time—powerless. Publicly he neither approved nor condemned the anti-Communist junta which Casado formed in Madrid on March 5. It turned upon itself in the internecine strife, and then collapsed. Juan Negrín simply went away, one more exile Spaniard in France.

He kept the title of Premier until 1945. The ghostly continuity of the Second Spanish Republic has been sustained by its nominal Presidents. Diego Martínez Barrio succeeded Manuel Azaña after his initial reluctance was overcome. When Martínez Barrio died in 1962, his place was taken by Luis Jiménez de Asúa, a jurist who lived in Buenos Aires. On his death in 1971, a professor of Spanish residing in Paris, José Maldonado, was named as President. The idea seems to be to preserve a legalistic framework at least until Franco dies.

The Basques, too, have a shadowy government-in-exile. It was headed until his death in 1960 by José Antonio Aguirre. The present incumbent is Jesús María de Leizaola.

One should, perhaps, say a word here about the Spaniards who went to Russia, including the hundreds of children sent off during the war "for safety." They met a grim fate, although on arrival in the months before the World War they were received with great fanfare. Then they were forgotten, and almost all fell into desperate straits. Harrison Salisbury, when he was *The New York Times* correspondent in Moscow, remembers the pitiful Spanish exiles who used to approach him for aid in getting to the United States. Many of the Spanish refugees starved to death during the World War, although so did many Russians, but even after the war, Salisbury says, the Spaniards were treated as "non-persons." They sought help from Latin American countries, and some were accepted as refugees, but most languished and many died of hardship. The United States would not help, as all the refugees were assumed to be Communists.

But let us return to Don Juan Negrín, who should not be left at the lowest point in his extraordinary career. He will live in Spanish history in a brighter light, once passions are spent and future historians weigh him in a true balance. Mistaken beliefs about Negrín have colored and distorted a great many histories, especially perhaps those of the most scrupulous postwar scholars, hardly any of whom had the opportunity of knowing Dr. Negrín. He was the key figure on the Republican side. Get his character and motives wrong and the history being written will be wrong. Even a scholar as discerning and shrewd as Hugh Thomas, whose portrayal of Dr. Negrín is quite fair and sympathetic, could not allow himself to believe that certain charges against Don Juan—that he yielded to Communist demands, for instance—were completely false.

In his book *The Spanish Revolution,* Professor Payne is wrong in saying: "That he [Negrín] was dedicated to the cause of a leftist victory irrespective of tactics or consequences seems without question." Dr. Negrín used and worked with the Communists simply for practical reasons which had nothing to do with "leftism" or any ideology. He had no political coloration or preference for any political party or movement as such. He wanted "a military victory for the Popular Front"—to cite Payne again—because it was the government of the Second Spanish Republic. Payne, whose scholarly work on the Spanish Civil War has been outstanding, singularly fails to understand Juan Negrín and therefore misunderstands much that was crucial about the last year of the war.

Negrín's Spanish enemies—Nationalist and Loyalist—were swayed by hatred, envy, timidity and, in some cases, cowardice, and by the strong emotions which this thorny, arrogant man aroused. Because Álvarez del Vayo's behavior in the war laid him open to the label of "fellow traveler" (as he, himself, concedes), his portrayal of Dr. Negrín in *The Last Optimist* is dismissed by historians as unreliable. In fact, Vayo's picture can be accepted as entirely true:

> Rarely has there been a politician less disposed to be anybody's puppet than Negrín. The Spanish Communists were the first to know this. They can tell of occasions during the Spanish war when only determination to carry on the fight to the end prevented a rupture. . . .
>
> Another point Negrín considered essential to the maintenance of good relations with the Russians was a clear understanding that he would not tolerate, from anyone, even

the suggestion of intervention in the affairs of the Republican Government or the internal policy of Spain. To the scrupulous observation of this principle Negrín attributes Spanish friendship with the Russians during the war. He was highly esteemed by them. But the Russians must have been the first to laugh over the charge of some Spanish leaders that overnight Negrín had become a "tool of Moscow."

Dr. Negrín became friendly with a few of the Russian civilian advisers, but not the police, intelligence, or Comintern officials. He kept his contacts with the Russian military advisers down to a minimum and was always very formal with them.

No one who knew him could underrate his intense, all-absorbing Spanishness and his inflexible pride, courage, and integrity. The same sort of mistake was being made during the Civil War by those who thought that Generalissimo Franco was taking orders from the Germans and Italians. Like Negrín, the Caudillo was dependent on foreign help, but he was never Hitler's or Mussolini's tool. He was too Spanish, for one thing. It is a strange feature of the historiography of the Spanish Civil War that Franco's independence of mind and character and his refusal to accept any outside dictation, are universally accepted, while the same characteristics on the part of Negrín are overlooked or disbelieved.

Of course, Dr. Negrín had no postwar opportunity to demonstrate his independence, as Franco did. However, he refused to go along with the Communists in crucial ways during the war. He blocked their dearest wish—to make a merger with the Socialists. He sought a negotiated peace in 1938 against the wishes of the Communist party and without their knowledge. In the central zone at the end of the war, he infuriated the Communists by seeking a settlement in which they were given no determining part.

Juan Negrín López was the son of a wealthy Canary Islands merchant. Professor Gabriel Jackson notes his modesty and unobtrusiveness in never seeking the limelight, and the unselfish way he let his students (he had the chair of physiology at the University of Madrid) get credit for their work. Negrín did much, and contributed generously from his private fortune, to build University City in Madrid, which was virtually destroyed in the war. Before the rebellion, he worked with the moderate Prieto Socialists whom he joined in 1929. As Minister of Finance under Largo Caballero from September 1936 to May 1937, he was fairly successful in restraining wartime inflation. During that period he reconstructed the *Carabineros* into a disciplined, alert police force, always loyal to him. I have mentioned how, during the days of terror in Madrid, he would go out in the streets and into the prisons at night, to get civilians, whose lives were threatened, into foreign embassies or out of the country.

The moderates admired and liked "this genial, immensely able bourgeois," as Jackson wrote, not that he was by any means always "genial." He was much the ablest figure to arise in the Republican zone, but he was not a good administrator and did not have close contacts with his subordinates, especially the Communists, who committed crimes and excesses of which he often had no knowledge at the time.

His major political problem as Prime Minister was to assert the authority of the central government against regionalism, which he disliked, and the factionalism of the revolutionary political parties. He was always contemptuous of party politics. The "infantile leftism" of Largo Caballero's Socialist faction especially irritated him. He and Largo never got along.

At the end of October 1937, Negrín moved the government from Valencia to Barcelona, where he thought it should have gone the year before from Madrid. This gave him a stronger control over Catalonia without, however, winning the Catalans over to a greater participation in the war. His aim was to concentrate exclusively on broad policies directed at waging the war.

Dr. Negrín demanded more of his associates and the Spanish people than ordinary human nature could stand, but because of his retiring and rather inarticulate nature, he could not build up the fervent loyalty which could have sustained a sacrificial drive in the bitter death struggle of the closing months. One of his weaknesses as a politician was that he could not suffer fools gladly or accept human failings that impaired the war effort. His own idiosyncrasies—a great fondness for women, food, and good living—were like fuel that stoked his immense energy. Like Churchill a few years later, he demanded "blood, toil, tears and sweat," but he did not have the marvelous oratorical gifts, the imagination, or the histrionic flair of that great extrovert. Where Churchill had an irresistible popular drive to carry him on a flood tide to victory, Negrín worked alone, assuming a burden greater than any man could sustain.

He never believed that defeat was inevitable, although his hopes were based on a great gamble—that the European situation, perhaps even a European war, would persuade Britain and France to change their policies. In any event, it was not in his nature to despair. He had the rare gift in a leader (in this he did resemble Winston Churchill) of being inspired by adversity. He believed that any price was worth paying to avoid the conquest of Spain by the Franco forces—and he saw it as a conquest. The mass of the war-weary, hungry, and frightened people in the Loyalist zone would naturally have wanted peace on any terms by that time.

With hindsight, one can argue that after the Insurgent breakthrough to the coast in the spring of 1938, Premier Juan Negrín faced a hopeless task. His strength was in the army, where he was heavily dependent on the Communists who held most of the commands, dominated the rank and file, and controlled military aid. There were Communist subsecretaries in the army, navy, and air force ministries and a Communist at the head of the War Commissars Corps. The quarreling between the Communists, Socialists, and Anarchists was irrepressible.

Professor Jackson put Negrín's dilemma well: "He himself was a patriot, a bourgeois and a democrat; but the international situation forced him to depend increasingly upon the Communists, and with the growth of their power, he inevitably alienated the non-Communist Left and made less likely than ever a change in the foreign policy of the Western powers."

Negrín had begun seeking a negotiated peace in mid-1938, first on reciprocal terms, and then from February 1939 onward in an effort to get Generalissimo Franco to agree not to take reprisals. It is extraordinary to think how many thousands of lives could have been spared and how much misery over many years could have been avoided if General Franco had been merciful and not vengeful. Negrín argued in the last year, when the military situation was hopeless, that more men would be killed by Franco if they surrendered than if they resisted. The terrible repression of 1939–1943 proved Negrín to have been right.

Churchill had prophesied: "The cruelties and ruthless executions extorted by the desperation of both sides, the appalling hatreds unloosed, the clash of creed and interest, make it only too probable that victory will be followed by the merciless extermination of the active elements of the vanquished and by a prolonged period of iron rule."

The surrender of Madrid and the central zone was a tragic farce in formal style. The Nationalists made the gesture of a military occupation of Madrid and other large cities, but it was against no opposition. The Casado Junta was rewarded for its services by being given permission to embark from or fly out of Spain. The old Socialist, Professor Julián Besteiro, dignified and honorable to the end, stayed on to die of tuberculosis in prison.

All over the central and southern zones Republican garrisons were surrendering between March 28 and 31. The next day—April 1, 1939—the conflict was over. In Anthony Eden's bitter jest, the "War of the Spanish Obsession" would no longer plague the statesmen of Europe and America, but its ghost must sometimes have risen to haunt them.

No Spaniard could have had more bitterness in his heart than Juan Negrín, and it was a lasting bitterness. I feel free now to print a poignant passage from a letter he wrote to me on September 5, 1952, from Mexico, four years before he died. It must be seen as his final and terrible indictment of his own people, in which he did not spare himself. The correspondence was about George Orwell, whose *Homage to Catalonia* had recently appeared in the United States. I had asked Dr. Negrín to tell me what he remembered of Orwell, which he did in his letter, but the memory stirred smoldering embers into flame.

> Spain was often a matter of conversation [he wrote of his meetings with Orwell], generally in connection with the daily developments of the World War, and occasionally recollecting bygone episodes of our Civil strife. I remember now that, when this point was touched, he was very eager to enquire about the policy, internal and external, of the government I headed; the changes in the line of conduct of the war which I introduced; our problems and difficulties; the many mistakes I later realized to have committed, which I frankly confessed to him though some of them were unavoidable and would have had to be repeated once more, even after the foregone experience; our way of handling the motley conglomeration of incompatible parties, labour unions and dissident groups and, also, the frequently self-appointed, largely unconstitutional local and regional "governments" with which we had to trade; our foreign policy, especially our relations with Russia, having to take into account that the U.S.S.R. was the only great power supporting us internationally, and prepared to provide us, on the basis of cash payment (we never demanded it gratuitously from anyone) with the necessary weapons; the causes of our defeat which I held, and still hold, as due more than to the shortage of armaments, to our incommensurable incompetence, to our lack of morale, to the intrigues, jealousies and divisions that corrupted the rear, and last, but definitely not least, to our immense cowardice. (When I say "our" I point, of course, not to the brave who fought to death or survived after all sorts of ordeals, nor to the poor hungering and starving civilians. I mean "we," the irresponsible leaders who, having been unable to prevent a war that was not inevitable, contemptibly surrendered when it could be still fought and won. And I make no discrimination among the "we." As with original sin, there is a solidarity in the responsibility, and the only baptism that can whitewash us is the acknowledgment of our common faults and wrongdoings.)

Professor Stanley Payne concludes his chapter on the defeat of the Loyalists in *The Spanish Revolution* with these words: "The [Franco] counterrevolution of 1939 . . . had become an iron-fisted military dictatorship that immediately incarcerated more than a quarter-million opponents, prosecuted and sentenced most of them to prison terms, and, during the next few years, brought tens of thousands of them before the firing squad. . . . The goal of this repression was to exact vengeance and to drown the revolution in its own blood."

In another book, *Politics and the Military in Modern Spain,* published three years earlier, Payne had put forward an interesting and more sinister thesis about the Franco repression.

"However many people it may have liquidated," he wrote, "the goal of this mass purge was not merely to exact justice or even to wreak vengeance, but to carry out a thorough social and political prophylaxis. The repression achieved this goal. It strengthened the dictatorship by decimating the opposition and cowing those who survived, while binding the members of the rebel movement firmly together in a partnership of slaughter."

If so, this was an even colder and crueler calculation than the military decision made by Franco and the rebel generals at the beginning of the war—that they had to terrorize the people by a mass slaughter of "leftists." A postwar decision such as Payne describes, taken in cold blood, would have been wanton cruelty without a military *force majeure.*

I have not seen this accusation against the Franco regime elsewhere, although it is arguable, and the result was what Payne described. This seems to me like too diabolical a calculation. Generalissimo Franco's character is unforgiving and vengeful, but it is not Machiavellian. Moreover, there is no need to seek any further than the convictions that Franco and his followers had of the enormity of the "crimes" committed by the Republicans in fighting for Communism, Socialism, liberalism, and even democracy. Payne also underrates the Caudillo's overwhelming self-righteousness, and he applies an Anglo-Saxon point of view to a Spanish mentality. The very religious Francisco Franco would not have the slightest Christian qualm about exercising ruthless "justice" instead of mercy and forgiveness. When the war ended, there was what Gerald Brenan in *The Spanish Labyrinth* called "a stupendous proscription." His estimate was that one million men and women were jailed. This figure is probably too high, but that hundreds of thousands were imprisoned is certain, as is the fact that Payne mentions, that "tens of thousands" were executed.

Americans who remember Abraham Lincoln's "with malice toward none; with charity for all," will find nothing comparable in Generalissimo Franco's heart or deeds.

On February 9, 1939, before the war ended but with victory in sight, a Law of Political Responsibilities was decreed. Its definition of "political" crimes was very broad and extended liability back to October 1, 1934. One of the offenses was "grave passivity," such as not helping the Nationalist cause or living neutrally abroad. All Freemasons were automatically and seriously guilty. A variety of prison terms were prescribed for a wide variety of offenses. Fines accompanied all sentences and could result in an offender's surviving relatives losing all their possessions.

One provision, in which the Generalissimo seemed to take a special interest, permitted a form of redemption under which the offender would get a day's remission of his sentence for every day spent at hard labor on roads, railways, construction and, in the course of time, the building of the greatest and most expensive mausoleum since the Pharoahs built the pyramids. It is called the Valley of the Fallen. On one side of the altar, the body of José Antonio Primo de Rivera has been placed. The other side, presumably, is reserved for the Generalissimo.

It does not appear that many prisoners were able to "redeem" themselves. The official *Anuario Estadístico* for 1941 listed 233,373 prisoners of whom only 8 per cent were rated eligible for *redención*. An interesting evidence of the psychology of the Caudillo was that, as he saw it, and as the preamble of the 1939 law asserted, he was not meting out stern punishment.

"The international magnitude and the material consequences of the crimes committed against Spain," it reads, "are so great that they prevent punishment and redemption reaching a proportionate scale, since this would be repugnant to the profound feelings of our National Revolution, which desires neither to punish cruelly, nor to bring misery into homes."

In reality, as Hugh Thomas wrote, "the victors showed no charity." Even Foreign Minister Count Ciano, who visited Madrid in July 1939, was shocked. "There are still a great number of shootings," he wrote of a conversation with Franco on July 19. "In Madrid alone between 200 and 250 a day; in Barcelona 150; in Seville, a town which was never in the hands of the Reds, 80. . . . During my stay in Spain, while more than 10,000 men already condemned to death awaited in the prisons the inevitable moment of their execution, only two, I repeat two, appeals for pardon were addressed to me by families. I may add that the Caudillo granted them forthwith."

According to Ciano, at that time there were "already 200,000 under arrest in the various Spanish prisons." Of the more than 300,000 Republican soldiers who surrendered and were at first put in concentration camps, about 100,000 were held prisoner and many shot.

The official figure for early 1940 was 270,719 political prisoners. In 1941, as stated above, the same source gave 233,373 prisoners. There were mass executions just after the war's end, with dozens of prisoners at a time slaughtered by machine-gun squads. "Justice" was at best summary, with the accused having little chance, and all denunciations accepted as proof of guilt. Embittered relatives were often allowed to take personal vengeance.

"The shootings did not end after the first year of peace," writes Professor Payne, "but went on in great volume throughout 1941 and part of 1942." In fact, while the number of executions gradually decreased, they continued through 1943. The reason they finally stopped, according to Payne, was not compassion, but because it became obvious to Generalissimo Franco that the Fascist powers, who "had seemed to provide a sort of sanction to mass murder," were losing the war. One can argue, even more cynically, that there were no more "Red criminals" left to execute. A simple explanation could be that the lust for vengeance and blood had been sated. There was no longer any purpose—political, social, or emotional—to keep on killing prisoners three and four years after the war ended. General Franco began to extend amnesties to surviving prisoners in 1942 and continued year after year until few or none were left.

Chronologically, the story of the postwar repression has come a little prematurely in our history because it was part of the Spanish Civil War—like a bloody curtain descending on the final act of the tragedy.

How many Spaniards killed each other in their terrible conflict? The figure of a million deaths out of a population of about 26,000,000 in 1936 has gone into the mythology of the Civil War. The Catalan novelist José María Gironella wrote a best-seller after the war called *Un millón de muertos (A Million Deaths)*. The figure is used incessantly, but it is obviously a rough guess without any scientific basis. Hugh Thomas's total is half a million, including 175,000 Republicans and 110,000 Nationalists killed in action. To these he adds the atrocities (50,000); the deaths of civilians from Insurgent bombings and artillery (24,-000); and 100,000 who died from disease and starvation.

Thomas's figure of 500,000 seems like a reasonable minimum; a million is undoubtedly a great exaggeration; but there could have been as many as 700,000 or 800,000. Whatever calculation one makes, the toll was a dreadful one, and Franco went on adding his "tens of thousands" in the postwar years. It was a fortunate Spanish family who did not mourn for their dead.

(The Spanish Civil War figures can be compared to those of the American Civil War when, out of a population of about 31,000,000, the dead numbered 617,000.)

Another credible source for the religious victims of the terror at the beginning of the war in the Loyalist zone (Antonio Montero, *History of the Religious Persecution in Spain*, Madrid, 1961) gives 6,800 out of a total of 30,000 priests, monks, and nuns.

By the end of the war, twenty-four classes (1919 to 1942, ages seventeen to forty) totaling more than 900,000 men, had been mobilized on the Republican side. In addition, there were about 100,000 police. The Nationalists also mobilized close to a million men, but this was from a steadily expanding population base. No men older than the class of 1927 (twenty-five years old) were conscripted. Thus, in all, something like 2,000,000 men out of Spain's population of 26,000,000 saw military service in the Civil War.

The diplomatic wind up of the Civil War had come like an anticlimax. Britain and France, who were concerned for their commercial interests and feared that Germany and Italy would not withdraw their forces, recognized the Franco government formally (as I mentioned) on February 27, 1939, a month before the war ended. The first French ambassador lent a touch of historic irony, for he was Marshal Henri Pétain. Actually, the Franco regime shook off the presence of Germany and Italy in a few months.

The United States had nothing at stake inside Spain. Washington's chief concern was the domestic American conflict between the Catholics and Protestants. The Roman Catholic community agitated for the recognition of the Franco government after the Insurgent conquest of Catalonia. Secretary of State Cordell Hull, consistent to the end, argued for the immediate recognition of Franco when the fighting stopped toward the end of March 1939. Ambassador William C. Bullitt in Paris was entrusted with the negotiations. Pro-Loyalist sympathizers in the United States could no longer muster the strength they had shown in fighting for the repeal of the arms embargo. The Catholic community was as strong and well-organized as ever.

I was told later by Ambassador Claude Bowers, who was still accredited to the Republican government at the end, that President Roosevelt was considering what to do when he left Washington (perhaps too conveniently?) for a weekend's rest. He gave orders, Bowers said, that nothing was to be done until he returned and could study the matter further. If so, the State

Department paid no attention; recognition was granted on April 1, the day the Civil War ended.

The United States had traditionally followed a policy of refusing to recognize governments established through the use of force. At the time, Washington had not recognized the Japanese seizure of Manchuria, the Italian conquest of Ethiopia, or the German occupation of Austria, Czechoslovakia, and Memel.

"Why?" asked Representative John Coffee, Democrat of Washington State. "In the past, when we asked to lift the [arms] embargo, our voices fell upon deaf ears. Now, no sooner is democracy driven from Spain than we join the dictators of the world."

Four hundred and seventy-three Protestant clergymen wrote President Roosevelt that official recognition of the Franco regime was "the crowning mistake on our part. . . . A decent self-respect, not to speak of a concern for our own welfare, should have prevented us from recognizing a government which announced and is carrying on a program of brutal reprisals against Republican leaders."

It is a valid indictment of the Roosevelt administration that no effort was made to restrain Generalissimo Franco's massive reprisal against the conquered Loyalists. Probably, no efforts would have succeeded, but the United States could have tried, if only for the historic record.

The clouds of a much greater war were now close and menacing. After the fall of Barcelona, Mussolini stood on the famous balcony of the Palazzo Venezia in Rome and told his followers: "Your shout of exultation, which is fully justified, blends with that rising in all cities of Spain, which are now completely liberated from the Reds' infamies, and with the shout of joy from all anti-Bolshevists the world over. General Franco's magnificent troops and our fearless Legionaries have not only beaten Negrín's government, but many others of our enemies are now biting the dust."

The Duce meant Britain, France, and the United States. He forgot to mention Germany's contribution to the victory.

The British had feared that a weakened Germany would mean a strengthened Russia. Many observers believed that London hoped to see Germany and the Soviet Union fight each other. This, if true, was stupid, since there was always the possibility, which became a dreadful reality, of a compact between Hitler and Stalin against Britain and France. It was, in fact, never plausible that the Fuehrer and Stalin would oblige the British and French by cutting each other's throats. With their realistic, totalitarian mentalities it stood to reason that they would not let ideological differences divide them against their common enemies—the democracies.

The fact that Germany, Italy, and the Soviet Union were using Spain as a testing ground for their soldiers, technicians, and matériel was always obvious. From the angle of their general staffs, the Spanish war was a golden opportunity. As a rule, they talked and wrote about it privately. Hugh Thomas cites one public slip made by German General Walther von Reichenau, commander of the Fourth Army Group, in a lecture which the London *News Chronicle* summarized on July 12, 1938. "Two years of real war experience," Reichenau said, "have been of more use to our yet immature *Wehrmacht,* to the offensive power of the people, than a whole ten years of peaceful training could have been." Goering was saying much the same thing about the experience the fledgling *Luftwaffe* was getting. General Hugo von Sperrle, commander of the Condor Legion, who masterminded the bombing of Guernica, was, in World War II, to direct the raids on Rotterdam, Coventry, and other open cities.

Of the three great powers who intervened in Spain—Germany, Italy, and the Soviet Union—it was the German military who profited most from the lessons learned in the Spanish conflict. The Condor Legion normally used old army and air force matériel, but as the war progressed, some of the latest planes and artillery were tried out. The historic bombing of Guernica was an exercise in saturation bombing, without any tactical advantage to the advancing troops. The most valuable lesson learned by the Germans was in the use of tanks. They discov-

ered the effectiveness of employing massed tanks as an attacking force to break through enemy lines, harassing the rear, and
opening up gaps for the infantry to pour through. The Russians
used their tanks throughout the war inefficiently as "cavalry,"
giving tactical support, in small groups, to the infantry.

Military historians of World War II have noted, with puzzle-
ment and condemnation, that the Russian commanders in the
early stages of the German onslaught did not grasp the value
of the German tank tactics. The Russians continued to rely on
their outmoded technique of scattering tank units as support
for the infantry. It was not until after Stalin's death and
Khrushchev's "de-Stalinization" that the mystery was solved.
Several high-ranking Russian commanders who had fought in
Spain and survived Stalin's purges published their memoirs.
The Russian military advisers in the Civil War, and especially
their able tank commander General Pavlov, had realized the
obvious advantages of the German tank tactics. On their return
to the Soviet Union, they reorganized the tank corps and
trained their units in the new technique of massing the tanks
and smashing through the lines to break up the enemy infantry
formations. However, just before the 1939 war Stalin, who was
in the midst of his paranoiac purge of the military, came under
other influences and turned the clock back. More Spanish veterans were liquidated. Pavlov survived only, ironically, to become a sacrificial victim of Stalin's need for scapegoats when
the Germans overran the Russian armies. All Pavlov had done
was to follow Stalin's orders strictly, knowing that they were
disastrous.

The French, incidentally, learned nothing about tank tactics
from the Spanish war and paid dearly for their blindness in
1940. Whatever the British learned was of no use to them. As in
so many respects, the Germans had profited most from the
Spanish Civil War and the accompanying era of appeasement.

One lesson that the Germans and Italians did not learn in
Spain was that the bombing of civilians in open cities did not
break their spirit, or make the inhabitants want to sue for
peace. On the contrary, such bombings embittered and in-

furiated the people and made them more determined to fight on. In World War II and Vietnam, air force strategists made a similar mistake.

The use of bombing against troops, military objectives, and lines of communication was, however, very effective. The Germans got much valuable practice in tactical bombing in Spain. So did the Italians, but they were to have no opportunity to use their knowledge. The Russians either did not have or did not send advanced planes to Spain, and in the latter half of the war the pilots and gunners were anyway all Spanish. According to Colonel Adolf Galland, the *Luftwaffe* learned a valuable lesson in the drive to the Mediterranean coast in 1938. This was the effectiveness of using some squadrons as combat planes to fight off enemy air support while sending in a separate force for bombing and strafing troop concentrations.

In a conversation between Joachim von Ribbentrop and Mussolini in Rome on March 10, 1940, recorded in Ciano's *Diplomatic Papers,* Ribbentrop said that when he was sent to London as ambassador in 1937, "he put the chances of a [European] war to the Fuehrer at ten to one. If he had been asked under what circumstances he would wish to conduct that struggle, his wildest fantasy could not have suggested to him a situation so favorable as that in which Germany finds herself today."

What was true for Germany was not true for Italy. The Duce had to tell Ribbentrop ruefully "that at the moment of the outbreak of war, on the 3rd of September [1939], Italy was not ready."

This was probably the greatest service that the Spanish Republicans performed for the Allies of World War II—and it is rarely noted for its worth by historians of that conflict. Italy "was not ready" simply because her armed forces and her supplies of war matériel had been exhausted in Spain. Even when she "stabbed France in the back" on June 10, 1940, Italy's intervention was derisory.

At the time of Munich, General Franco had been so frightened at the thought of what a European war could mean to him that he hastily put thousands of prisoners to work building fortifications along the border with France and the frontier between Spanish and French Morocco. He at first offered to help the Germans, but Hitler ignored him. A timely word from the Foreign Office in London made the Generalissimo realize, prudently, that his best policy was neutrality. In fact, he even promised to keep the Germans and Italians in Spain away from the French frontier. The Italians were openly disgusted; one can only guess at German feelings. Neither of them had anything to worry about; they had Neville Chamberlain on their side.

The Caudillo began preparing for the oncoming conflagration before the war ended in Spain. On March 17, 1939, he concluded a pact of friendship and nonaggression with Portugal; on March 27 he joined the Anti-Comintern Pact; on March 31 he also signed a Treaty of Friendship with Germany; on May 8 Spain withdrew from the League of Nations. When the war began on September 3, 1939, Spain was where Generalissimo Franco wanted her to be—neutral, in favor of the Axis.

11

FRANCO KEEPS THE PEACE

THE FIGHTING STOPPED ON APRIL 1, 1939, but the Spanish Civil War is not over. For one thing, Generalissimo Francisco Franco Bahamonde, "by the Grace of God" is still Caudillo of Spain. He will not be there much longer in the nature of things, having been born in 1892, but for the purposes of a book published in 1972, he is the great, durable symbol of the Spanish conflict. One cannot look back over the Civil War that he joined, fought, and won without thinking of General Franco, nor can one think of the decades since 1939 without his dominating figure.

Because of him and *his* ideas, the Spain that fought the Civil War still lives. It has changed less than any nation in Europe, except neighboring Portugal, which also had a long-lasting dictatorship rooted in the past. The dynamism—good or bad—that could have come to Spain from liberal democracy, social democracy, Communism, or Fascism, was blocked by the Caudillo. It will not be held back after he is gone. Behind the dam which the Generalissimo has erected much has been happening. A new generation has come along and one knows (it is all that one can know about Spain today) that when Francisco Franco dies, there will be great changes.

That will be a story for future historians to write. Today, one has to recognize that in many fundamental ways, the political, social, and religious structures of pre-Republican Spain have been perpetuated. The economy has progressed greatly, one might almost say in spite of the Generalissimo, for he was most reluctant to take the steps in the 1960's that belatedly set the country on the path to modern progress and national prosperity. But within that prosperity the traditional gap between the few wealthy and the many poor remains, and Spain's historic need for agrarian reform has not been met.

General Franco has given his nation more than three decades of internal peace, but at the price that a reactionary dictatorship demands. Even economically, compared to other European nations devastated by war—Germany, Italy, Holland, Belgium, for instance—Spain has progressed little. The fretful "peace" which Franco has imposed on Spain is simply a lull before she enters the storm of our turbulent times—our world in revolution—and she will enter it poorly prepared.

Under any kind of regime the effects of the terrible wounds of the Civil War would have lasted. We in the United States still live with the consequences of the War Between the States. France lives with her great Revolution of nearly two centuries ago. Civil wars and revolutions are traumatic experiences for nations.

To retrace the path that Spain has followed since 1939 is rather like crossing a wasteland. It has been one of those periods when Spaniards, having expended their energies in a furious burst of violence, calm down, exhausted, almost apathetic, as if gathering strength for another supreme effort. No one ever threatened Franco's power during the Civil War or doubted that he would be the dictator afterward. No one has threatened his power since 1939. He has performed one of the most extraordinary feats of political finesse, shrewdness, and personal ascendance in this century.

Hitler misjudged him badly. He is quoted in his *Table Talk* as saying that Franco did not have "the personality to face up to the political problems of the country." He also thought Franco "incapable of freeing himself from the influence of Serrano Suñer"—the brother-in-law who had his period of power as Foreign Minister in World War II, until it suited Franco to dismiss him.

Foolish Ciano wrote in his *Diplomatic Papers:* "Franco is

completely dominated by the personality of Mussolini and feels that he requires him to face the peace just as he did to win the war. . . . He expects from the Duce . . . instructions and directives."

When World War II began, Captain Liddell Hart wrote in *The Defense of Britain* (1939): "The direct assistance which Italy gave with aircraft and which Germany gave with warships, in transporting Franco's troops across from Africa to Spain, were the first operations of the present war."

A lurid thread ran through the pattern woven by the Spanish generals in the course of the Civil War that they started: intervention by foreign powers. Now one of the generals was facing the consequences. To begin with, he was not at all unhappy, for he expected his Civil War allies to win, and that Spain, which would help them, would profit by their victory. When the tide turned against the Axis, General Franco turned with it.

Many historians and commentators rate the Caudillo's feat in keeping Spain out of World War II as the greatest service that he performed during his regime. It was a case where the cautiousness and canniness, which are such strong features of his character, paid off. The contrast between Francisco Franco and Benito Mussolini explains a great deal about the histories of their countries in World War II. For Sir Samuel Hoare, Britain's wartime ambassador in Madrid and a sour commentator on the Generalissimo and his regime, the reasons Spain stayed out of the war were "a mixture of self-interest, fear and complacency" on Franco's part; his belief that "he could obtain everything he wanted without fighting," and "the overriding fact that the Spanish people were opposed to war." Hoare rather gloatingly cites documents which the American Army of Occupation discovered in Germany, containing confidential correspondence between Hitler, Mussolini, and Franco and accounts of interviews between the dictators and their ministers. The State Department published them in a volume entitled *The Spanish Government and the Axis*. There is, for instance, a letter from Franco to Hitler dated February 26, 1941.

"I want to dispel all shadow of doubt," Franco wrote, "and declare that I stand ready at your side, entirely and decidedly at your disposal, united in a common historical destiny, desertion from which would mean my suicide and that of the Cause which I have led and represent in Spain. I need no confirmation of my faith in the triumph of your Cause and I repeat that I shall always be a loyal follower to it."

According to Hoare, Franco gave Hitler "a free hand in the Spanish police, press and censorship. . . . There was to be no German army of occupation. The system was to be control without occupation, but control no less complete and pervasive." Madrid, the ambassador claimed, also became "the European center of the Japanese secret service."

Franco officially changed Spain's neutrality to "nonbelligerency" on June 13, 1940. He told U.S. Ambassador Carlton Hayes that this was "a form of national sympathy with the Axis." France was being overrun at the time. In a memorandum to the Germans on June 19 Franco wrote: "Should England continue the war after France has ceased fighting, Spain would be willing to enter the war after a short period of preparing the public."

However, the Caudillo was more cautious with his deeds than his words. Franco met Hitler at Hendaye, on the French frontier, on October 23, 1940. Five days later, the Fuehrer saw Mussolini in Florence and, speaking of his nine-hour talk with Franco, he called it, Ciano wrote, "a conversation of such kind that 'rather than go through with it again the Fuehrer would prefer to have three or four teeth taken out.' "

Actually, Franco simply stalled, keeping all avenues open, but refusing to permit the German Army to go through Spain to attack Gibraltar. On that point the Generalissimo was adamant throughout the war.

"The Fuehrer expressed himself in very harsh terms on the subject of Generalissimo Franco," Ciano wrote on April 20, 1941. On the twenty-fifth, Hitler and Mussolini met again. "The Fuehrer," said Ciano, "employed bitter terms against Spain and affirmed that this country has proved a real disappointment to him."

The alliance between Hitler and Stalin was a great embarrassment to Franco. When, on June 22, 1941, the Germans invaded Russia, a barrier was lifted. Serrano Suñer, then Foreign Minister and a Falangist leader, proposed that a volunteer Spanish division be sent to the Russian front, and Franco agreed. However, not enough volunteers were forthcoming, so the Foreign Minister made up a "Blue Division" of 17,000 men, composed mostly of regular soldiers, with some Falangists and adventurers. They went to Russia the following year, 1942, and fought well for about a year, but they were ill-equipped and reportedly had a rough time of it. Casualties were heavy.

Meanwhile, on November 8, 1942, "Operation Torch," the American landing in North Africa, took place. Serrano Suñer had been removed as Foreign Minister in September and replaced by the relatively pro-Ally Count Jordana. The Blue Division was brought home in October 1943, at which time Franco changed back from non-belligerency to neutrality. Even before the Normandy landing in June 1944, it was clear who was going to win the war. In April 1944, for instance, the Generalissimo cut down on Spanish exports to Germany of wolframite, the mineral from which tungsten is extracted. Spain was the second largest producer of wolfram in Europe and her shipments to the Nazis were one of the best services that Franco offered in the war. The Spaniards were making enormous profits, as wolfram fetched fantastic prices.

"Germany and Italy will fall," Herbert Feis, economic adviser to the U.S. Embassy in Madrid wrote of American feelings in 1944, "but Franco would stand, his past behind him. He would remain part of our universe, an affront to our sense of justice."

President Roosevelt was now (March 1945) able to say what he thought and felt. It was an ironical postscript to the issue of diplomatic recognition which he had shirked in April 1939.

"Having been helped to power by Fascist Italy and Nazi Germany, and patterned itself along totalitarian lines," the President wrote to U.S. Ambassador Norman Armour in Madrid, "the present regime in Spain is naturally the subject of distrust by a great many American citizens, who find it difficult to see the justification for this country to continue to maintain relations with such a regime. . . . The fact that our government maintains formal diplomatic relations with the present Spanish regime should not be interpreted by anyone to imply approval of that regime and its sole party, the Falange, which has been openly hostile to the United States and which has tried to spread its Fascist party ideas in the Western Hemisphere."

The United Nations was shaping up. At the preliminary San Francisco conference, membership was barred to regimes "established by Axis aid." The Big Three (the United States, Great Britain, and the Soviet Union), meeting in Potsdam in June 1945, made it clear that they would not favor any application for membership in the United Nations "put forward by the present Spanish Government, which, having been founded with the support of the Axis powers does not, in view of its origin, its nature, its record, and its close association with the aggressor States, possess the qualifications necessary to justify such membership."

A report of the General Assembly of the U.N. in 1946 rubbed it in by saying that: "In origin, nature, structure and general conduct the Franco regime is a Fascist regime patterned on, and established largely as a result of aid received from Hitler's Germany and Mussolini's Fascist Italy."

The final decision was made on December 12, 1946, when the General Assembly voted to bar Spain from the United Nations, threatened sanctions, and recommended that its members withdraw their ambassadors from Madrid. Many nations did so, including the United States, but the U.N.'s attitude was what Spaniards call "counterproductive." It was just what Generalissimo Franco needed to bolster his faltering image inside Spain. Spanish pride was affronted; nationalism was aroused. Franco held a monster rally at which he received a great ovation. And Spain withdrew into her historic isolationism.

Franco's complacency and self-righteousness were unshaken. He calculated that since he was right and the other countries wrong, all he had to do was to wait, and they would come to him and make amends. This is what happened. The Generalissimo did make some gestures toward world opinion, but they were no more than that. The mandatory Fascist salute was dropped. The Cortes were revived, but the legislature has never been anything but a rubber stamp for the regime's policies. A bill of rights was promulgated in July 1945, but it has remained a dead letter.

When NATO came along in 1948, Spain was excluded, as she was from the European Economic Community (The Common Market). The barriers have, in part, been broken down, largely thanks to the Cold War and the United States all-absorbing policy of anti-Communism. An American ambassador was back in Madrid in 1950, along with envoys from most other countries. That was the year the Korean War began and the United Nations Security Council (which had voted to intervene in Korea during the absence of the Russian delegate) and the General Assembly reversed the U.N. policy about the recognition of Spain. The mountain had moved to Mohammed.

Franco's great year—his triumph over all his enemies—was 1953, when the United States made a military pact with Spain and the Vatican granted a new Concordat. In both cases the terms for the Franco regime were very favorable and the prestige which the agreements brought effectively ended Spain's role as "the pariah of the Western world." The agreement with the United States provided for the building of five military air bases and a great naval base at Rota, near Cádiz. With the development of long-range and Polaris missiles, the air bases lost much of their value, but Rota remains important as a naval base for operations in the Mediterranean.

It cannot be said that Franco Spain, even in the 1970's, has been accepted as a charter member of Western Europe's community of nations. It will not be, so long as the Generalissimo is the dictator of Spain. Not only the smaller democratic nations—Norway, Holland, Denmark, Belgium—but even France and Britain are opposed, or reluctant, to allow the Franco regime to become a full member of NATO or the Common Market. She does play a role in the Organization for European Cooperation and Development (OECD) and the International Monetary Fund. Franco disapproved of both, and only reluctantly yielded to the necessity of joining the contemporary economic world in 1964, since which time there has been a spectacular improvement in the economy. Generally speaking, Spain is still on the margin of the Western European economic and defense systems.

Spain still has one of the strongest and most domineering dictatorships of modern times—and one of the most reactionary. To the Generalissimo, this would not be a criticism, for he disapproves of democracy, liberalism, Marxism, egalitarianism, permissiveness, and other manifestations of our revolutionary age. He believes in law, order, hierarchy, religious orthodoxy, the supremacy of the military over civilian authority, strict government and church control over education, and a heavily censored press and literature. Foreign attacks and ostracism are used by him to arouse the always latent Spanish xenophobia.

The Generalissimo knew that he simply had to sit tight and make sure that no rival or potential oppositionist movement became strong enough to overthrow him. In a speech in March 1946 he referred to himself as "the sentinel who is never relieved; the man who receives the unwelcome telegrams and dictates the solutions; the man who watches while others sleep."

The army officers, the church hierarchy, the Monarchists, the landowners, the bankers, and businessmen never deserted him, for they profited by his regime and they feared the chaos, if not the revolutionary effects, of any other government. The most important cohesive factor of all was that nobody—literally no Spaniard in his right senses—could bear the thought of another civil war. Faced with the alternative of a resumption of internecine strife, even the most determined opponents would think of Generalissimo Franco as a necessary evil, the Devil they knew.

Franco's technique, for which political scientists give him a high rating, was to keep his nation politically divided. "For twenty years," Professor Payne wrote in his book on the Falange, "Franco had carefully fostered all the hatreds, enmities, divisions, and infantile fixations which beset Spanish politics in 1936." A less exaggerated and more positive way of putting much the same idea appears in a recent biography by an English historian, J. W. D. Trythall. "To General Franco," he writes, "the art of politics is to avoid by force and by subtlety the polarisation of opinion and the clash of ideas that is the life of liberalism."

For Sir Samuel Hoare, writing in wartime, Franco had "one of the most inefficient governments that anyone could conceive." But in 1965, for the American scholar Gabriel Jackson, "In sober truth it may be said that General Franco built the most powerful and repressive regime to exist in Spain since the reign of Philip II."

Jackson is much nearer the truth. The power structure that Franco erected and manipulated after World War II has never been seriously shaken. It has been under growing strain as a younger generation became more and more restive. This has forced the aged Caudillo into concessions he would never have made earlier, but thus far this opposition is not remotely strong enough to threaten the governmental structure.

General Franco's claim to constitutional legitimacy lies in a "Law of Succession," approved by the customary huge majority of a popular referendum in July 1947. It designated Franco as Caudillo and Chief of State for life, abolished the Second Republic and restored the monarchy—in theory. Franco left it open to himself to decide when and who. The "when" is to be within eight days of Franco's death, and the "who" is Prince Juan Carlos de Borbón, son of Don Juan, Count of Barcelona, who was the legitimate Pretender.

The Generalissimo disapproved of Don Juan, the third son of

King Alfonso XIII. In 1936, Don Juan tried to volunteer in the Nationalist forces under General Mola, but he was rejected. However, in World War II he was pro-Ally. In 1945, he made the mistake of calling on the Spanish people to oust Franco, and in 1948 he quarreled with the Caudillo over the latter's desire to turn the monarchy into a continuation of the Franco regime. Meanwhile, he had let Juan Carlos, Prince of Asturias (now officially called the Prince of Spain) return to Spain to be educated and trained militarily. The result was that on July 22, 1969, Franco designated Juan Carlos as the future king in place of Don Juan.

It seems to be Franco's hope that when Juan Carlos ascends the throne, which will be when the Caudillo decides that the time is ripe, or after he dies, he will rule as well as simply reign. The prince has already been given the power, by decree, to act as head of government whenever Franco is ill or absent. (The Caudillo has not left Spain since 1936.) On accepting the role of future king, Juan Carlos swore "an oath of loyalty to his Excellency the Head of State and fidelity to the Principles of the National Movement and other Fundamental Laws of the country."

The prince is running a risk in basing his legitimacy on the Nationalist victory in the Civil War and not on the historic legitimacy derived from the Bourbon dynasty. However, he had no choice and he seems to have a reasonable chance of saving the Spanish Bourbons from the fate which the House of Savoy met in Italy in 1944. Juan Carlos is a serious, dedicated young man who will certainly try hard.

The Bourbon dynasty was completely discredited well before the Republican revolution of 1931. It had lost authority and popular appeal everywhere in Spain except in Navarre and Old Castile. In these post-World War II years there has been a monumental indifference to the monarchy. This may well permit Prince Juan Carlos to be crowned, but he, himself, has no experience or capacity to be head of the government. He would have to "rule" through strong ministers and generals. The monarchy could exist on sufferance, but if it really represents the old order, for which Franco stands, it will not last.

The regime Franco constructed is a façade which he has propped up. He started by exalting the Falange—the "Movement," as it was called, the only permitted political party—but he never gave it any effective power. It was a vast bureaucratic structure, dispensing patronage of all kinds and providing a means of harnessing the working class through a variation of national socialism or syndicalism. In such ways, it was enormously useful to Franco until recent years.

The Generalissimo ruled through a cabinet that was not changed from 1945 to 1957, when the Falangists were eliminated. The second cabinet saw the introduction to governmental power of the Opus Dei, the secret Catholic religious and lay order which is often called "White Masonry." It was founded by a Spanish priest in 1928 and soon won unprecedentedly high Vatican approval. Although a worldwide organization, it is a political power only in Spain. Its secular goals are economic development and political stability along corporative, conservative lines. It is pro-monarchist and anti-leftist. All of which is fine for General Franco, who doubtless also rather enjoys the fact that Opus Dei is anti-Falangist and anti-Jesuit. It has been especially strong in recent years. Membership is secret. It probably has about 10,000 followers in Spain, which is not many, but they come from an élite. Franco provided the organization with its own university in Pamplona, the first new Spanish university since 1925 and only the third new one in the twentieth century, which is an indication of the poverty of Spanish higher education.

After the Civil War, the church's privileges and properties were immediately restored everywhere in Spain. Civil marriages had to be repeated in church to be valid. Divorce was abolished. The church was given a key role in education and the right to censor morals and literature. Not for centuries has the Spanish Roman Catholic hierarchy had such power and privileges. The church is known to receive a very large, tax-exempt subsidy from the government, but the amount is secret.

On April 12, 1931, Manuel Azaña had rashly announced that Catholic Spain ceased to exist. Yet, it was, in a sense, "Catholic Spain" which triumphed in the end.

Under the Concordat of 1953, the "Catholic, Apostolic and Roman" religion is the "only" recognized religion in Spain. The Head of State (i.e., Franco) has a unique, traditional privilege, which is to name three bishops who will naturally be politically acceptable to him. This is a provision which the Vatican does not like and it will probably disappear after Franco dies.

Spain is as close to 100 per cent Roman Catholic as any country in the world. Benjamin Welles, former *New York Times* correspondent in Madrid, in his book, *The Gentle Anarchy* (1965), put the Spanish Protestant community at 32,000 of whom 20,000 were children. Jews numbered 8,000 (5,000 in Barcelona, 3,000 in Madrid, none in the rural areas). In a population now over 30,000,000, this would make Spain more than 99.8 per cent Roman Catholic. Nevertheless, Welles points out, Spain is eighth in Europe in proportion of priests to the Catholic population. Fewer and fewer young Spaniards have been feeling a call to the priesthood. The younger priests have been very restive in recent years, balking against the rigid, reactionary policies of the hierarchy and, in the Basque country, often openly supporting the regional discontent.

Richard Eder, *New York Times* correspondent in Madrid until 1972 (who is a Roman Catholic), believes that the church in Spain has already turned against the Franco regime. Like all observers, he was startled and impressed by the liberalism of the assembly of bishops and priests from all over Spain in September 1971. They were a minority, but the then Primate of Spain, Cardinal Enrique Tarancón, presided at the conference, whose resolutions were remarkably bold and progressive.

One of the proposals stated that Christians in Spain "must be preoccupied by the insufficient scope given to human rights and the persistence of grave economic and social inequalities." Among these it listed freedom of expression and association and the right of people to govern themselves. The resolutions argued that Spaniards did not have sufficient guarantees of "the right to physical integrity—that is, protection from bodily or mental torture."

Generalissimo Franco soon showed who was master in Spain. In his New Year's message on December 30, he ordered the Spanish church sharply to restrict its activities to spiritual matters. "The State will oppose any interference with its sovereignty which aims at perturbing the peaceful living together of Spaniards," he said. A harder and, in this case, unexpected blow came on March 11, 1972, when the Holy See addressed a letter to the Spanish clergy asking that most of the key texts and motions adopted by the assembly, including those mentioned above, be revoked.

It was a disappointing setback to the most hopeful church development of recent years, but the assembly's resolutions are on record. They represent the beliefs and desires of a large sector of the Spanish clergy. The signs are unmistakable that the Spanish church, like all of Spain, is in transition from its almost medieval ossification to the dynamic and revolutionary world of today. It is even possible that it will be the church that leads Spain into the welfare society of the contemporary West. Meanwhile, one should not expect miracles. The Roman Catholic Church of Spain was built on solid, medieval, hispanic foundations which will take time to refashion from the top down. The voice of the dead past will still be heard for years to come. Besides, the church will not lightly surrender the great privileges and wealth which the present system guarantees.

In no country is proselytism so feared and so fiercely combated. Protestants and Jews in recent years have been allowed to meet in worship, but there must be no "external" signs that the place of worship is a chapel or a synagogue. "A Protestant pastor who said grace at meals in a private home was breaking Spanish law," Welles writes. The King James and other English versions of the Bible have been banned. No Protestant can be an officer in the Spanish Army.

In 1959, the first synagogue to be opened in Spain since 1492 was consecrated in Madrid. One has to know that it is there. Spaniards have long been tolerant of Jews for the simple reason that there are so few Spanish Jews; they never proselytize; and they have no political coloration. Some 30,000 Jews fled from Germany and France into Spain during World War II and were given refuge or helped on their way by the Franco regime. In recent years the government has helped Jews to migrate from North Africa into Israel.

Welles, like Hoare, believes that Franco "almost certainly has Jewish blood in his veins" because his mother's name—Bahamonde—is of Sephardic origin.

It is strange to think that perhaps not one Spaniard in a hundred who has lived all his life in Spain has ever met a Jew. When one remembers how rich and powerful the Jews were in medieval centuries (until their expulsion in 1492), how much culture, erudition, and philosophy they contributed to Spanish life, and how much Jewish blood must still flow in Spanish veins, one must say that this could only have happened in Spain.

Of course, even Spain could not escape contemporary moral permissiveness, but relatively to her past. A man can bathe on the beach at San Sebastián without a top to his suit. The police do not spring into shocked action when they see a woman in a bikini. Girls, who could never go without chaperones up to ten years ago, are beginning to be trusted alone by their parents. Scandinavian and British girls in revealing clothes cannot go into churches, but they can walk the streets of Madrid without being arrested.

None of these freedoms yet applies to politics. "Our regime," as Franco once said, "is based on bayonets and blood, not on hypocritical elections." The Cortes were made a little more representative in 1958, but they have never ceased to be a passive, obedient instrument for the Caudillo. Only 104 out of 554 members are elected as "family representatives," but these come from carefully picked, pro-regime candidates. The other 450 members are ex officio or appointed, and they nominally belong to the Falangist "Movement." No member (who theoretically should be called by the medieval name of *procurador* and not *diputado*) is allowed to express "judgments of a political character." In short, no opposition is allowed, but one can wonder how many crypto-Socialists, Communists, Anarchists, and Republicans are among them. The appalling Nationalist bloodbath of 1936–1943 had done its job in crushing any open leftist opposition. Anyway, neither in the underground nor among the Spanish exiles is there any less disunity and mutual antagonism than during the Civil War.

Both of the recent *New York Times* correspondents in Madrid, Welles and Eder, consider the Socialists to be the strongest opposition element. They are, as Welles wrote, "reformist, antimilitary and anticlerical," but they are split into the old Republican element in exile, with headquarters in Toulouse, France, and the internal group led by Professor Enrique Tierno Galván, who is in constant trouble with the authorities.

Both correspondents rate the Communists as the "best organized" of the national movements and, thanks to Moscow, the best financed. The underground "workers' commissioners" are Communist controlled. They are also the most fiercely persecuted and, when caught, they can expect police torture as well as imprisonment. Welles estimates their numbers at about 5,000, but membership is, of course, secret. A popular revulsion from, and fear of, Communism certainly exists, partly as a hangover from the Civil War and partly as a result of nearly four decades of Franco regime propaganda. The Communists would seem to have no chance to achieve power after Franco dies except in some possible future recrudescence of a Popular Front, which is still official Spanish Communist policy. The nominal leader and president of the *Partido Comunista Español* in exile is still *La Pasionaria.*

Anarchism, according to Welles, "now has little appeal," but an Anarchist movement does exist and probably always will. Anarchism will never cease to have a pseudo-religious appeal to the Spanish temperament, but Franco has seen to it that there are no proselytizers.

The best organized and strongest group in a regional sense are the Basques, who are the most restive and discontented of Spaniards and the most cruelly treated. The Basque language, like Catalan, is banned for official use. The sensational Basque trials in Burgos toward the end of 1970 drew such worldwide attention and condemnation after some of the prisoners were not only condemned to death by an army court-martial but given *two* death sentences each, that the Generalissimo felt constrained to commute the sentences. A sadistic police chief had been kidnapped and murdered by Basque revolutionaries.

"One can describe the kidnappers as thugs and terrorists," a Basque priest said to his parishioners from the pulpit during the trial, "but words fail to describe men who torture prisoners, record their screams, play the recordings to wives and mothers and tell the distraught women that they must turn informers if they wish to save their loved ones."

The police, like the military, still employ torture, but they are considered less ferociously brutal than in the immediate post-Civil War period. They are more efficient, as Franco's relatively peaceful reign has proved.

The army is the real guardian of law and order, except for the control of straightforward social crimes. In a near-totalitarian regime like Franco's, any kind of open and violent opposition is political and a form of treachery. Many Nationalist Civil War officers are still serving. There are about 200 active generals, just as there were in the time of the Second Republic. And they are the same types: reactionary, narrow-minded, anti-intellectual, religious.

"Being dogmatists by education and inclination," writes Welles, "the anti-Communist Spanish officers extend Marxism to mean liberalism, progressivism, even the bourgeois Socialism practiced by the British Labor party. To them, any Spaniard who is not pro-Franco is *ipso facto* a *Rojo,* a Red."

Surprisingly and unhappily, the younger officers are just as much reactionaries and hardliners as the older generation. This bodes ill for Spain's future, since it is hard to see any alternative in the immediate post-Franco era to military rule—under the monarchy or through a military junta, or both.

Now that most of the Spanish possessions in North Africa are irrevocably gone, only one cause for irredentism remains: Gibraltar. It has been one of Franco's failures, but he keeps trying and so will his successors. Gibraltar has been an English crown colony since the Treaty of Utrecht in 1713. The Generalissimo began a determined campaign to get it back in 1950, when he saw that the British intended to make Gibraltar self-governing. There was no chance of it willingly opting for Spain, as the population is now of Italian, Maltese, and Moroccan descent, with a Spanish minority.

One can say that Spain still has the ghost of an empire, for seventeen Latin American countries and Puerto Rico are linguistically and culturally Spanish. In the Far East, there are the Philippines. They are reminders of past glory and greatness.

How much have Spaniards changed since the 1930's? Two generations have grown up ignorant of the world, not even knowing the true history of their own Civil War. More than 60 per cent were born after the Civil War. Their education has been poor, for the system is poor. Spaniards up to the age of forty have known and can remember nothing but the Franco regime. They have had no civic freedoms; they could not practice politics in a democratic sense; they have not been able to read, see, or hear about the world outside except by stealth. Partly as a reaction to the agonies of the Civil War and partly through indoctrination and deprivation, Spaniards have shown little interest in politics. Their lives have forced them into an unnatural preoccupation with materialism, comfort, and personal security.

A great new difference is the expansion of the hitherto small, but always influential, middle class. "More and more key positions," Richard Eder wrote in a dispatch to *The New York Times* in March 1970, "—technicians in the ministries, professors, doctors, lawyers, journalists, businessmen—are being held by Spaniards in their thirties and early forties, who are keenly alive to the criticisms of the opposition and know that Spain will never be fully accepted by Europe until it finds a way to give this opposition a legally protected position."

Hundreds of thousands of Spanish laborers have gone to France and Germany for long spells, living in an atmosphere of freedom and relative well-being. They could not have a-voided absorbing some ideas which stirred hopes and desires for better things than their native country could offer them. The economic betterment in Spain has seeped downward to many workers and even peasants, stirring up the well-known phenomenon of rising expectations.

Spain is stagnant only on the surface, as if General Franco were sitting on a lid under which Spanish society seethed and boiled. It will not blow him off, but when his weight has gone, there will be a release. The changes which always take place in all societies are working feverishly in Spain, but not visibly. A writer in *The Economist* of London made a distinction between "official Spain" and "real Spain." So long as Franco lives, the world can see and know only "official Spain."

The nation doubtless needed a long breathing spell and the advent of a new generation of potential leaders who did not know the horrors of the Civil War or feel its intense emotionalism. The Spanish youth of the last few decades think that their fathers and grandfathers must have been mad.

Francisco Franco has now been a Chief of State longer than any statesman in the West. "I do not find the burden of rule heavy. Spain is easy to govern," he told Don Juan in 1954. One is tempted to feel that only Franco in all of Spain's history from the ancient Romans to today would have said that.

There is no such thing as *Franquismo*—no ideology, no system, no line, no more political coloration than to be rightist. Franco has been compared to Charles de Gaulle as a "patriot" devoted to the unity and glory of Spain, but he has brought Spain neither unity nor glory. He lacked the sort of intense emotional dedication to the *grandeur* of France which de Gaulle had and, above all, he lacked the *grandeur* of character which made the French general one of the great figures of our age. Franco is a little man with a few fixed ideas, a rocklike character, and an astonishing run of luck. He has been sustained by one overwhelming national determination: at all costs to avoid another civil war.

There were so many changes of ministers after 1957 that it serves little purpose to name names at any given time. Franco plays his cards close to his chest. Any cabinet minister or, indeed, all of them, can be here today and gone tomorrow. The men who are "here" on the day Generalissimo Franco dies will be key figures, but they will have been lucky. Franco has managed to survive dozens of ministers, generals, and journalists who go to the Madrid post hoping to be there when the Caudillo finally gives up or dies. He boasts, with reason, that he comes of a long-lived family.

Yet—go he must. He hopes for continuity; he does not say, "After me the flood," although there can be no second Franco. This paradoxical, enigmatic man, who has longed so fervently to see the Spain that he ruled after his fashion, perpetuated, did not prepare Spaniards for self-government, nor did he allow any potential rival to win popular support. His parting gift, politically, is Prince Juan Carlos, an ineffectual, inexperienced, mediocre young man for one of the most vital and divided people in Europe.

The end of an era approaches: the end of the Spanish Civil War. As the coins say, Francisco Franco is "Caudillo of Spain by the Grace of God"—a throwback to the divine right of kings and an indication of what the Generalissimo thinks of himself. He has often referred to God's intervention on his behalf, for he came to believe that he had a God-given mission. Therefore, those who criticize him are not only committing a crime against the Head of State but, in theory, an act of impiety. It has always been risky for his ministers to give him unwelcome advice. When the advice is good and he follows it, he still resents the rash person who disagreed with him. Ever since 1939 he has lived in partial seclusion and increasing aloofness in the former royal villa of El Pardo outside of Madrid. He has been called "a king in all but name."

I wrote of him in 1956: "Franco has achieved the extraordinary position of being, on the whole, neither hated nor loved in Spain. To those who know the Spaniards, this is the highest form of condemnation."

Until incapacitated by illness or accident, Generalissimo Francisco Franco Bahamonde will remain in power, as he put it on October 1, 1971, the thirty-fifth anniversary of his rule, "while God gives me life and a clear mind." Meanwhile, Spain's political stability will continue. But afterward? There must and will be significant political and social changes which cannot be toward more authoritarianism. When those changes come, the Republican heritage will be felt along liberal and constitutional lines. Spain will awake, as after a long sleep which has been part nightmare, part rest.

BIBLIOGRAPHY

THE READER OF ENGLISH who is interested enough to want a broader, but not excessively detailed, account of the Spanish Civil War can find it without too much difficulty.

Gerald Brenan's *The Spanish Labyrinth* (New York: Cambridge University Press, 2nd ed., 1950–1960), is universally accepted as the best standard work on the political and social background of the war. A valuable and more extensive study is Antonio Ramos Oliveira's *Politics, Economics and Men of Modern Spain* (London: Gollancz, 1946). E. Allison Peer's *The Spanish Tragedy* (London: Methuen, 1936) is a solid, rather anti-Republican study.

Dozens of books appeared in English during the course of the war. Among the important ones were Franz Borkenau's *The Spanish Cockpit* (Ann Arbor: University of Michigan Press, 1937); Arthur Koestler's account of his dramatic prison experience, *Spanish Testament* (London: Gollancz, 1937); Frank Jellinek's left-wing but well-documented *The Civil War in Spain* (New York: Fertig, 1969); and George Orwell's famous but misleading *Homage to Catalonia* (New York: Harcourt Brace Jovanovich, 1969). My own *Two Wars and More to Come* (New York: Carrick & Evans, 1938) is a journalistic work which makes the link between Abyssinia, Spain, and World War II.

The best general study of the Civil War, a pioneer, standard, and incomparable work of scholarship, is Professor Hugh Thomas's *History of the Spanish Civil War* (New York: Harper, 1961). It should be read in the revised 1965 Penguin paperback. Professor Gabriel Jackson's *The Spanish Republic and the Civil War* (Princeton: Princeton University Press, 1965) is a splendid work which, as its title indicates, gives full treatment to the Second Spanish Republic. The outstanding American scholar on the Civil War and contemporary Spain is Profes-

263

sor Stanley G. Payne, whose three books are models of scholarship. They tend to be anti-Republican and pro-Franco. They are: *Falange: A History of Spanish Fascism* (Stanford: Stanford University Press, 1961); *Politics and the Military in Modern Spain* (Stanford: Stanford University Press, 1967); and *The Spanish Revolution* (New York: Norton, 1970). One of the best and most authoritative books by an observer who saw the war from beginning to end, and who knew Spain well, is by Reuter's correspondent, Henry Buckley: *Life and Death of the Spanish Republic* (London: Hamish Hamilton, 1940).

The role of the United States is best covered in F. Jay Taylor's *The United States and the Spanish Civil War* (New York: Bookman Associates, 1956). Another excellent study is Allen Guttmann's *The Wound in the Heart* (Glencoe, N.Y.: Free Press, 1962). Of the books written about the American volunteers, the one by Edwin Rolfe, the poet, who was a volunteer, is most highly recommended: *The Lincoln Battalion* (New York: Random House, 1939). A thoroughly researched, but hostile and critical account, lacking in understanding, is Professor Cecil Eby's *Between the Bullet and the Lie* (New York: Holt, Rinehart & Winston, 1969). It is valuable for otherwise unobtainable information.

Burnett Bolloten's *The Grand Camouflage* (London: Pall Mall Press, 1961, rev. ed. 1968), assembles a great mass of information to support his thesis that the Spanish Republican government and its war operations were run from Moscow. The case is unproven but the information he gathered is useful.

Personal histories and memoirs of the war are legion. They have all been culled by later scholars, although there is a valuable recent group of Russian memoirs yet to be translated.

The best political book on the postwar Franco regime is Ben Welles's *The Gentle Anarchy* (New York: Praeger, 1965). My earlier, *The Yoke and the Arrows* (New York: Braziller, 1956), was put out in paperback in 1970.

There has been no biography of Juan Negrín, but many of General Franco, all but one so completely laudatory as to be useless. The exception is *El Caudillo* (New York: McGraw-Hill, 1970), by J. W. D. Trythall, which is worth reading.

Many novels have taken the Civil War as their scene. The most famous is Ernest Hemingway's *For Whom the Bell Tolls* (New York: Scribners, 1940). A neglected but splendid novel which should not be missed is Alvah Bessie's *Men in Battle* (New York: Scribners, 1939). André Malraux's *Man's Hope* (New York: Random House, 1938), like the two American novels, tells much truth about the war in the form of fiction. A vivid picture of the events leading up to the war is to be found in the first of a series of novels by the Catalan author, José María

Gironella, translated as *The Cypresses Believe in God* (New York: Knopf, 1956).

Two documentary films on the war have become classics. Joris Ivens's *The Spanish Earth,* for which Ernest Hemingway did the script, was made in and around Madrid in 1937. The hauntingly sad and beautiful French film *Pour Mourir à Madrid* is an enduring monument to those who died in Spain.

INDEX

Rota, 248
ROWAK, 169

Saavedra Lamas, Carlos, 134
Salazar de Oliverira, Antonio, 166
Salisbury, Harrison, 225
San Sebastían, 3
Sanjurjo, José, 70, 76–78, 86–87
Santander, 11, 91, 92, 143
Sarabia, Hernández, 93
Saragossa, 14, 75
Schmutchkievich, Jacob, 152, 161, 196
Segovia, battle of, 12
Segura, Cardinal Pedro, 50
Seguridad, 76, 90
Serrano Suñer, Ramón, 77–78, 98, 102, 243, 246
Servicio de Inteligencia Militar (SIM), 38–39, 109, 111, 112
Seville, 87, 89
Sheehan, Vincent, 213
Shuster, George, 119
Sierra de Guardarrama, 2, 5
Social classes, 28–29, 258
Socialist party (France), 184
Socialist party (Spain), 8, 44, 56, 70–71, 126, 127, 256
  Communist party and, 66–67
  elections of 1936, 62
  formation of, 53
  labor unrest and, 54
  Largo Caballero and, 52
  and Popular Front, 61
  in Second Republic, 50
  split in, 13, 55, 64
Society of Jesus, *see* Jesuits
Sorel, Georges, 43
Soviet Union, *see* Union of Soviet Socialist Republics
Spanish Battalion, 211
Spanish Civil War, The (Thomas), 164
Spanish Cockpit, The (Borkenau), 33, 124
Spanish Government and the Axis, The, 244
Spanish Labyrinth, The (Brenan), 233
Spanish Revolution, The (Payne), 226, 232
Spanish Testament (Koestler), 116
Sperrle, Hugo von, 10, 238, 240

Squadristi, 64
Stalin, Joseph, 19, 56, 139, 215
  aid to Republicans, 4, 154–158, 160–164, 170
  alliance with Hitler, 148, 238
  and International Brigades, 194
  non-intervention, 6–7, 130, 135, 156, 158–159
  purges, 4, 162–163
  Spanish gold, 170–171
Standard Oil Company, 179
Stefani, 146
Stern, General (Grigorovitch), 15
Stern, Lazar, *see* Kléber, Emil
Stimson, Henry L., 185–187
Stohrer, Eberhard von, 103
Strikes, 28, 44, 54, 64
Strunk, Captain, 113
Sturzo, Don Luigi, 119
Swierczewski, Karol, 195, 196, 199, 209

Table Talk (Hitler), 84, 136, 155, 243
Tagüeña, Manuel, 20, 93
Tarancón, Enrique, 38, 253
Tarragona, 20
Taylor, F. Jay, 174–175, 185
Tercios, see Foreign Legionaries
Teruel, battle of, 14–15, 209
Tetuán, 85
Texas Oil Company (Texaco), 179
Third Communist International, *see* Comintern
Thirteenth Brigade, 201
Thirty-fifth Division, 201
This I Remember (Roosevelt), 188
Thomas, Hugh, 19, 20, 23, 37, 61, 62, 65, 69, 87, 104, 105, 110, 111, 128, 139, 148, 163–165, 196–200, 208, 215, 226, 234, 235, 238
Thorez, Maurice, 163, 193
Thorning, Joseph, 183
Tierno Galván, Enrique, 256
Time for Decision, The (Welles), 187
Tito, Marshal, 194, 219
Togliatti, Palmiro, 193–196
Toledo, 3–4
Trades Union Congress (TUC), 184
Traditionalists, *see* Carlists
Trevor-Roper, Hugh, 31
Tribunales de Guardia, 113
Trotsky, Leon, 196
Trotskyism, 13, 125

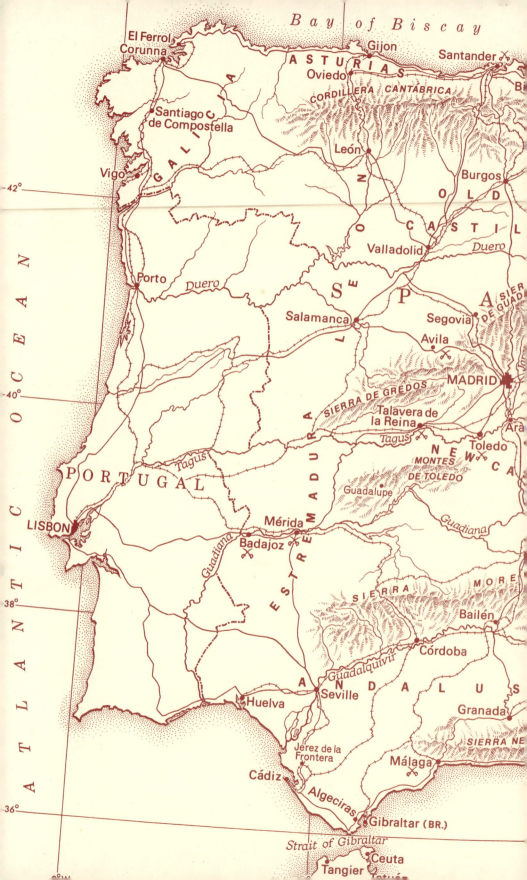